How To Use This Plan Book

Square Footage Calculations

Square footage calculations are made from the outside face of exterior wall construction and include all walls. Window, fireplace and room projections are included only when the floor joists are extended under that area.

Construction Drawings

Construction drawings include the following:
1. Cover sheet with general specification design notes.
2. Exterior elevations of all four views.
3. Building sections and details as required to construct that design.
4. Interior elevations of cabinets and wall with unique conditions.
5. Some, but not all plans include a list of building materials. When the lists are included, they help determine construction costs, but are not recommended for use in ordering materials.
6. Schematic electrical plans with suggested switch, outlet and light-fixture locations.

Note: Mechanical and plumbing drawings are not included. Me [illegible] s and design considerations vary widely across the country; there [illegible] n is left to the contractor—as is frequently done throughout the [illegible] s include information and details builders need to make an app [illegible] it at the local inspector's office. Plans are drawn to meet standard [illegible] a- tions for local code variations or peculiar structural requiremen [illegible] al level.

The diagrams presented in this issue constitute only floor plans and elevations. Purchasers are advised to consult their state and local building regulations and a state-certified architect prior to any construction to these plans.

Purchasing Of Prints

You may purchase complete sets of construction drawings of these designs in either of the following two ways:

1. **Direct purchase of blueline prints**
Right reading or "mirror image." Mirror image sets are reverse images—including the lettering. They are useful in building a reversed plan when they accompany a right-reading set.

2. **Direct purchase of mylar sepia or vellum prints**
These print may be used as an original tracing. They may be printed as drawn as often as required, or the builder may make alterations to suit his specific client, site, material selections, individual construction methods or local code requirements.

3. **Two ways to order working drawings**
There are two ways to order working drawings—by mail or by telephone. To order by mail, complete an order form and mail it with payment to: *Professional Builder & Remodeler,* 1350 E. Touhy Avenue, P.O. Box 5080, Des Plaines, Ill. 60017-5080. For faster service, Visa, MasterCard, and American Express credit-card holders may call a TOLL-FREE number—1-800-323-7379.

Order forms appear in the back of this book.

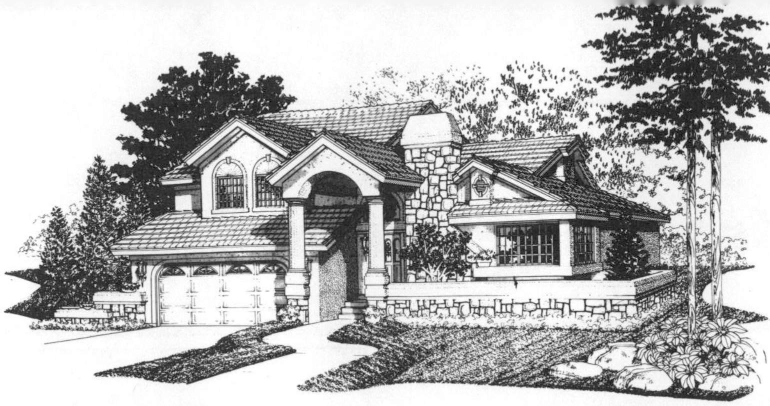

Plan number DPI-2383-9002-SW93

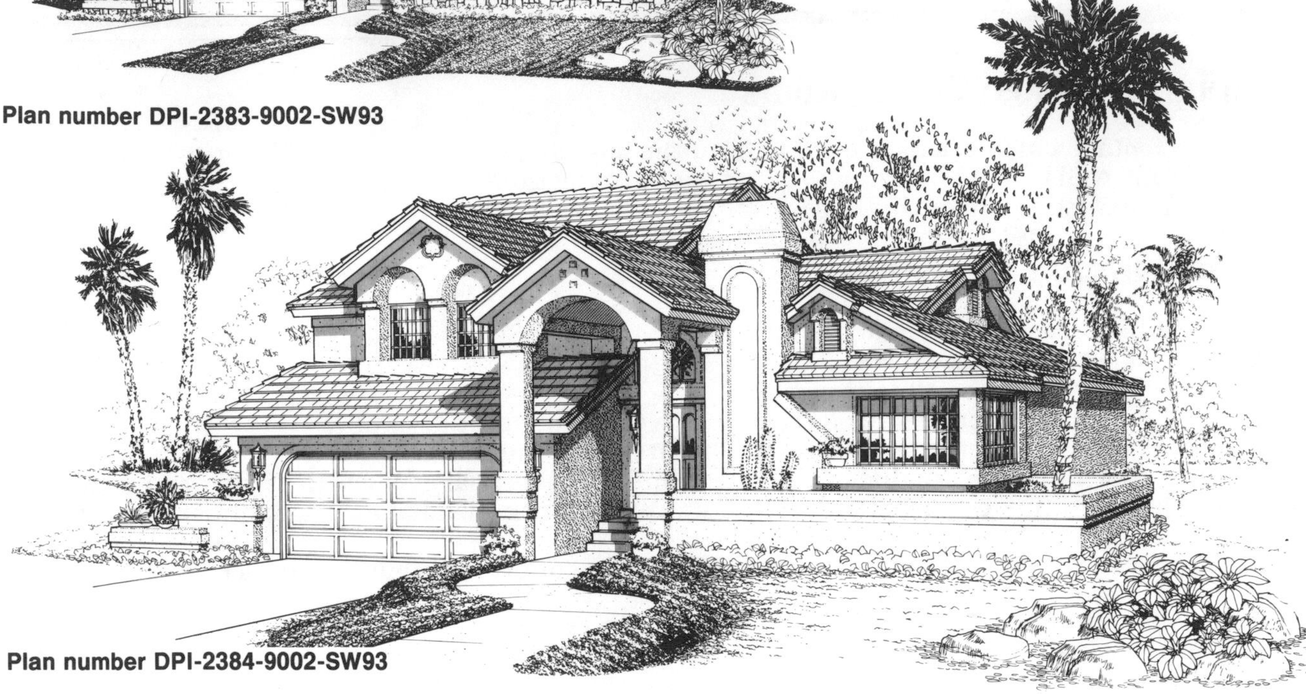

Plan number DPI-2384-9002-SW93

Walk-Out Family Room Makes Expandable Split Level Extra Special

Main floor—1170 sq. ft.
Lower floor—397 sq. ft.
Total living space—1567 sq. ft.
3 bedrooms, 2½ baths
Shown with a basement

- Elevated foyer features a handy coat closet.
- Living and family rooms have fireplaces.
- Kitchen island provides space for informal seating as a snack bar.
- Unfinished expansion space includes a large game room.
- Order each elevation separately.

The plan price is $300.00. You may choose either five sets of bluelines or a reproducible mylar. Plan by Design Profile, Inc.

The diagrams presented here constitute only floor plans and elevations. Purchasers are advised to consult their state and local building regulations and a state-certified architect prior to any construction related to these plans.

Main Floor

Lower Floor

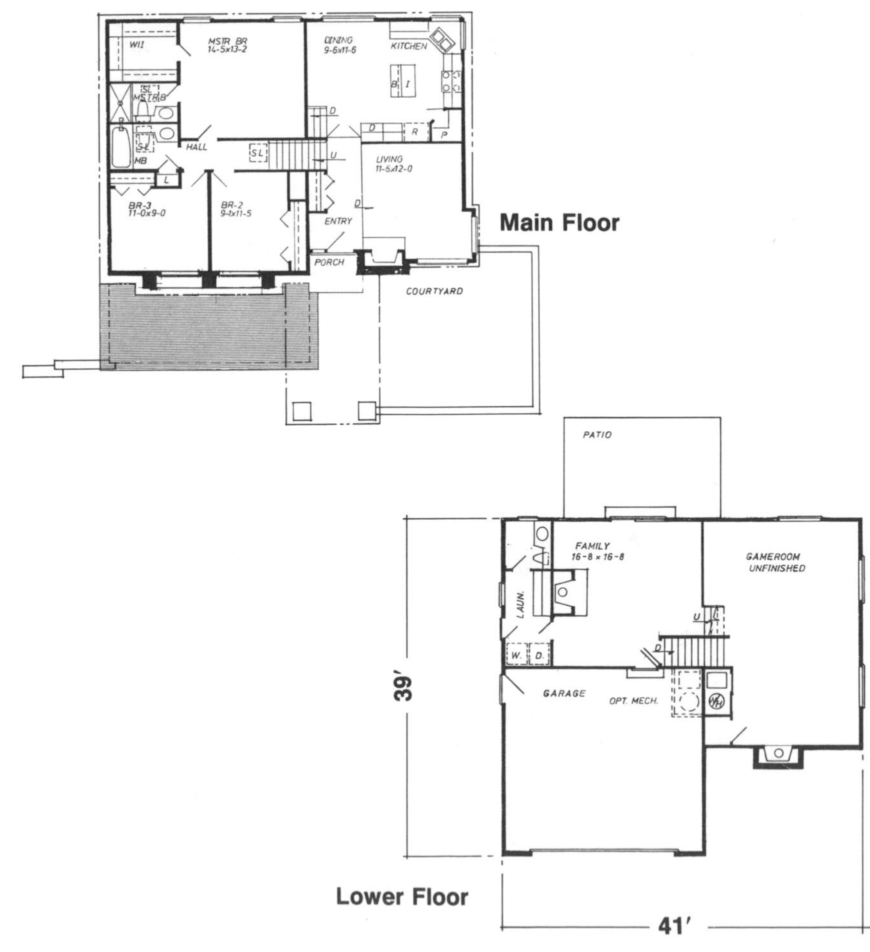

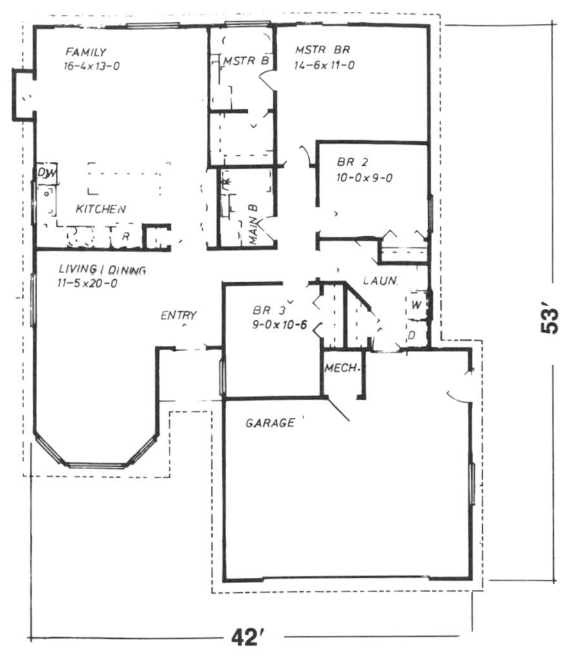

Open Interior Makes The Most Of Available Space

Total living space—1371 ft.
3 bedrooms, 2 baths
Shown with concrete slab construction

- Large living room is enhanced by the view offered by a bay window.
- Efficient kitchen includes plenty of counter space and a pantry.
- Family room includes a fireplace.
- Private bath and walk-in closet are included in the master bedroom.
- Order each elevation separately.

The plan price is $300.00. You may choose either five sets of bluelines or a reproducible mylar. Plan by Design Profile, Inc.

The diagrams presented here constitute only floor plans and elevations. Purchasers are advised to consult their state and local building regulations and a state-certified architect prior to any construction related to these plans.

Plan number DPI-2303-8906-SW93

Plan number DPI-2303A-8906-SW93

Second-Floor Deck Adds A Touch Of Romance To Master Suite

First floor—1350 sq. ft.
Second floor—1108 sq. ft.
Total living space—2458 sq. ft.
4 bedrooms, 2½ baths
Shown with a basement

- Exciting, two-way fireplace serves as the focal point in the living and family rooms.
- Dining room features a very formal, out-of-the-way location.
- Skylights brighten the second floor, including the double vanity in the master bathroom.
- Laundry room doubles as a mud room with access from the back yard.
- Large, three-car garage includes a handy storage closet.

Plan number DPI-M2302-8906-SW93. The plan price is $368.70. You may choose either five sets of bluelines or a reproducible mylar. Plan by Design Profile, Inc.

The diagrams presented here constitute only floor plans and elevations. Purchasers are advised to consult their state and local building regulations and a state-certified architect prior to any construction related to these plans.

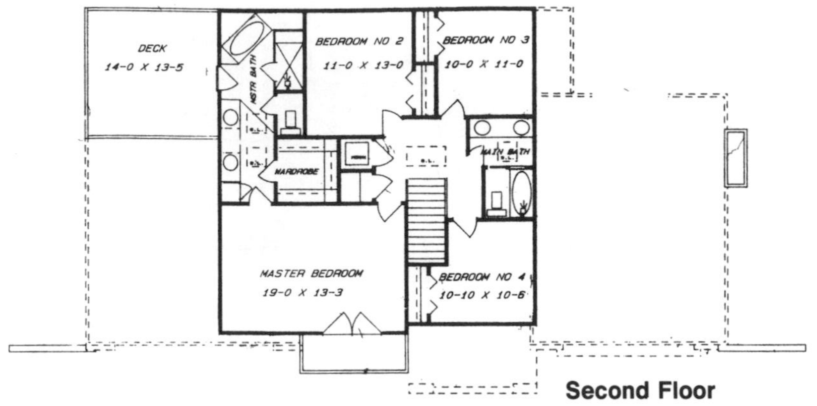

Second Floor

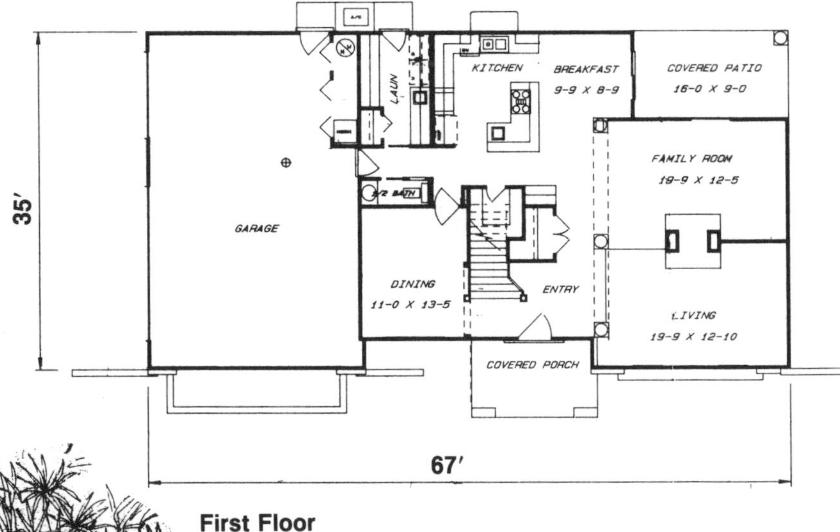

First Floor

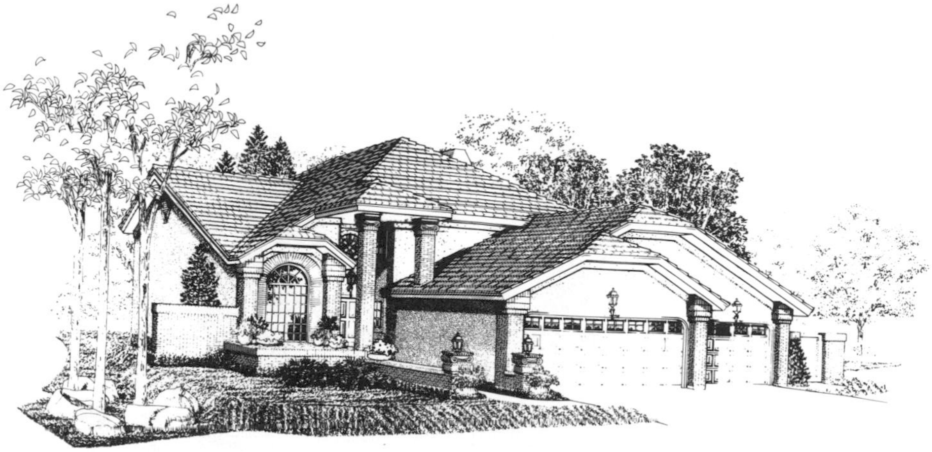

Plan number DPI-M2396-9002-SW93

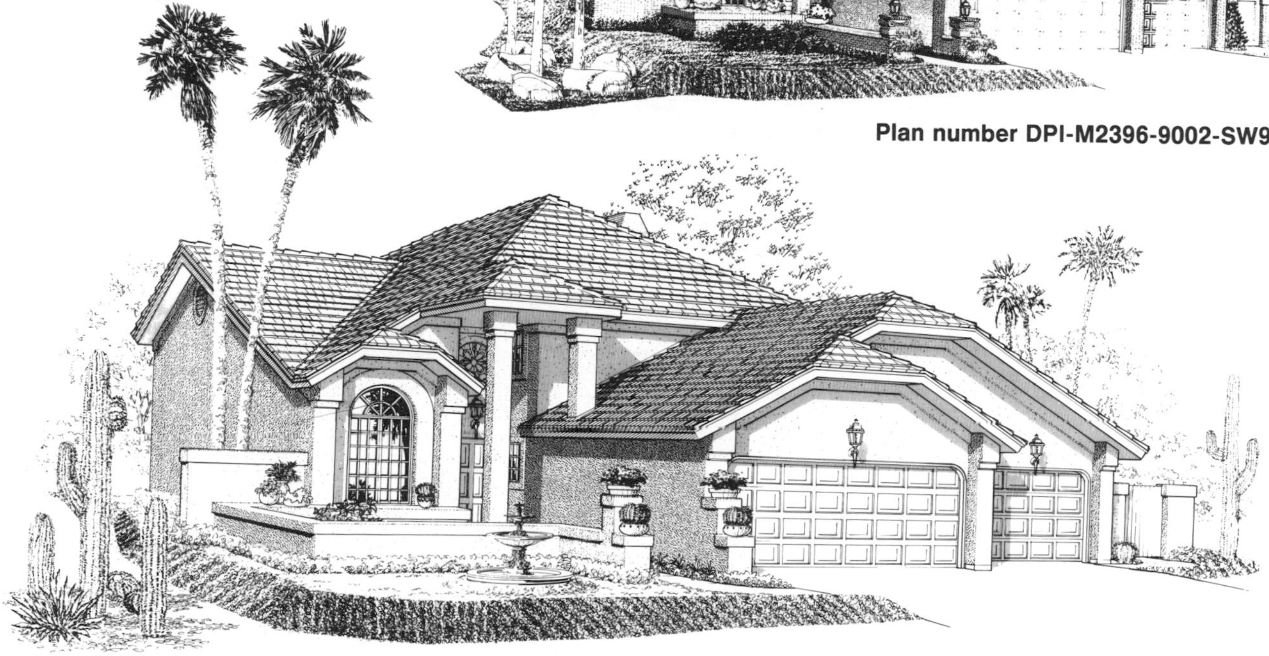

Plan number DPI-M2397-9002-SW93

Second Floor

First Floor

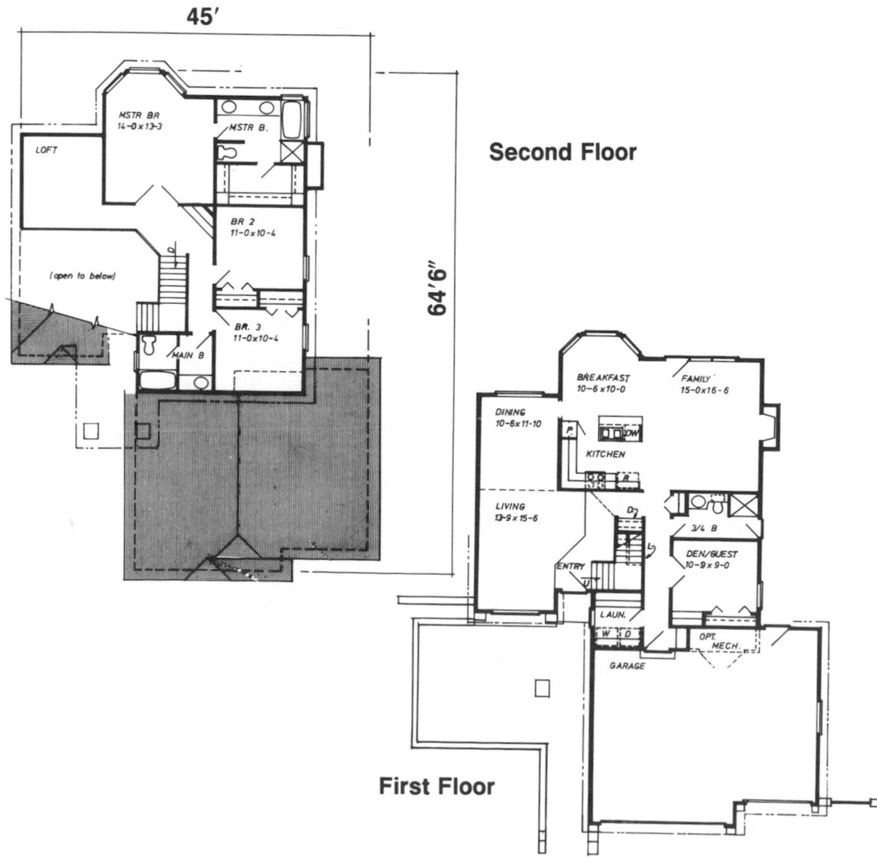

Secluded Den Provides The Ideal Hideaway For At-Home Office

First floor—1252 sq. ft.
Second floor—979 sq. ft.
Total living space—2231 sq. ft.
3-4 bedrooms, 3 baths
Shown with a basement

- Open design of the formal and informal living area creates a spacious environment.
- Easy access to a full bath gives den the ability to adapt as a guest room.
- Second-floor loft is a bonus multi-purpose area.
- Order each elevation separately.

The plan price is $334.65. You may choose either five sets of bluelines or a reproducible mylar. Plan by Design Profile, Inc.

The diagrams presented here constitute only floor plans and elevations. Purchasers are advised to consult their state and local building regulations and a state-certified architect prior to any construction related to these plans.

Family Area Offers 'Wall Of Glass' Overlook Of The Back Yard

First floor—1926 sq. ft.
Second floor—1708 sq. ft.
Total living space—3634 sq. ft.
4 bedrooms, 2½ baths
Shown with a basement

- Formal courtyard sets the stage for the grand foyer with its two-story ceiling and angled staircase.
- Generous use of windows promote outdoor views, especially in the informal family zone at the back.
- Island kitchen offers the option of a built-in desk, planning center.
- Fireplace is a dramatic element of the master suite .
- Mud room includes built-in lockers and a bench.

Plan number DPI-2350-SW93. The plan price is $545.10. You may choose either five sets of bluelines or a reproducible mylar. Plan by Design Profile, Inc.

The diagrams presented here constitute only floor plans and elevations. Purchasers are advised to consult their state and local building regulations and a state-certified architect prior to any construction related to these plans.

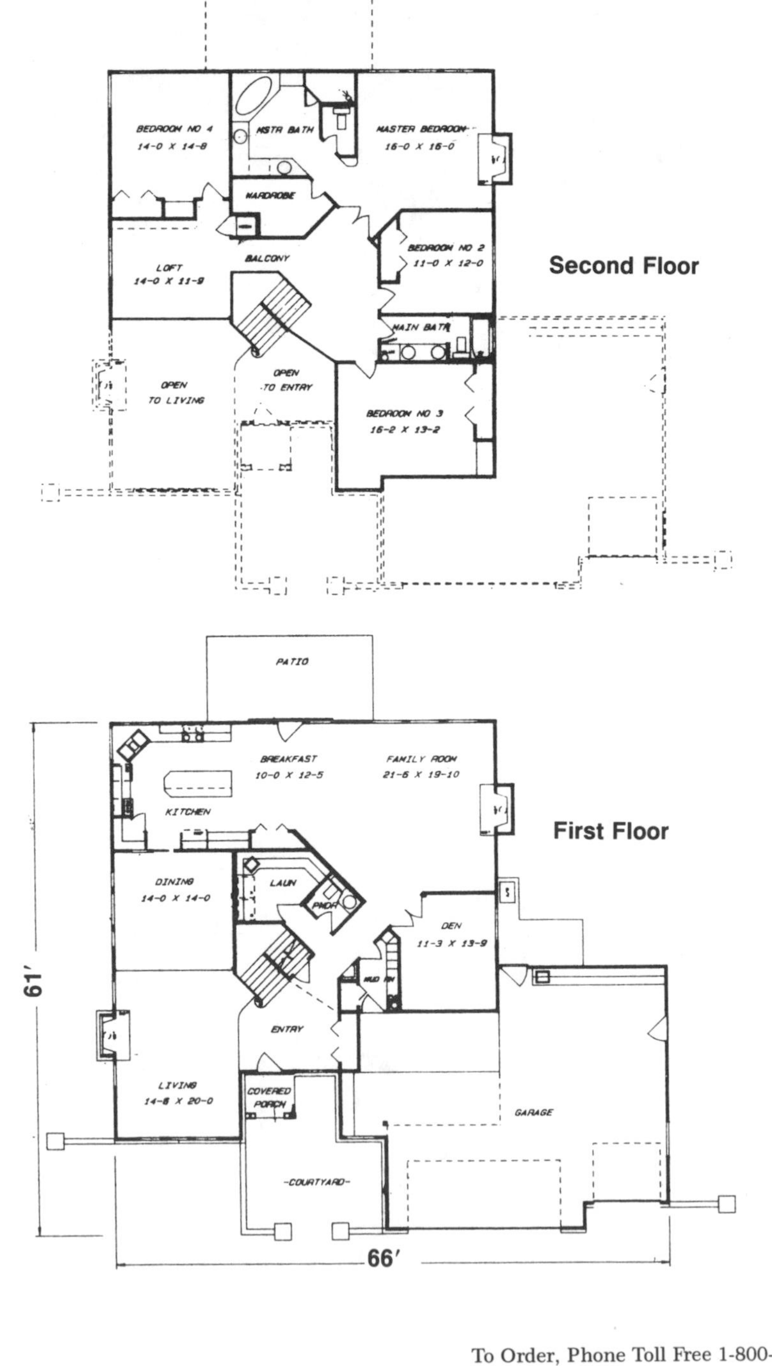

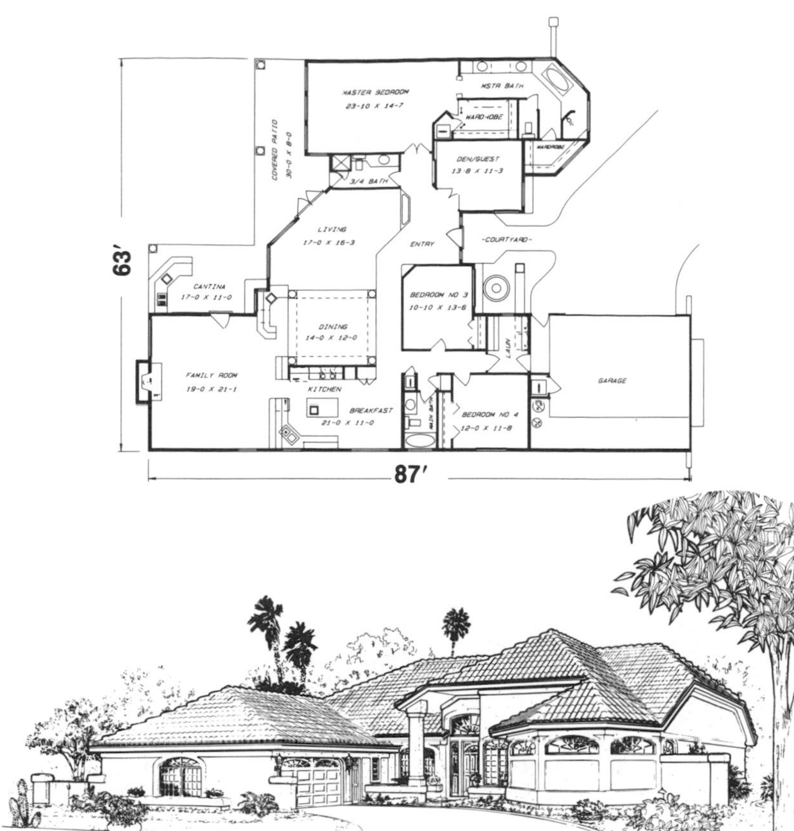

Top-Notch Master Suite Boasts Of Every Amenity

Total living space—2894 sq. ft.
3-4 bedrooms, 2-3 baths
Shown with concrete slab construction

- Grand bay provides a dramatic setting for the master bath.
- Pillars and planters define the room transitions without restricting interior views.
- Kitchen features a center island and a breakfast area.
- Large wet bar provides service to the living, dining and family rooms.

Plan number DPI-L2392-9002-SW93. The plan price is $434.10. You may choose either five sets of bluelines or a reproducible mylar. Plan by Design Profile, Inc.

The diagrams presented here constitute only floor plans and elevations. Purchasers are advised to consult their state and local building regulations and a state-certified architect prior to any construction related to these plans.

Pass The Time In The Kitchen Of This Attractive Ranch

Total living space—1673 sq. ft.
3 bedrooms, 2 baths
Shown with concrete slab construction

- Main bath features an efficient, compartmented design.
- Master suite offers the option of a bay window sitting area.
- Generous closet space is provided throughout.
- Vaulted ceilings are featured throughout the interior.

Plan number DPI-2319-9011-SW93. The plan price is $300.00. You may choose either five sets of bluelines or a reproducible mylar. Plan by Design Profile, Inc.

The diagrams presented here constitute only floor plans and elevations. Purchasers are advised to consult their state and local building regulations and a state-certified architect prior to any construction related to these plans.

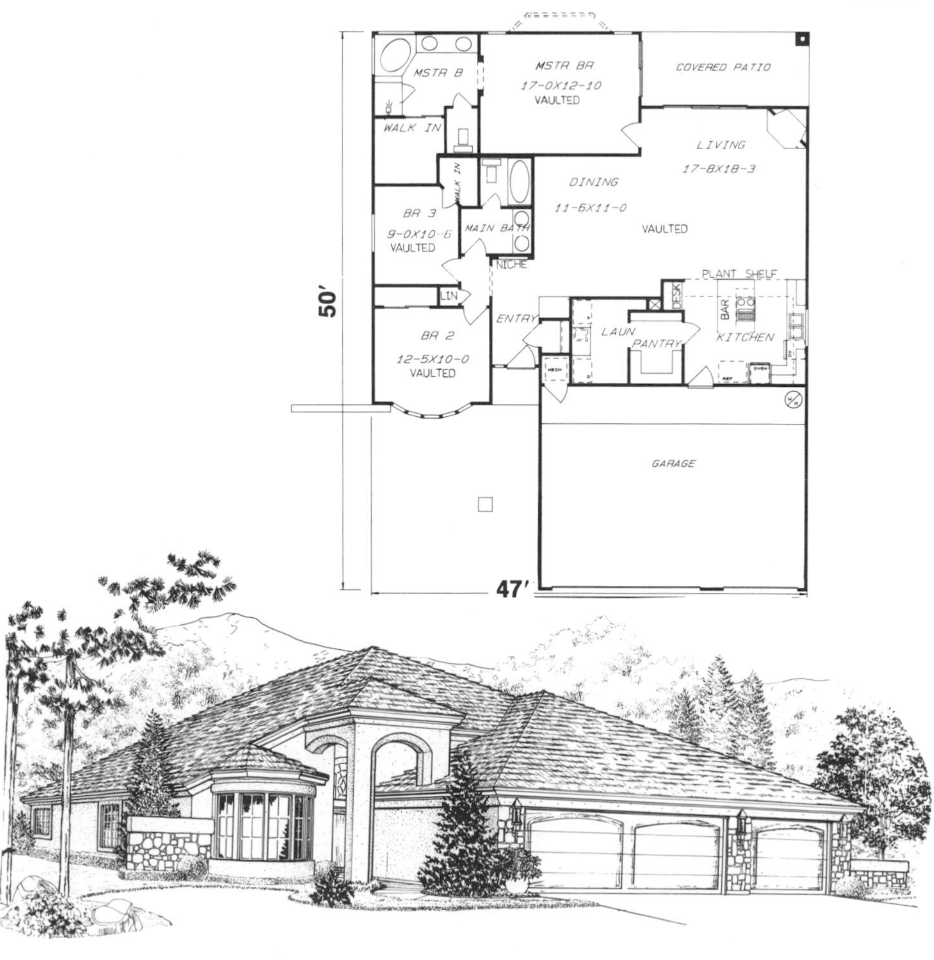

Plan number DPI-2381-AJ91-SW93

Plan number DPI-2382A-AJ91-SW93

Plan number DPI-2382-AJ91-SW93

Vaulted Ceilings Let Compact Ranch Live Large

Total living space—1423 sq. ft.
Unfinished basement—1404 sq. ft.
3 bedrooms, 2 baths
Shown with a basement

- Master bedroom has a private, compartmented bath.
- Entry includes a coat closet, direct access to the living room.
- Fireplace provides the focal point in the family room.
- Kitchen snack bar provides seating for informal dining.
- Order each elevation separately.

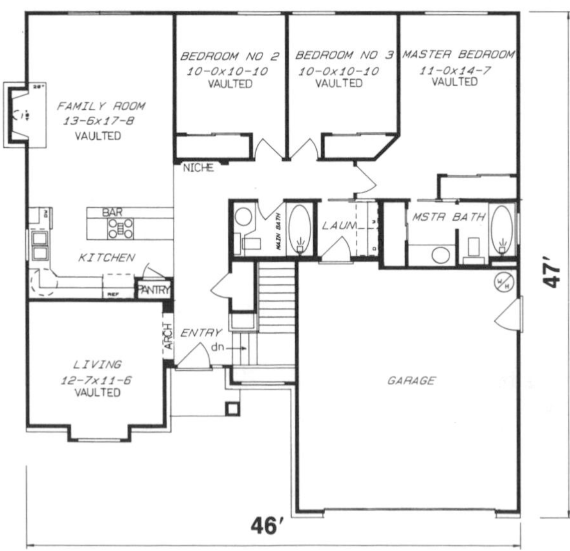

The plan price is $300.00. You may choose either five sets of bluelines or a reproducible mylar. Plan by Design Profile, Inc.

The diagrams presented here constitute only floor plans and elevations. Purchasers are advised to consult their state and local building regulations and a state-certified architect prior to any construction related to these plans.

Interior Angles Give Luxury Two Story Singular Appeal

Second Floor

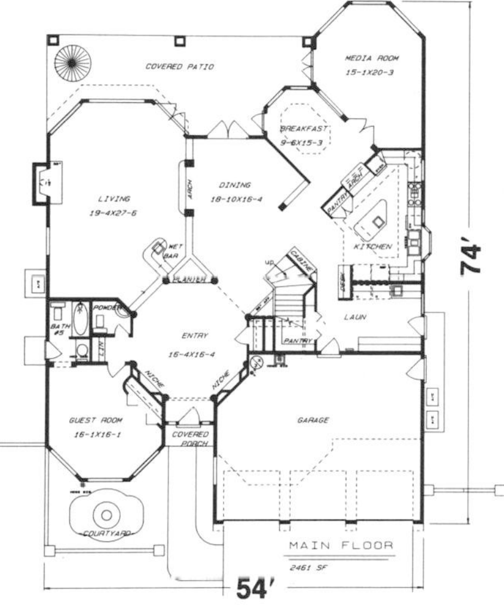

First Floor

First floor—2461 sq. ft.
Second floor—2655 sq. ft.
Total living space—5116 sq. ft.
4 bedrooms, 4½ baths
Shown with concrete slab construction

- Grand entry includes soaring columns, display niches and a planter.
- Arches, columns and a wet bar are featured in the living/dining areas.
- Functional kitchen includes a built-in desk and a pass-through to the breakfast area.
- Two master suites provide plenty of luxury.
- Spiral staircase on the rear deck leads to the second floor.

Plan number DPI-2333-SW93. The plan price is $767.40. You may choose either five sets of bluelines or a reproducible mylar. Plan by Design Profile, Inc.

The diagrams presented here constitute only floor plans and elevations. Purchasers are advised to consult their state and local building regulations and a state-certified architect prior to any construction related to these plans.

Master Suite Occupies Its Own Floor, Has Private Deck

First floor—2824 sq. ft.
Second floor—818 sq. ft.
Total living space—3642 sq. ft.
4-5 bedrooms, 4 baths
Shown with concrete slab construction

- Vaulted ceilings are featured in the entry, living and dining rooms, kitchen, breakfast bay and family room.
- Attractive plant shelves top the columns which define the living room's borders.
- Accessible wet bar serves both the living and dining rooms.
- Main-floor den may be put into service as an extra bedroom.
- Extra-large laundry room has access from the yard or the three-car garage.

Plan number DPI-2319-90MO-SW93. The plan price is $546.30. You may choose either five sets of bluelines or a reproducible mylar. Plan by Design Profile, Inc.

The diagrams presented here constitute only floor plans and elevations. Purchasers are advised to consult their state and local building regulations and a state-certified architect prior to any construction related to these plans.

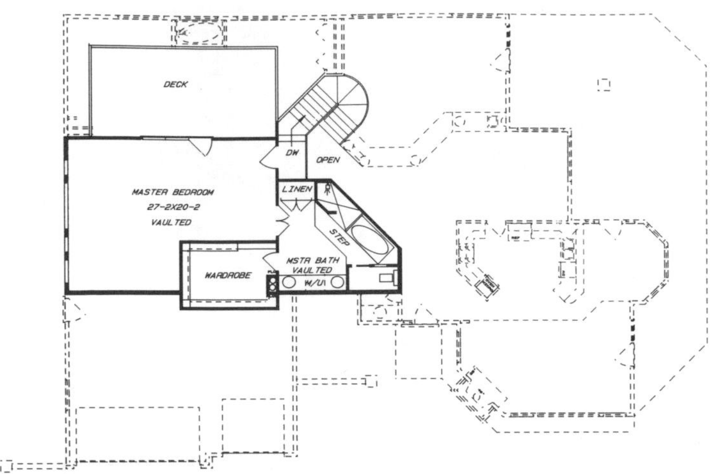

Second Floor

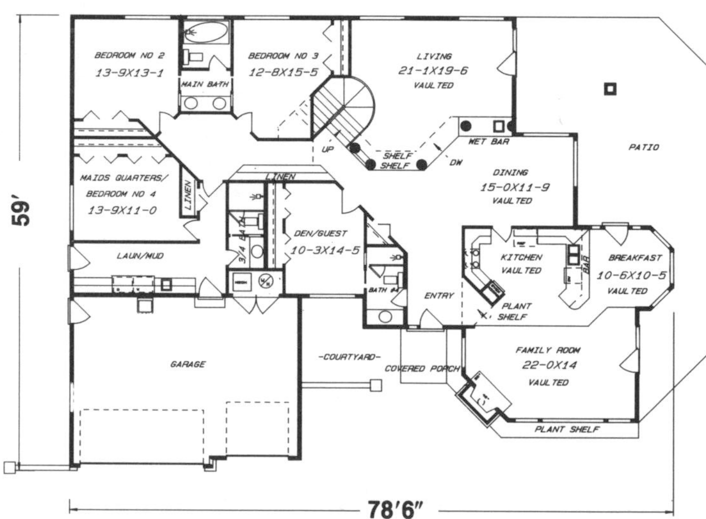

First Floor

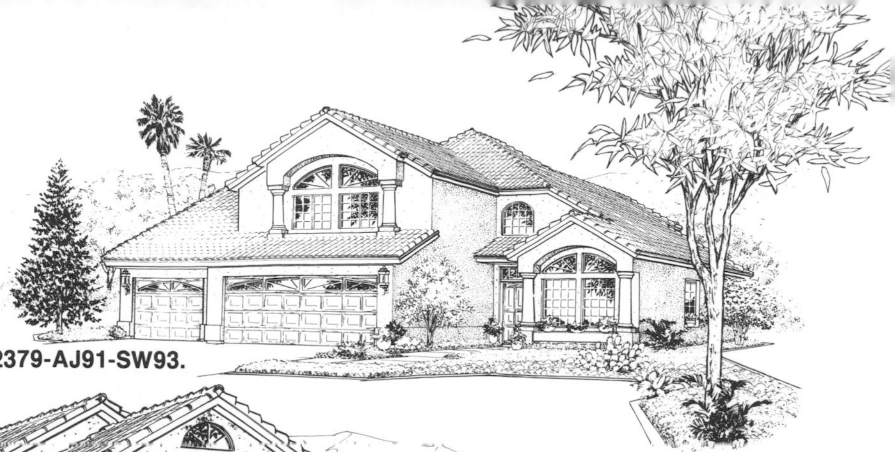

Plan number DPI-2379-AJ91-SW93.

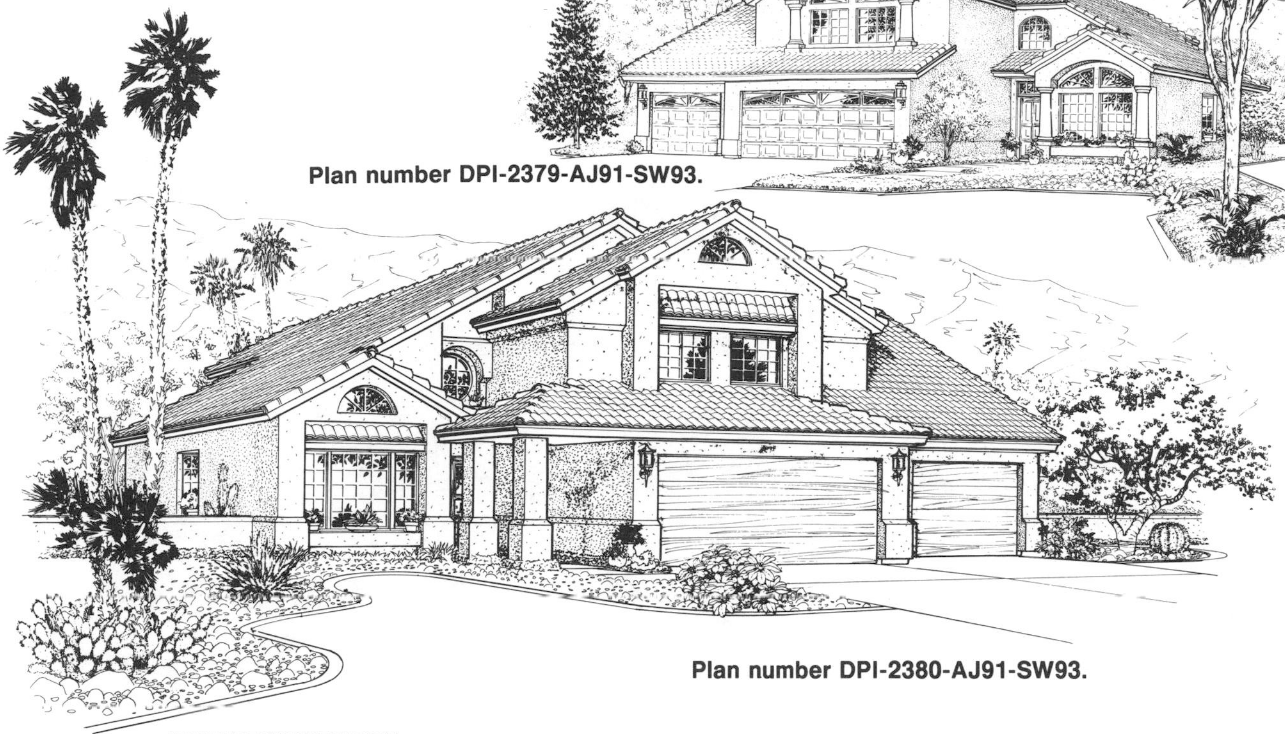

Plan number DPI-2380-AJ91-SW93.

Second Floor

First Floor

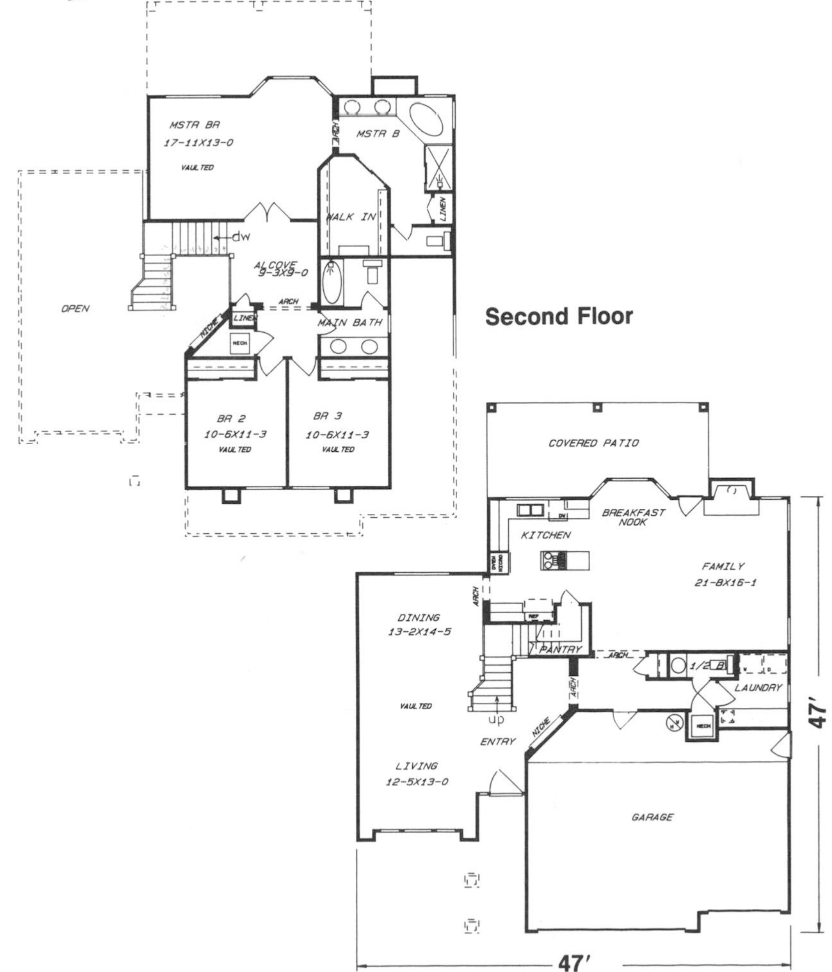

Roomy Interior Promises Comfortable Living

First floor—1055 sq. ft.
Second floor—1247 sq. ft.
Total living space—2302 sq. ft.
3 bedrooms, 2½ baths
Shown with concrete slab construction

- Vaulted ceilings highlight the foyer, living and dining rooms and the entire second floor.
- Practical kitchen island can be used as a snack bar.
- Master suite features a bay window sitting area and a commodious, compartmented bath.
- Spacious, three-car garage expands storage possibilities.
- Order each elevation separately.

The plan price is $345.30. You may choose either five sets of bluelines or a reproducible mylar. Plan by Design Profile, Inc.

The diagrams presented here constitute only floor plans and elevations. Purchasers are advised to consult their state and local building regulations and a state-certified architect prior to any construction related to these plans.

Plan number DPI-2389-9002-SW93.

Plan number DPI-2390-9002-SW93.

Bay Windows Create Bright, Custom Interior

First floor—988 sq. ft.
Second floor—922 sq. ft.
Total living space—1910 sq. ft.
4 bedrooms, 2½ baths
Shown with a basement

- Shared space of the living, dining rooms provides a large formal entertaining area.
- Patio door is incorporated into the breakfast bay.
- Fireplace highlights the family room.
- Master suite features a bay window sitting area, a private bath and a walk-in closet.
- Order each elevation separately.

The plan price is $300.00. You may choose either five sets of bluelines or a reproducible mylar. Plan by Design Profile, Inc.

The diagrams presented here constitute only floor plans and elevations. Purchasers are advised to consult their state and local building regulations and a state-certified architect prior to any construction related to these plans.

Fireplace Serves As An Attractive Room Divider

First floor—1005 sq. ft.
Second floor—930 sq. ft.
Total living space—1935 sq. ft.
Unfinished basement—1005 sq. ft.
3-5 bedrooms, 2½-3½ baths
Shown with a basement

- Display niches and arches accent the foyer and entry to the living room.
- Dramatic staircase features a lovely bay-windowed landing.
- Generous storage space is provided by multiple linen closets.
- Formal and informal dining space is provided.
- Order each elevation separately.

The plan price is $300.00. You may choose either five sets of bluelines or a reproducible mylar. Plan by Design Profile, Inc.

The diagrams presented here constitute only floor plans and elevations. Purchasers are advised to consult their state and local building regulations and a state-certified architect prior to any construction related to these plans.

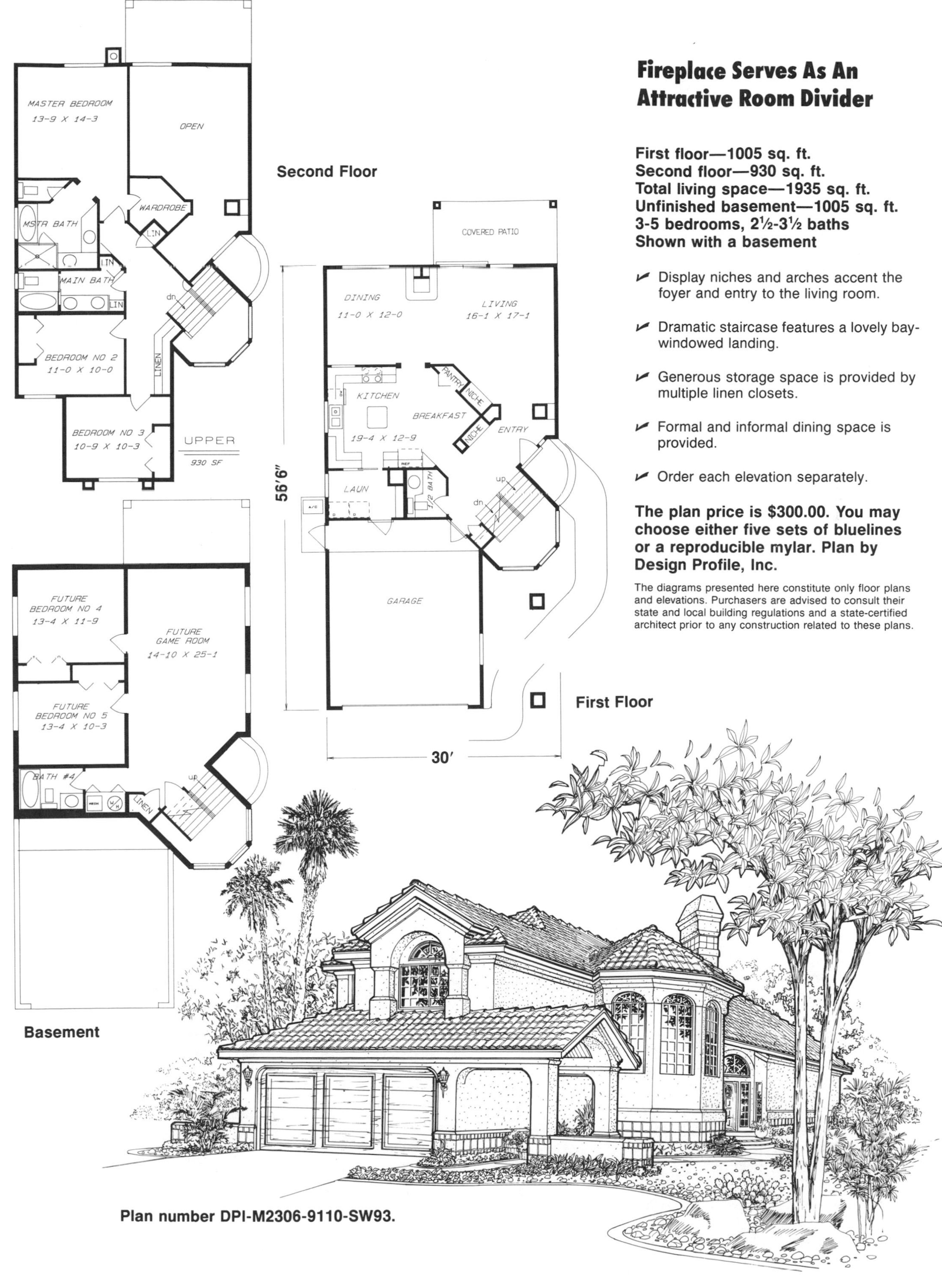

Plan number DPI-M2306-9110-SW93.

Separate Formal, Informal Zones, Comfortable Bedrooms In First-Class Family Home

First floor—1522 sq. ft.
Second floor—1400 sq. ft.
Total living space—2922 sq. ft.
5 bedrooms, 3 baths
Shown with concrete slab construction

- Double doors hide the den retreat, giving it appeal as an at-home office.
- Lovely bay window highlights the living room.
- Family room and master suite both feature a fireplace plus access to a patio or deck.
- Convenient breakfast bay adjoins the kitchen.
- Oversized laundry includes generous counter/cabinet storage space.

Plan number DPI-2379-AJ92-SW93. The plan price is $438.30. You may choose either five sets of bluelines or a reproducible mylar. Plan by Design Profile, Inc.

The diagrams presented here constitute only floor plans and elevations. Purchasers are advised to consult their state and local building regulations and a state-certified architect prior to any construction related to these plans.

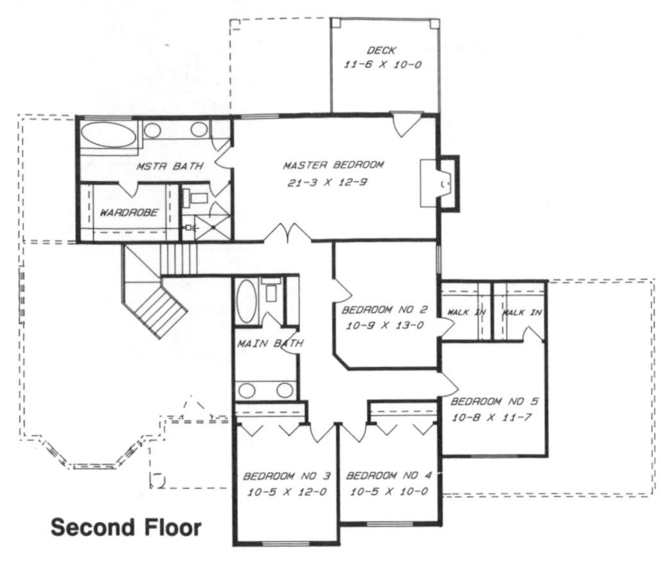

Second Floor

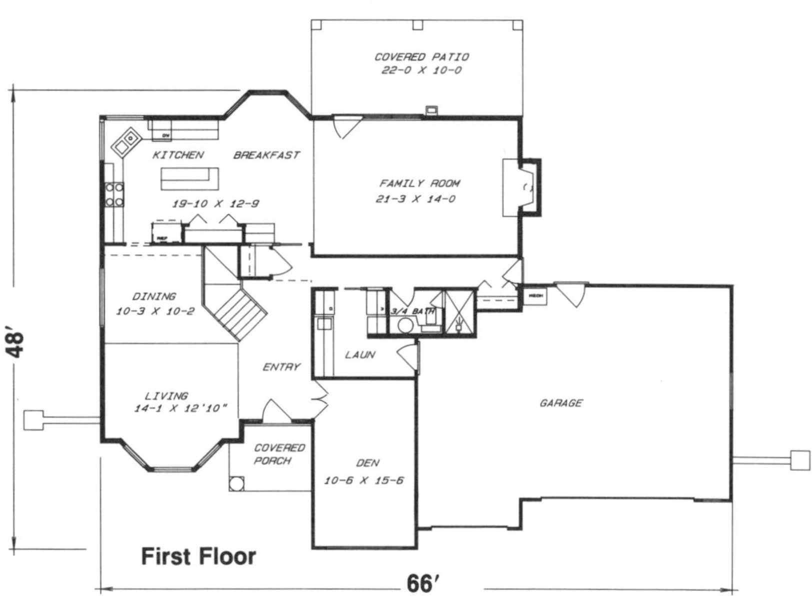

First Floor

Plan number DPI-2340-SW93

Plan number DPI-2341-SW93

Plan number DPI-2342-SW93

Downsized Ranch Is Modest In Size, Not Design Excitement

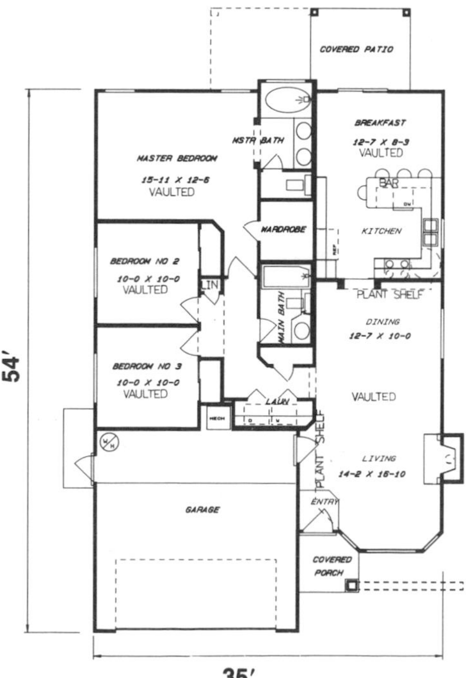

Total living space—1346 sq. ft.
3 bedrooms, 2 baths
Shown with concrete slab construction

- Space-expanding vaulted ceilings are used throughout the interior.
- Archways add a custom element to the entries to the dining room and the master bath.
- Seating is provided at the kitchen counter/snack bar.
- Breakfast area provides access to a covered patio.
- Order each elevation separately.

The plan price is $300.00. You may choose either five sets of bluelines or a reproducible mylar. Plan by Design Profile, Inc.

The diagrams presented here constitute only floor plans and elevations. Purchasers are advised to consult their state and local building regulations and a state-certified architect prior to any construction related to these plans.

Plan number DPI-2398-9002-SW93

Plan number DPI-2399-9002-SW93

Exceptional Ranch Features Comfortable Gathering Areas, Privacy Too

Total living space—1743 sq. ft.
3-4 bedrooms, 2 baths
Shown with concrete slab construction

- Versatile den/guest room boasts of a quiet, yet accessible location.
- Master suite has a large bath with an adjoining walk-in closet.
- Handy snack bar separates the kitchen and the breakfast nook.
- Main bath features a very handy dual sink vanity.
- Order each elevation separately.

The plan price is $300.00. You may choose either five sets of bluelines or a reproducible mylar. Plan by Design Profile, Inc.

The diagrams presented here constitute only floor plans and elevations. Purchasers are advised to consult their state and local building regulations and a state-certified architect prior to any construction related to these plans.

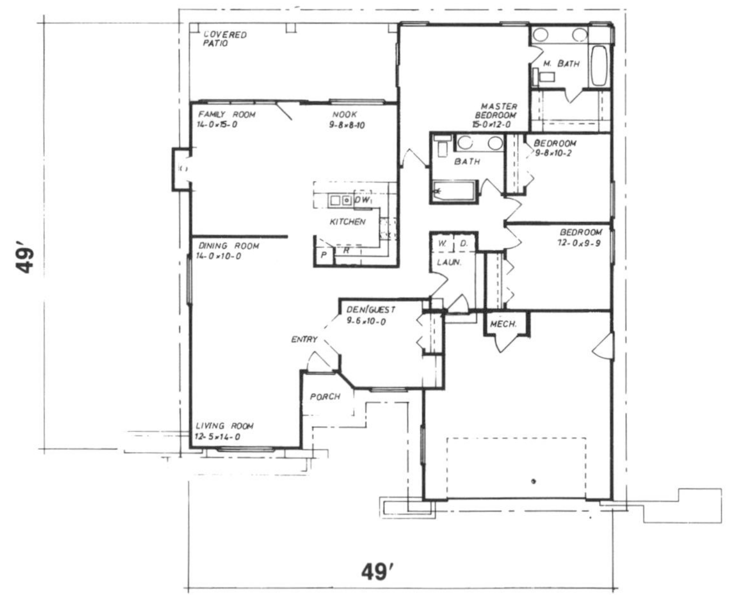

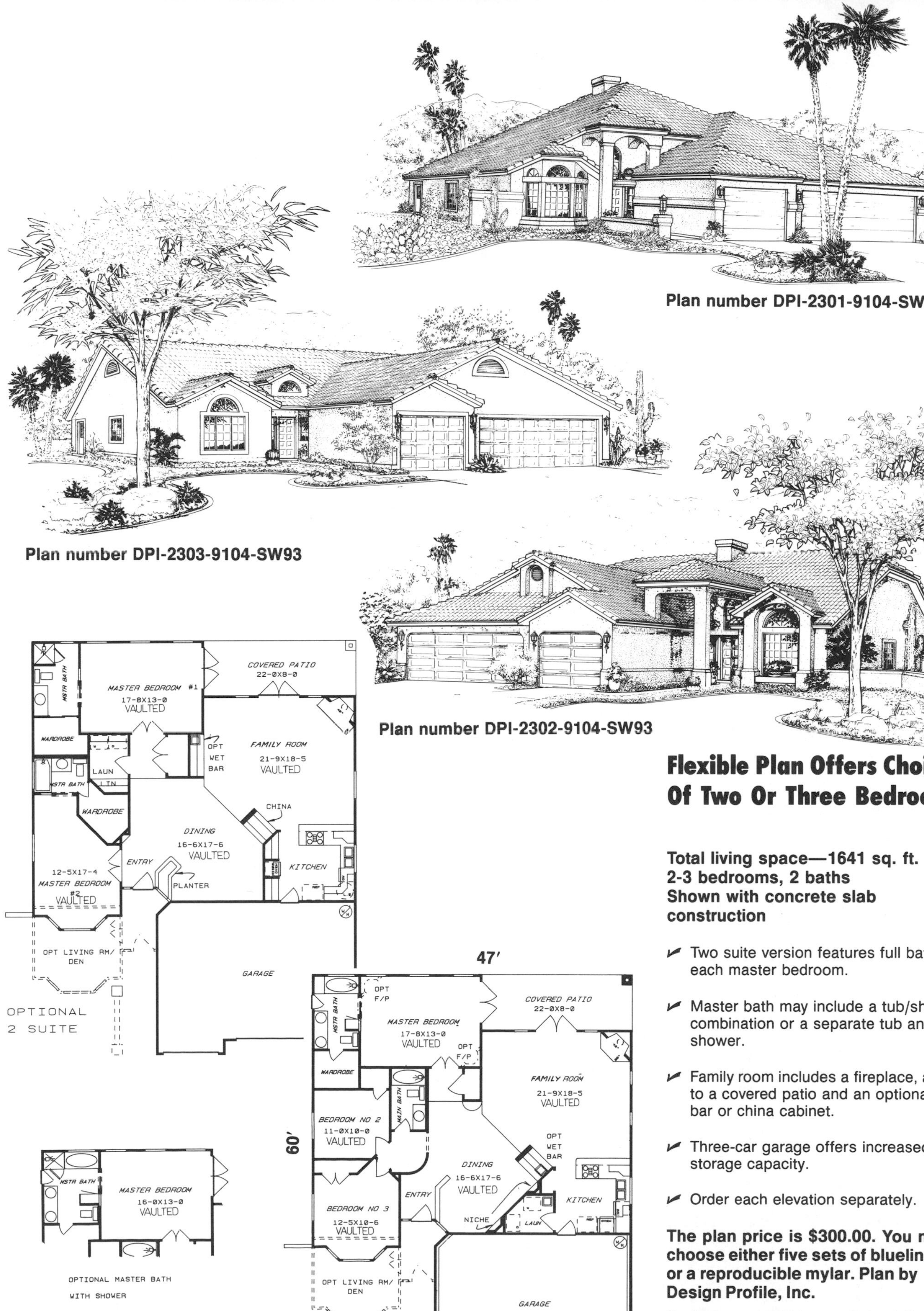

Plan number DPI-2301-9104-SW93

Plan number DPI-2303-9104-SW93

Plan number DPI-2302-9104-SW93

Flexible Plan Offers Choice Of Two Or Three Bedrooms

Total living space—1641 sq. ft.
2-3 bedrooms, 2 baths
Shown with concrete slab construction

- Two suite version features full baths in each master bedroom.
- Master bath may include a tub/shower combination or a separate tub and shower.
- Family room includes a fireplace, access to a covered patio and an optional wet bar or china cabinet.
- Three-car garage offers increased storage capacity.
- Order each elevation separately.

The plan price is $300.00. You may choose either five sets of bluelines or a reproducible mylar. Plan by Design Profile, Inc.

The diagrams presented here constitute only floor plans and elevations. Purchasers are advised to consult their state and local building regulations and a state-certified architect prior to any construction related to these plans.

Plan number DPI-2325A-9012-SW93

Plan number DPI-2325-9012-SW93

Plan number DPI-2325C-9012-SW93

Choice Of Exteriors, Unfinished Basement Gives This Ranch Plenty Of Options

Main floor—1465 sq. ft.
Basement—1475 sq. ft.
Total living space—2940 sq. ft.
6 bedrooms, 3 baths
Shown with a basement

- Railings with newel posts separate the entry and formal room which can be used as a living or dining room.
- Informal zone is created by the combined space of the family room, breakfast bay and kitchen.
- Master bath includes a separate shower and a corner whirlpool tub.
- Pantry and built-in desk are included in the kitchen.
- Order each elevation separately.

The plan price is $441.00. You may choose either five sets of bluelines or a reproducible mylar. Plan by Design Profile, Inc.

The diagrams presented here constitute only floor plans and elevations. Purchasers are advised to consult their state and local building regulations and a state-certified architect prior to any construction related to these plans.

Plan number DPI-2325D-9012-SW93

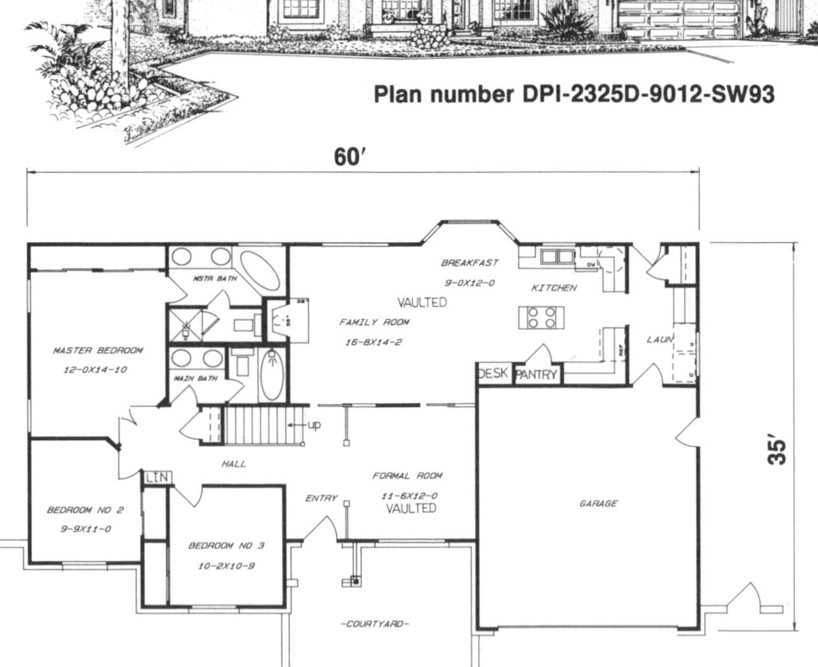

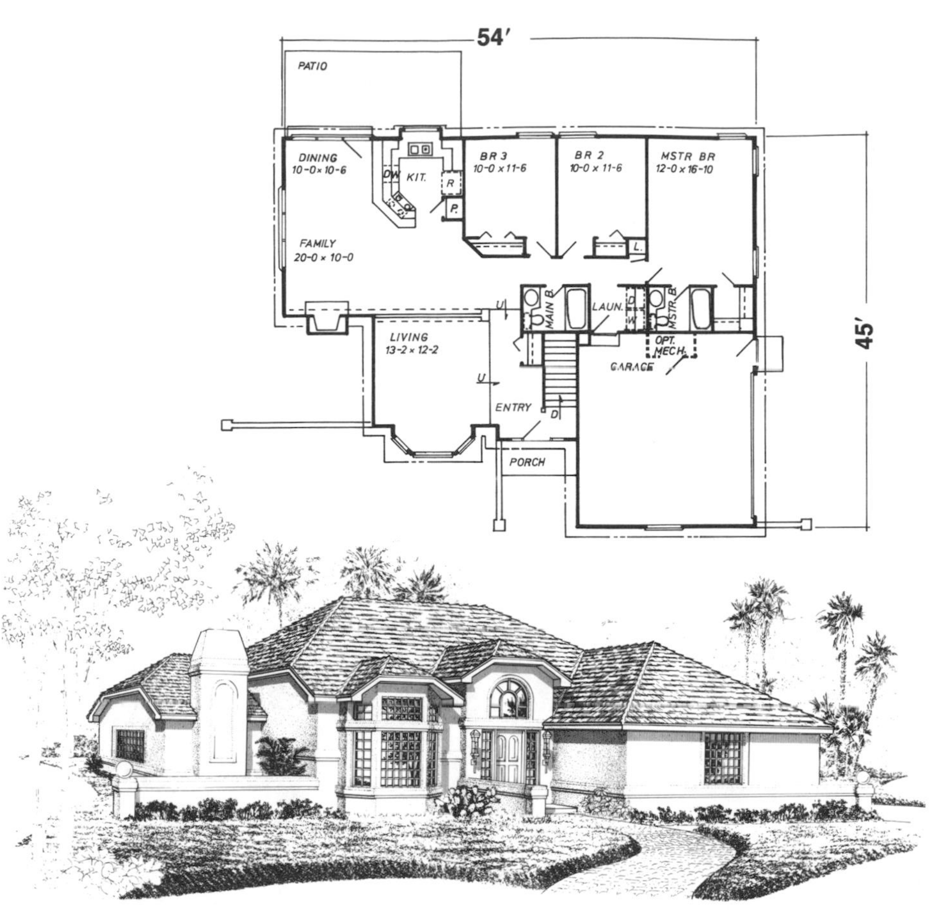

Lovely Bay Window Highlights Living Room In Cozy Ranch

Total living space—1452 sq. ft.
3 bedrooms, 2 baths
Shown with a basement

- Elevated foyer includes a convenient coat closet.
- Open rail with a plant shelf above separates the living and family areas.
- Family room has a fireplace and a view through the dining area to the patio beyond.
- Master bedroom has a private bath and a walk-in closet.

Plan number DPI-2392-AJ92-SW93. The plan price is $300.00. You may choose either five sets of bluelines or a reproducible mylar. Plan by Design Profile, Inc.

The diagrams presented here constitute only floor plans and elevations. Purchasers are advised to consult their state and local building regulations and a state-certified architect prior to any construction related to these plans.

Master Suite Is Totally Private, Luxurious

Total living space—1930 sq. ft.
3 bedrooms, 2 baths
Shown with concrete slab construction

- Attractive columns define the area of the formal dining room.
- Family room features a fireplace as its focal point.
- Kitchen sink is incorporated into a bay window.
- Master bath includes a tub, shower, dual vanity and adjoining walk-in closet.
- Extra-deep, two-car garage offers additional storage space.

Plan number DPI-M2395-9002-SW93. The plan price is $300.00. You may choose either five sets of bluelines or a reproducible mylar. Plan by Design Profile, Inc.

The diagrams presented here constitute only floor plans and elevations. Purchasers are advised to consult their state and local building regulations and a state-certified architect prior to any construction related to these plans.

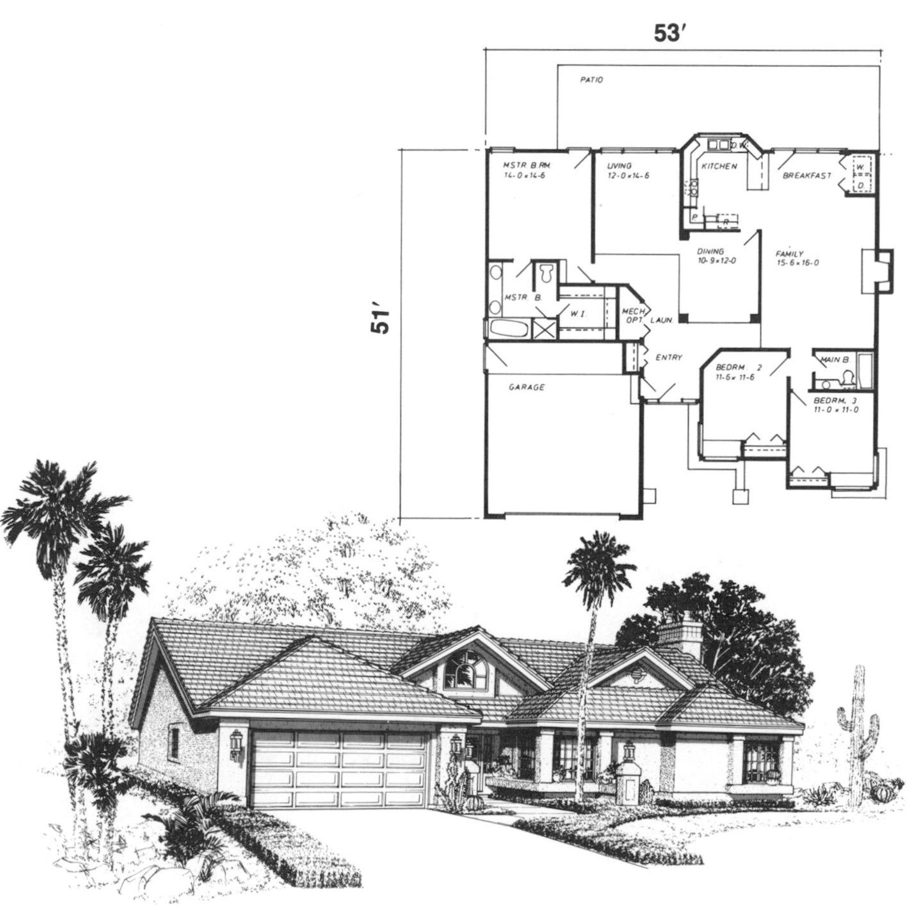

Unfinished Basement Offers Ranch Room To Grow

Total living space—1535 sq. ft.
Unfinished basement—729 sq. ft.
3-5 bedrooms, 2-3 baths
Shown with a basement

- Archways and plant shelves customize the interior.
- Vaulted ceilings are included in the living and dining rooms and the kitchen.
- Master suite has an enormous walk-in closet.
- An optional fireplace can be included in the living room.
- Order each elevation separately.

The plan price is $300.00. You may choose either five sets of bluelines or a reproducible mylar. Plan by Design Profile, Inc.

The diagrams presented here constitute only floor plans and elevations. Purchasers are advised to consult their state and local building regulations and a state-certified architect prior to any construction related to these plans.

Plan number DPI-2329-SW93

Plan number DPI-2396-AJ92-SW93

Plan number DPI-2397-AJ92-SW93

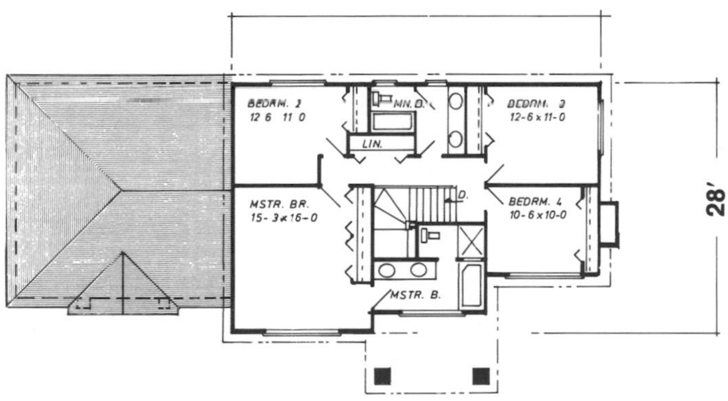

Second Floor

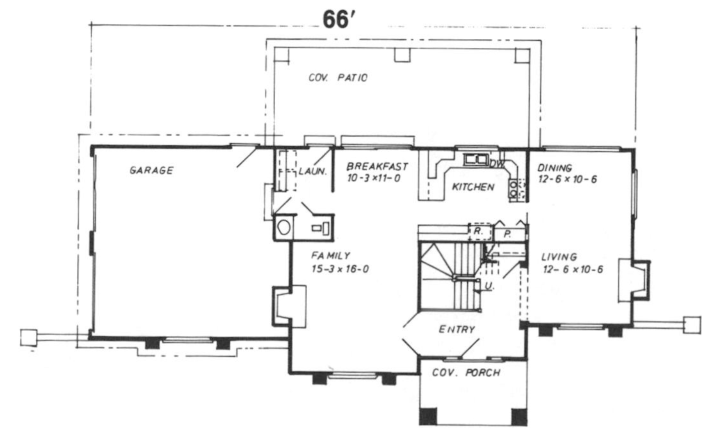

First Floor

Separate Entertaining Spaces, Equally Exciting

First floor—1048 sq. ft.
Second floor—1038 sq. ft.
Total living space—2086 sq. ft.
4 bedrooms, 2½ baths
Shown with a basement

- Double doors can be used to close off the family area from the entry foyer.
- Living, dining rooms combine their space, creating a large formal zone.
- Kitchen virtually surrounds you with counter and cabinet space.
- Fireplaces are featured in the family and living rooms.
- Well-placed laundry room serves as a mud room entry from the garage or the outdoors.

Plan number DPI-M2309-90M5-SW93. The plan price is $312.90. You may choose either five sets of bluelines or a reproducible mylar. Plan by Design Profile, Inc.

The diagrams presented here constitute only floor plans and elevations. Purchasers are advised to consult their state and local building regulations and a state-certified architect prior to any construction related to these plans.

Finished Basement Means Plenty Of Space For Fun And Games

Main floor—1461 sq. ft.
Unfinished lower floor—1404 sq. ft.
3-4 bedrooms, 2-3 baths
Shown with a basement

- Space enhancing vaulted ceilings are featured throughout the main floor.
- Master suite includes a built-in bookcase, and a make-up table in its amenity-packed bath.
- Kitchen boasts of a center island, a breakfast bay and a large, corner pantry.
- Bedroom two features a built-in desk.
- Basement plan calls for a spacious game room, plus two large bedrooms and the utility room.

Plan number DPI-2354-SW93. The plan price is $300.00. You may choose either five sets of bluelines or a reproducible mylar. Plan by Design Profile, Inc.

The diagrams presented here constitute only floor plans and elevations. Purchasers are advised to consult their state and local building regulations and a state-certified architect prior to any construction related to these plans.

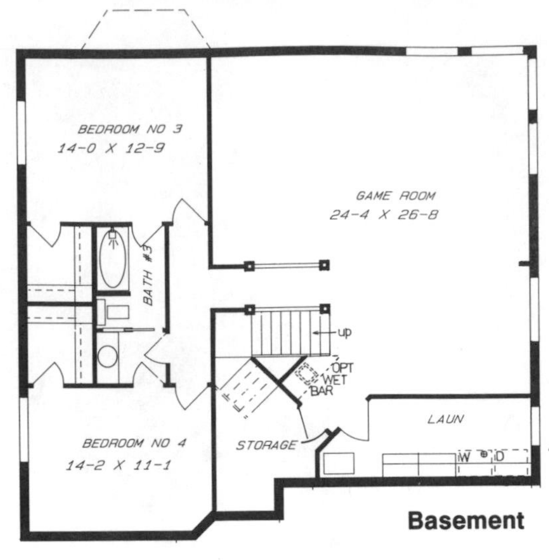

Basement

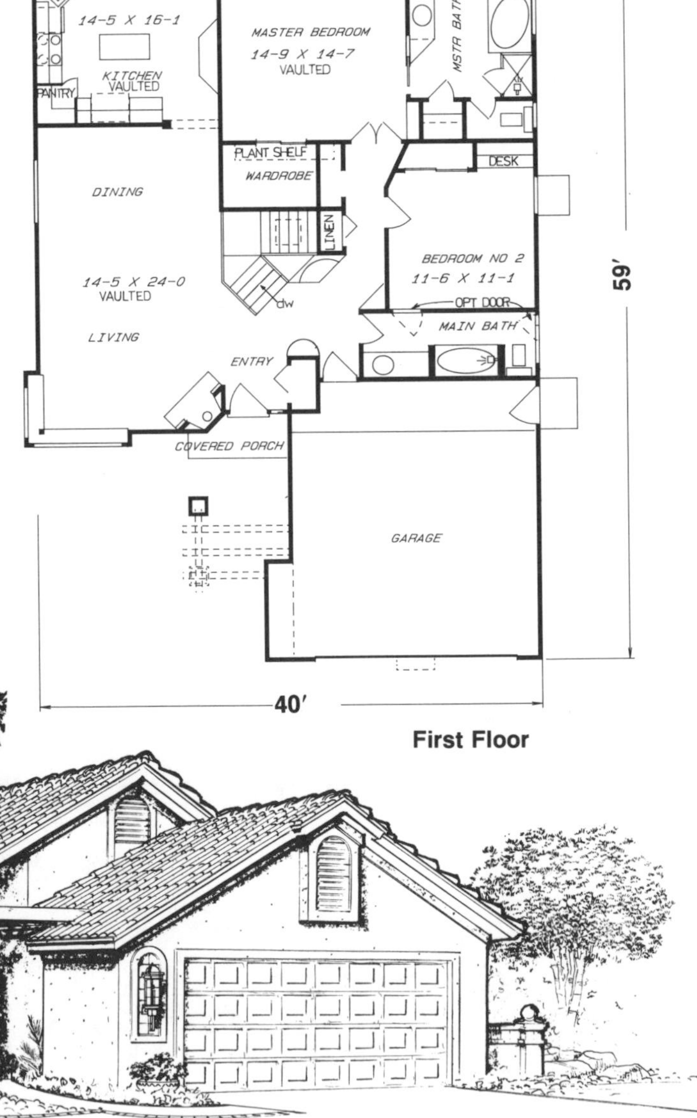

First Floor

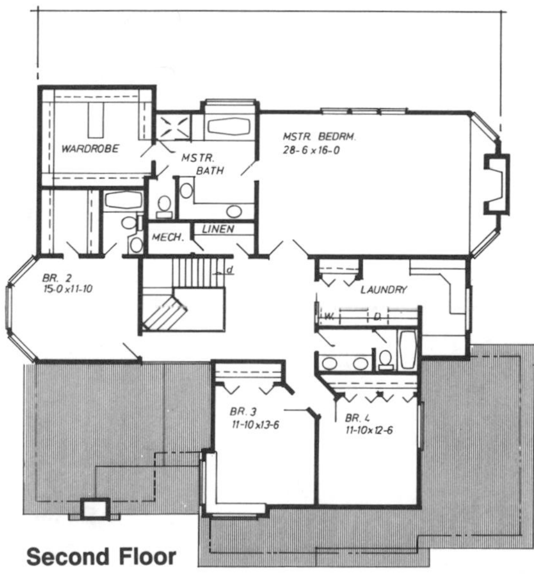

Second Floor

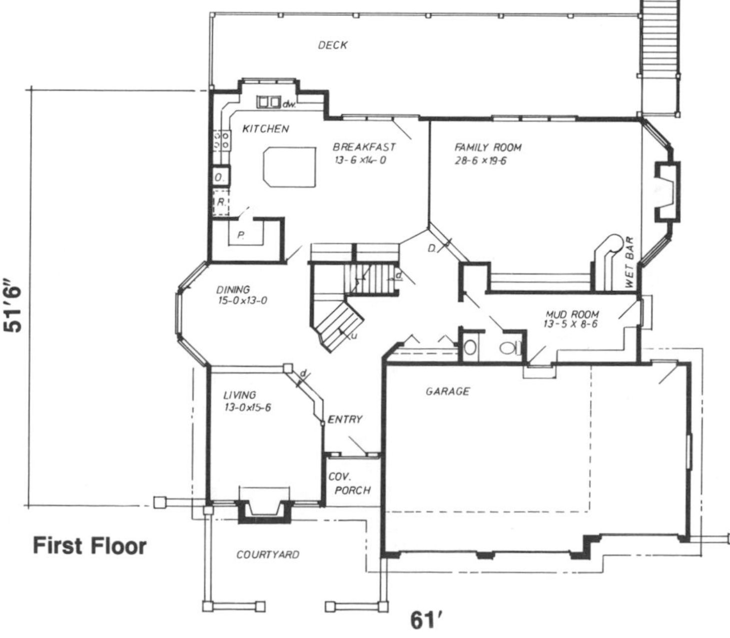

First Floor

Sprawling Executive Home Offers Every Luxury

First floor—1920 sq. ft.
Second floor—2082 sq. ft.
Total living space—4002 sq. ft.
Unfinished basement—1962 sq. ft.
4-6 bedrooms, 3-4½ baths
Shown with a basement

- Main floor mud room features a built-in bench and a drinking fountain.
- Exceptional second-floor laundry is both convenient and spacious offering bonus storage.
- Island kitchen boasts of a center bar, a walk-in pantry, built-in ovens and a hutch and phone desk.
- Dramatic windows flank the family room's fireplace, with adjoining wet bar.
- Double doors open into the glamorous master suite.

Plan number DPI-2349-SW93. The plan price is $600.30. You may choose either five sets of bluelines or a reproducible mylar. Plan by Design Profile, Inc.

The diagrams presented here constitute only floor plans and elevations. Purchasers are advised to consult their state and local building regulations and a state-certified architect prior to any construction related to these plans.

Three-Way Fireplace Shares Its Charm With Living, Dining Rooms

First floor—938 sq. ft.
Second floor—472 sq. ft.
Total living space—1410 sq. ft.
Unfinished basement—600 sq. ft.
1-3 bedrooms, 2-3 baths
Shown with a basement

- Split-level floor plan divides the living space maximizing privacy in minimal space.
- Den is well suited for use as a second bedroom or guest room.
- Master suite occupies the entire second floor.
- Handy closet in the kitchen hides the washer and dryer.
- Finishing the lower floor will add a large bedroom plus a game room.

Plan number DPI-2353-SW93. The plan price is $300.00. You may choose either five sets of bluelines or a reproducible mylar. Plan by Design Profile, Inc.

The diagrams presented here constitute only floor plans and elevations. Purchasers are advised to consult their state and local building regulations and a state-certified architect prior to any construction related to these plans.

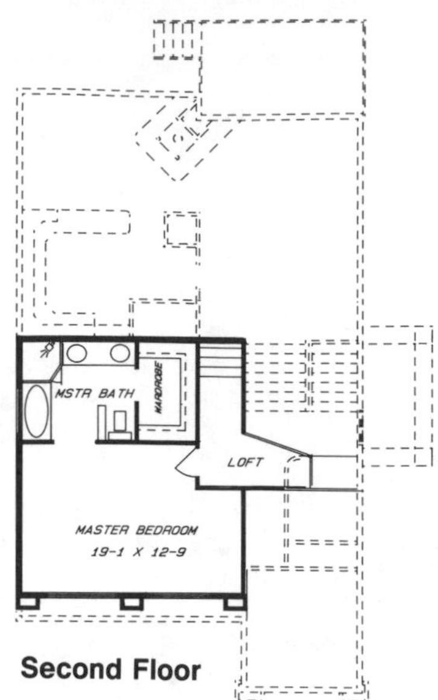

Second Floor

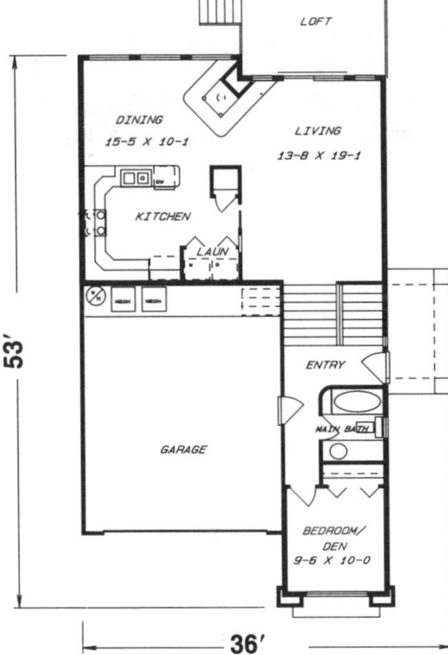

First Floor

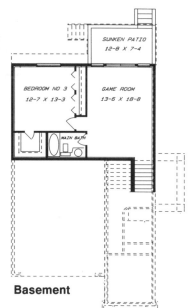

SUNKEN PATIO
12-8 X 7-4
BEDROOM NO 3
12-7 X 13-3
GAME ROOM
13-6 X 18-8
MAIN BATH

Basement

Second Floor

First Floor

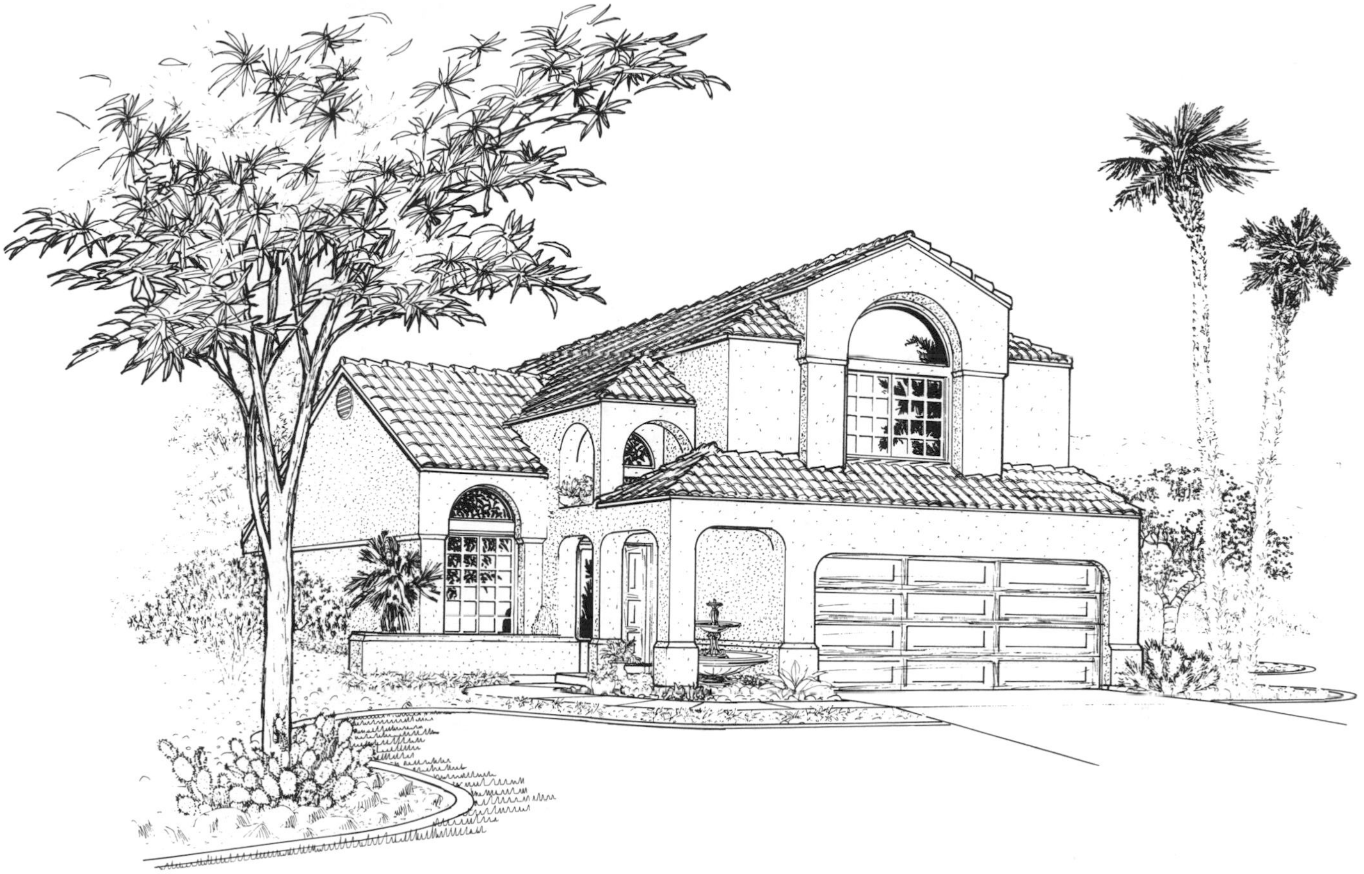

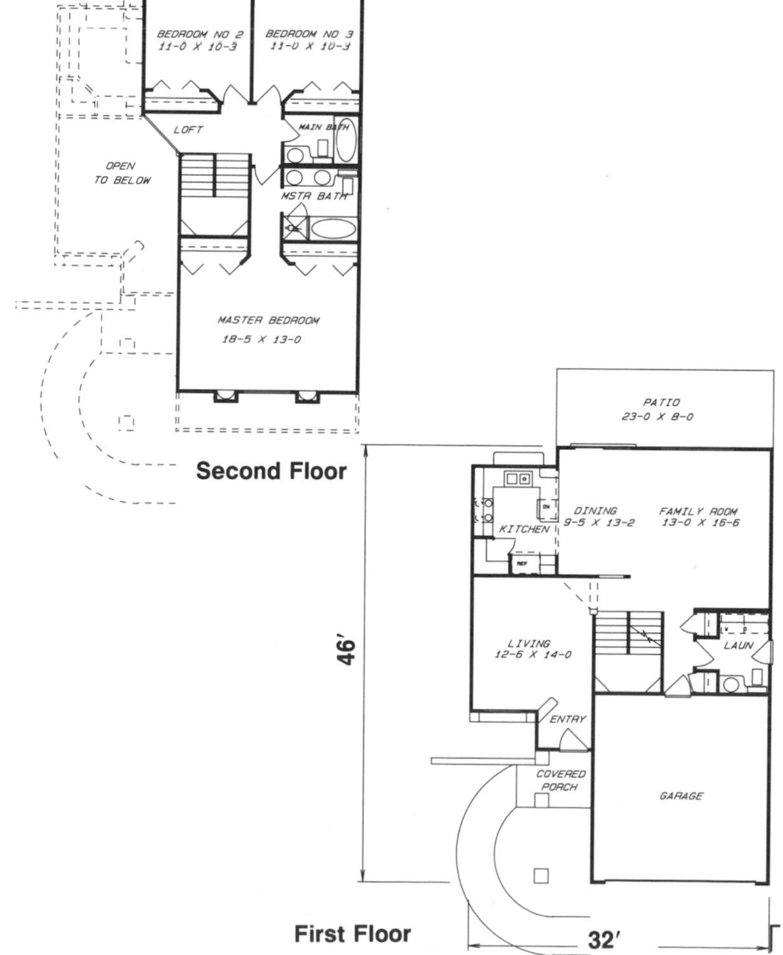

Loft Offers A View Into Lovely Living Room Below

First floor—866 sq. ft.
Second floor—798 sq. ft.
Total living space—1664 sq. ft.
3 bedrooms, 2½ baths
Shown with a basement

- Formal entry is separated from the actual living room by a half wall.
- Family and dining rooms combine visual space to create a large recreation area.
- Corner pantry in the kitchen provides generous storage potential.
- Master bedroom includes his-and-hers closets and its own bathroom with a separate tub and shower.
- Staircase landing is accented by display niches.

Plan number DPI-2352-SW93. The plan price is $300.00. You may choose either five sets of bluelines or a reproducible mylar. Plan by Design Profile, Inc.

The diagrams presented here constitute only floor plans and elevations. Purchasers are advised to consult their state and local building regulations and a state-certified architect prior to any construction related to these plans.

Courtyard Creates Private Entry, Lovely View From Dining Room

Total living space—1647 sq. ft.
3 bedrooms, 2 baths
Shown with a basement

- Handy coat closet is included in the main foyer.
- Skylights provide natural illumination inside.
- Great room views are concentrated to the rear deck through plentiful windows.
- Master suite has a private bath/dressing area and access to the rear deck.

Plan number DPI-2387-AJ92-SW93. The plan price is $300.00. You may choose either five sets of bluelines or a reproducible mylar. Plan by Design Profile, Inc.

The diagrams presented here constitute only floor plans and elevations. Purchasers are advised to consult their state and local building regulations and a state-certified architect prior to any construction related to these plans.

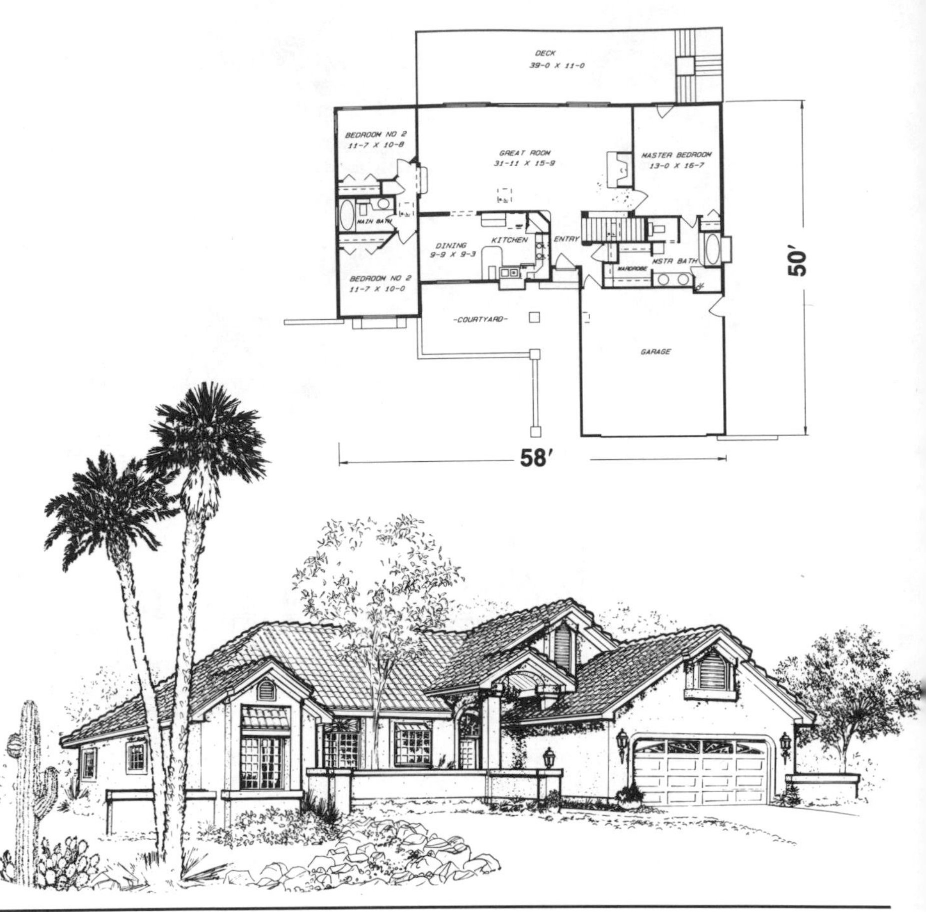

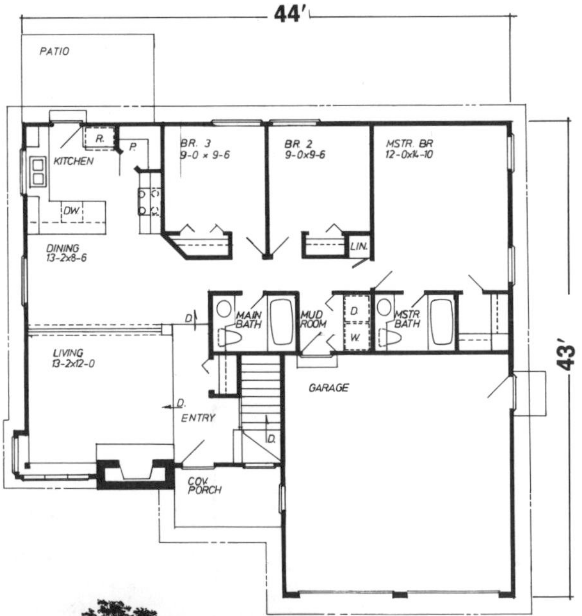

Private Bath, Walk-In Closet Make Master Bedroom Special

Total living space—1154 sq. ft.
3 bedrooms, 2 baths
Shown with a basement

- Elevated entry includes a handy coat closet.
- Bright corner window, fireplace are included in the living room.
- Separate dining area is provided, or choose to sit at the kitchen snack bar.
- Walk-in pantry in the kitchen provides plenty of storage space.
- Central location of the main bath is convenient to the bedrooms, living areas.

Plan number DPI-2389-SW93. The plan price is $300.00. You may choose either five sets of bluelines or a reproducible mylar. Plan by Design Profile, Inc.

The diagrams presented here constitute only floor plans and elevations. Purchasers are advised to consult their state and local building regulations and a state-certified architect prior to any construction related to these plans.

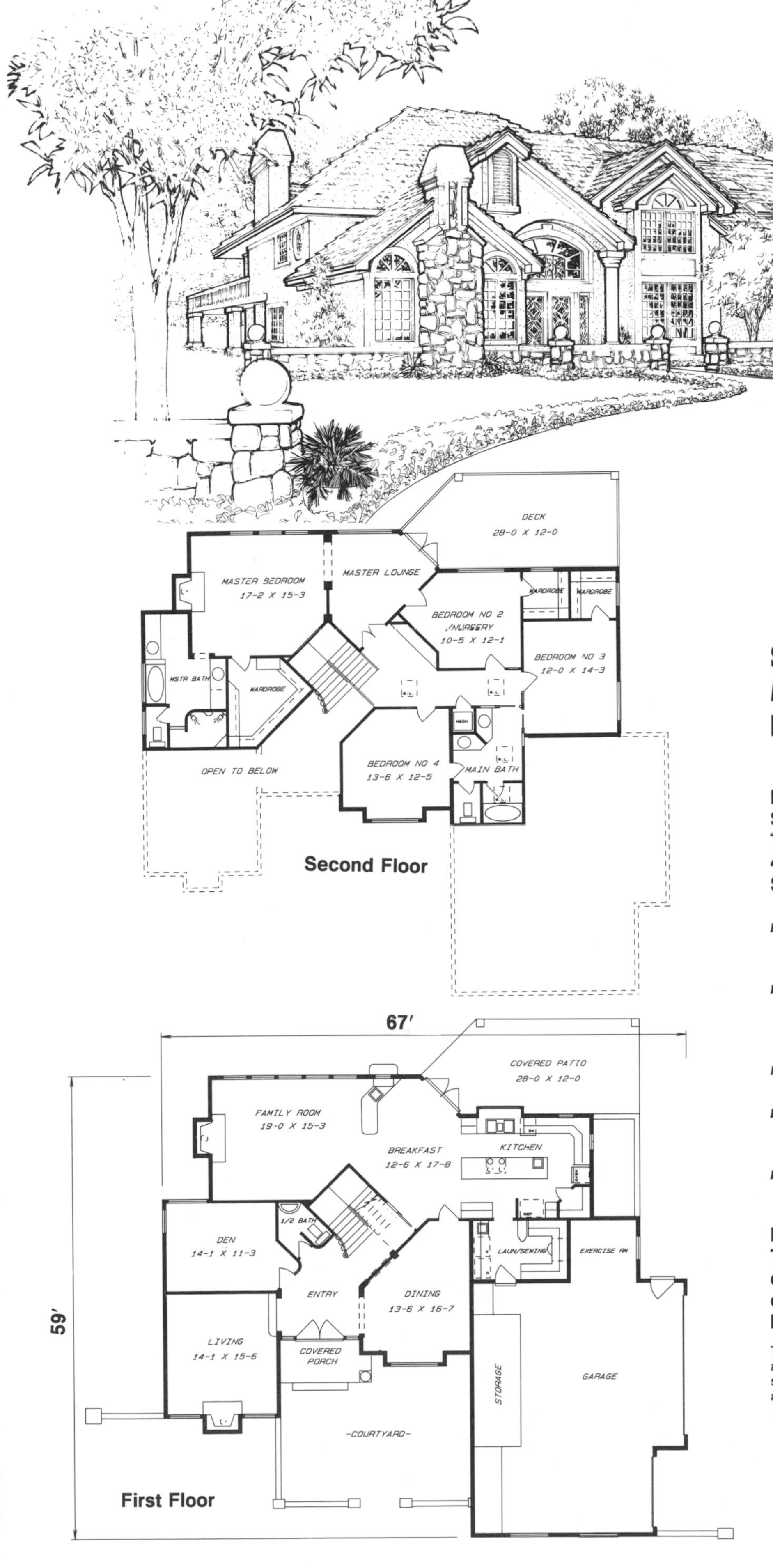

Separation Of Space Means Plenty Of Privacy In Luxury Two Story

First floor—1731 sq. ft.
Second floor—1587 sq. ft.
Total living space—3318 sq. ft.
4 bedrooms, 2½ baths
Shown with a basement

- Separate living and dining rooms create a formal atmosphere when entertaining.
- Plush master suite includes a lounge complete with French doors leading to a private deck.
- Living and family rooms have fireplaces.
- Skylights illuminate the interior hallways and main bath on the second floor.
- Abundant storage space is incorporated into the three-car garage.

Plan number DPI-L2303-89MJ-SW93. The plan price is $497.70. You may choose either five sets of bluelines or a reproducible mylar. Plan by Design Profile, Inc.

The diagrams presented here constitute only floor plans and elevations. Purchasers are advised to consult their state and local building regulations and a state-certified architect prior to any construction related to these plans.

Spacious Family Room Offers Comfort With Style

First floor—1175 sq. ft.
Second floor—899 sq. ft.
Total living space—2074 sq. ft.
3-4 bedrooms, 2½ baths
Shown with a basement

- Display niche adds a custom touch in the foyer.
- Large windows, volume ceilings and an open design make the living and dining rooms seem spacious.
- Eye-catching plant shelf surrounds the family room.
- Versatile second-floor offers the possibility of three or four bedrooms.

Plan number DPI-2373-SW93. The plan price is $311.10. You may choose either five sets of bluelines or a reproducible mylar. Plan by Design Profile, Inc.

The diagrams presented here constitute only floor plans and elevations. Purchasers are advised to consult their state and local building regulations and a state-certified architect prior to any construction related to these plans.

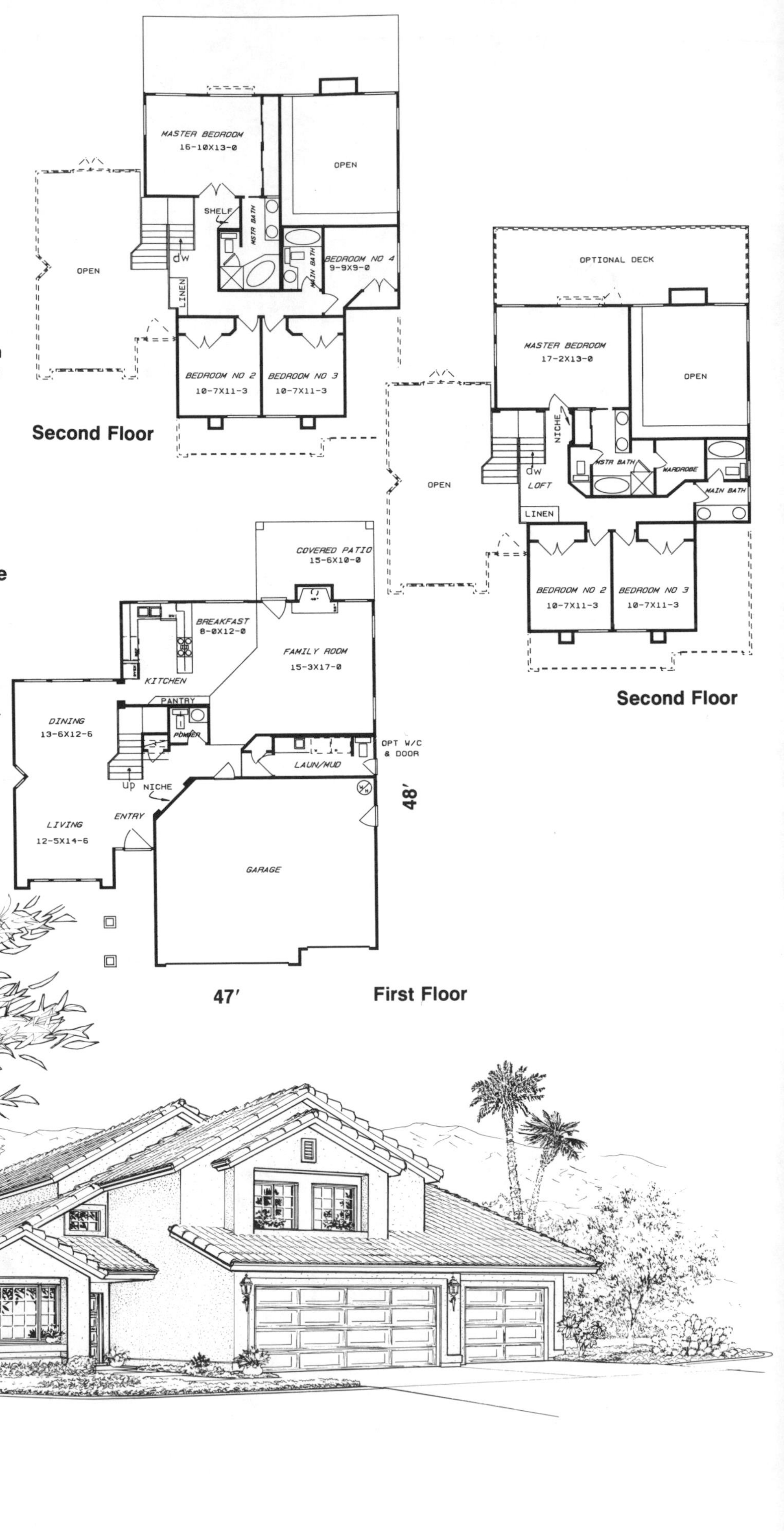

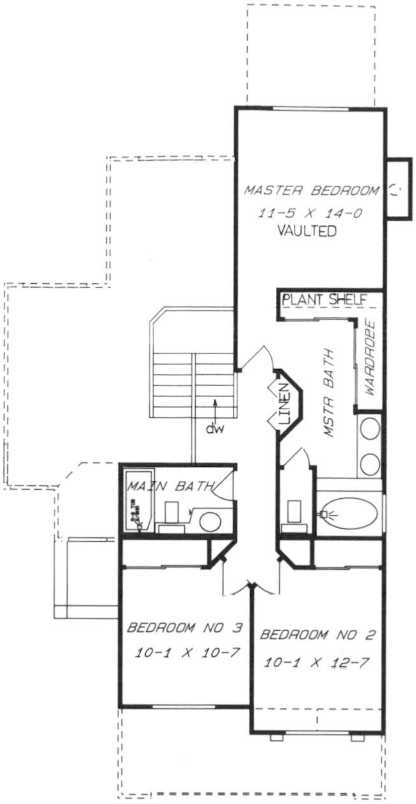

High Ceilings Turn Up The Volume In Attractive Two Story

First floor—837 sq. ft.
Second floor—766 sq. ft.
Total living space—1603 sq. ft.
3 bedrooms, 2½ baths
Shown with a basement

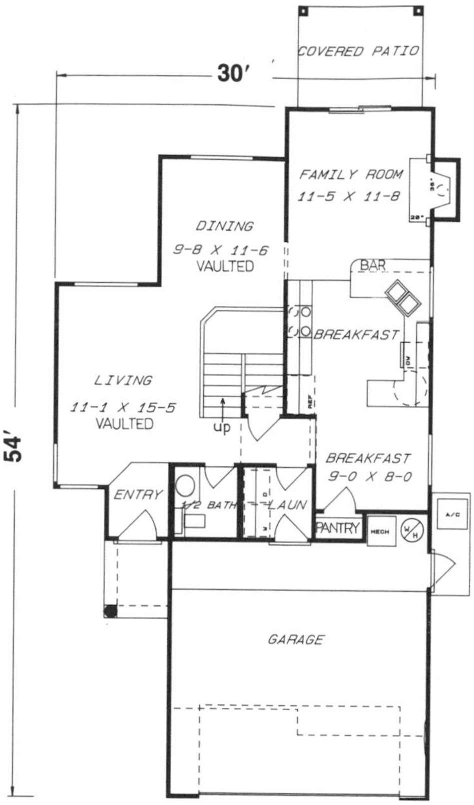

- Sliding glass doors in the family room lead to a covered patio.
- Arches highlight the entry to the dining and breakfast areas.
- Special kitchen features include a snack bar, a lazy Susan and a pantry.
- Plant shelf accents the L-shaped closet arrangement in the master suite's dressing area.
- Order each elevation separately.

The plan price is $300.00. You may choose either five sets of bluelines or a reproducible mylar. Plan by Design Profile, Inc.

The diagrams presented here constitute only floor plans and elevations. Purchasers are advised to consult their state and local building regulations and a state-certified architect prior to any construction related to these plans.

Second Floor

First Floor

Plan number DPI-2366-SW93

Plan number DPI-2368-SW93

Plan number DPI-2367-SW93

Covered Patio Expands Living Space To The Outdoors

Total living space—1992 sq. ft.
Unfinished basement—1982 sq. ft.
3-4 bedrooms, 2 baths
Shown with a basement

- Both the master suite and the family area have access to the covered rear patio.
- Storage lockers and a bench are included in the laundry.
- Built-in desk plus a closet makes the den/guest room especially versatile.
- Extra-deep, three-car garage opens into the home via a mud room.

Plan number DPI-M2396-AJ91-SW93. The plan price is $300.00. You may choose either five sets of bluelines or a reproducible mylar. Plan by Design Profile, Inc.

The diagrams presented here constitute only floor plans and elevations. Purchasers are advised to consult their state and local building regulations and a state-certified architect prior to any construction related to these plans.

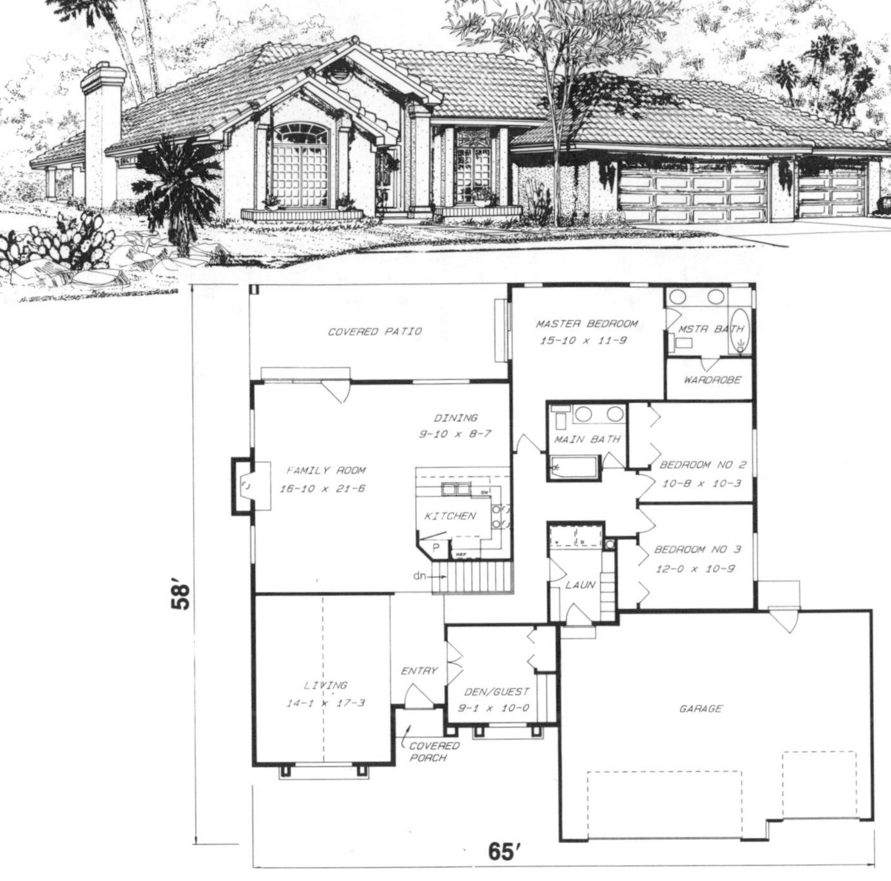

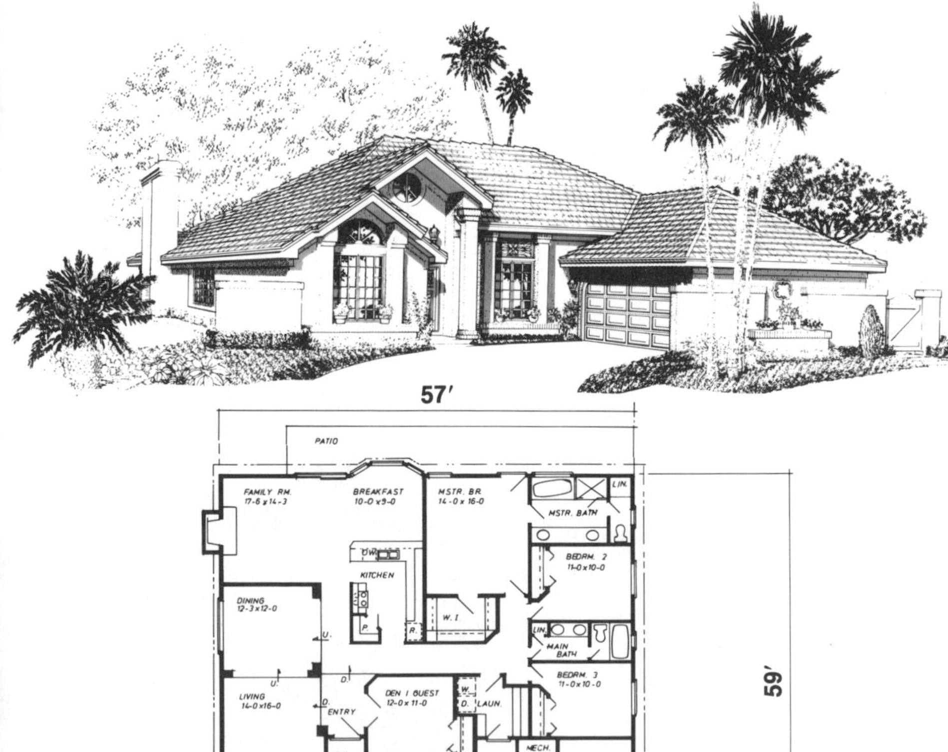

Choose Three Bedrooms Or Four In Adaptable Ranch

Total living space—2177 sq. ft.
3-4 bedrooms, 2 baths
Concrete slab construction

- Elevated dining room creates a distinctive environment for formal entertaining.
- Convenient, central kitchen has a walk-in pantry and a snack bar.
- Fireplace provides an appealing focal point in the family room.
- Compartmented main bath includes a linen closet and a dual vanity.
- Mud room/laundry entry from the garage keeps the interior spaces clean.

Plan number DPI-M2310-8908-SW93. The plan price is $326.55. You may choose either five sets of bluelines or a reproducible mylar. Plan by Design Profile, Inc.

The diagrams presented here constitute only floor plans and elevations. Purchasers are advised to consult their state and local building regulations and a state-certified architect prior to any construction related to these plans.

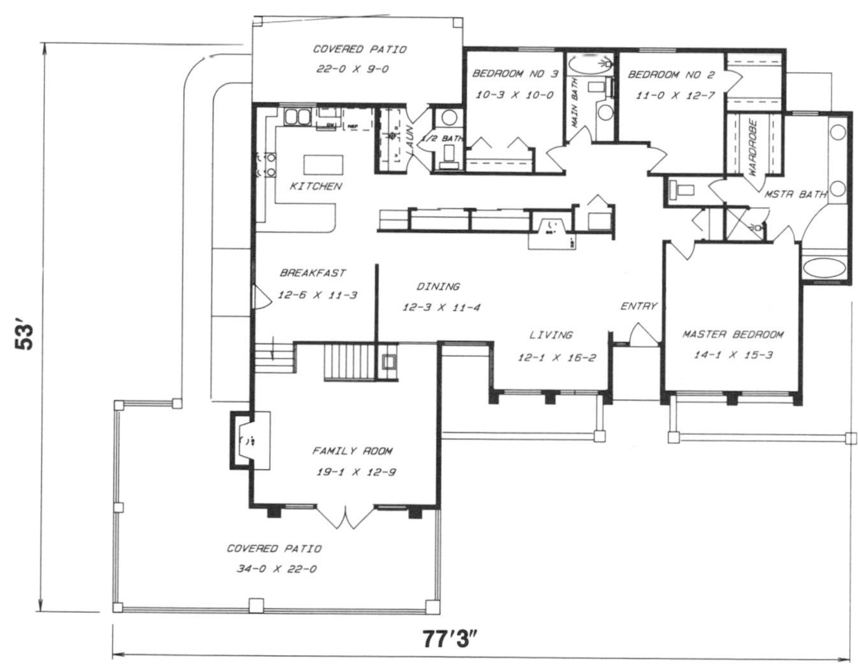

Team Attractive Split Level With A Hillside Site

Total living space—2156 sq. ft.
3 bedrooms, 2½ baths
Shown with a basement

- Foyer opens directly into the formal living room.
- Dramatic custom windows complement volume ceilings inside.
- Master bath/dressing room includes a separate tub and shower, his-and-hers vanities.
- Generous storage space is provided in the bedrooms and the kitchen.
- Fireplaces are featured in the living and family rooms.

Plan number DPI-M2302-9003-SW93. The plan price is $323.40. You may choose either five sets of bluelines or a reproducible mylar. Plan by Design Profile, Inc.

The diagrams presented here constitute only floor plans and elevations. Purchasers are advised to consult their state and local building regulations and a state-certified architect prior to any construction related to these plans.

French Doors Accent The Luxury Of Master Suite

First floor—2066 sq. ft.
Second floor—471 sq. ft.
Total living space—2537 sq. ft.
3 bedrooms, 2½ baths
Shown with a basement

- Vaulted ceilings add impact to the foyer, kitchen, living and dining rooms, and loft.
- Built-ins include display niches and a china hutch in the dining room and a desk in the kitchen.
- Handy serving buffet connects the dining areas with the living room.
- Large master suite has an oversized walk-in closet.
- Generous storage space is available on the second floor.

Plan number DPI-M2395-AJ91-SW93. The plan price is $380.55. You may choose either five sets of bluelines or a reproducible mylar. Plan by Design Profile, Inc.

The diagrams presented here constitute only floor plans and elevations. Purchasers are advised to consult their state and local building regulations and a state-certified architect prior to any construction related to these plans.

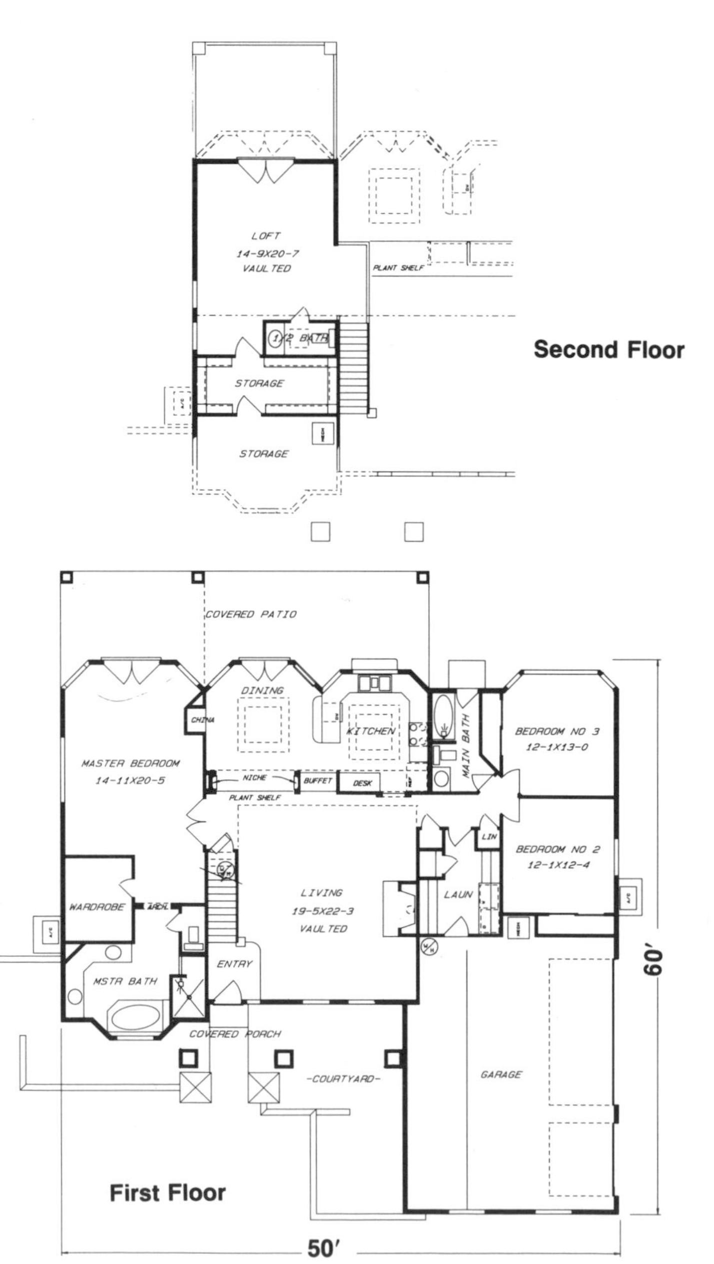

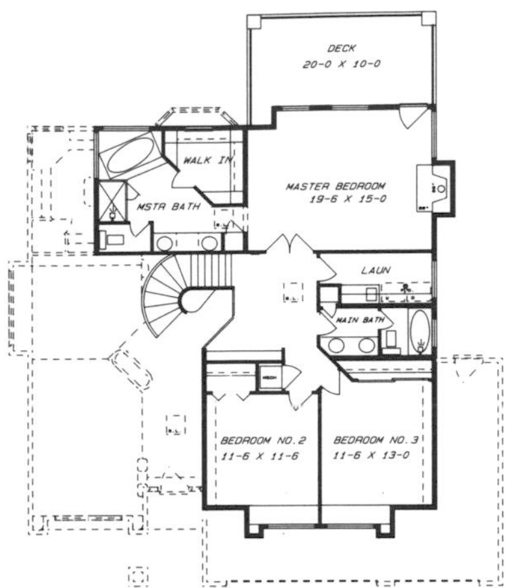

Second Floor

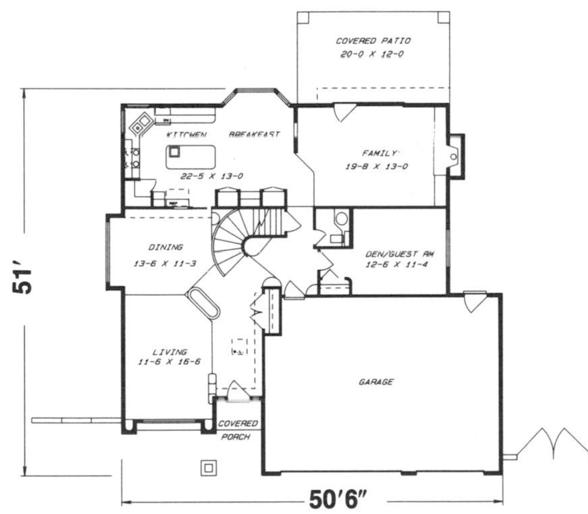

First Floor

Versatile Den/Guest Room Adds To Two Story's Appeal

First floor—1385 sq. ft.
Second floor—1184 sq. ft.
Total living space—2569 sq. ft.
3-4 bedrooms, 2½ baths
Shown with a basement

- Formal living and dining rooms share visual space, yet remain separate entertainment areas.
- Sliding interior door separates the kitchen and dining room for extra privacy.
- Walk-in corner pantry, generous counter space and a breakfast bay highlight the kitchen.
- Plush master suite includes a luxurious bath and a private deck.
- Skylights illuminate interior hallways.

Plan number DPI-M2310-90M5-SW93. The plan price is $385.35. You may choose either five sets of bluelines or a reproducible mylar. Plan by Design Profile, Inc.

The diagrams presented here constitute only floor plans and elevations. Purchasers are advised to consult their state and local building regulations and a state-certified architect prior to any construction related to these plans.

Easy Living Ranch Revolves Around Central Kitchen

Total living space—2226 sq. ft.
4 bedrooms, 2½ baths
Shown with concrete slab construction

- Covered porch leads to the dramatic foyer, which offers views into the living and dining rooms.
- Double doors open into the den and master suite.
- Family room features a built-in bookcase and a fireplace.
- Three-car garage provides generous storage space, or room for an extra vehicle.

Plan number DPI-M2385-9002-SW93. The plan price is $333.90. You may choose either five sets of bluelines or a reproducible mylar. Plan by Design Profile, Inc.

The diagrams presented here constitute only floor plans and elevations. Purchasers are advised to consult their state and local building regulations and a state-certified architect prior to any construction related to these plans.

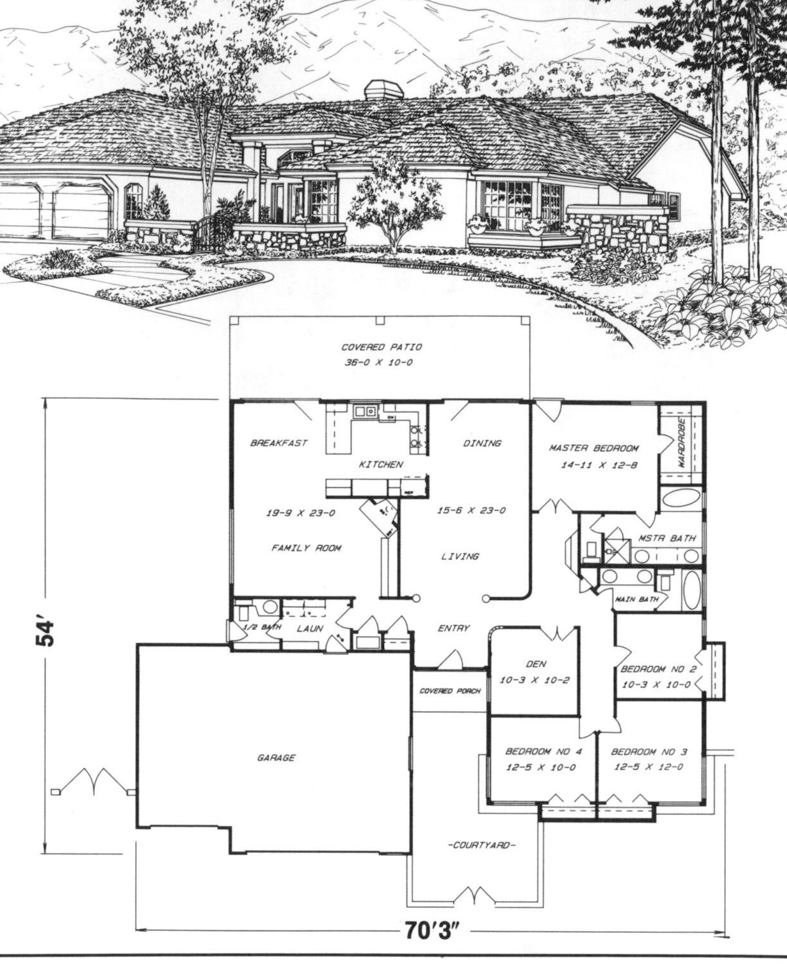

Master Suite Designed To Pamper

Total living space—2350 sq. ft.
3-4 bedrooms, 2 baths
Shown with concrete slab construction

- Master bath's spa tub features a corner setting brightened by oversized windows.
- Separate living and dining rooms are ideal for entertaining, or privacy, purposes.
- Spacious family area includes the family room, kitchen and breakfast bay.
- Skylight keeps the bedroom hallway bright and cheerful.

Plan number DPI-M2301-9003-SW93. The plan price is $352.50. You may choose either five sets of bluelines or a reproducible mylar. Plan by Design Profile, Inc.

The diagrams presented here constitute only floor plans and elevations. Purchasers are advised to consult their state and local building regulations and a state-certified architect prior to any construction related to these plans.

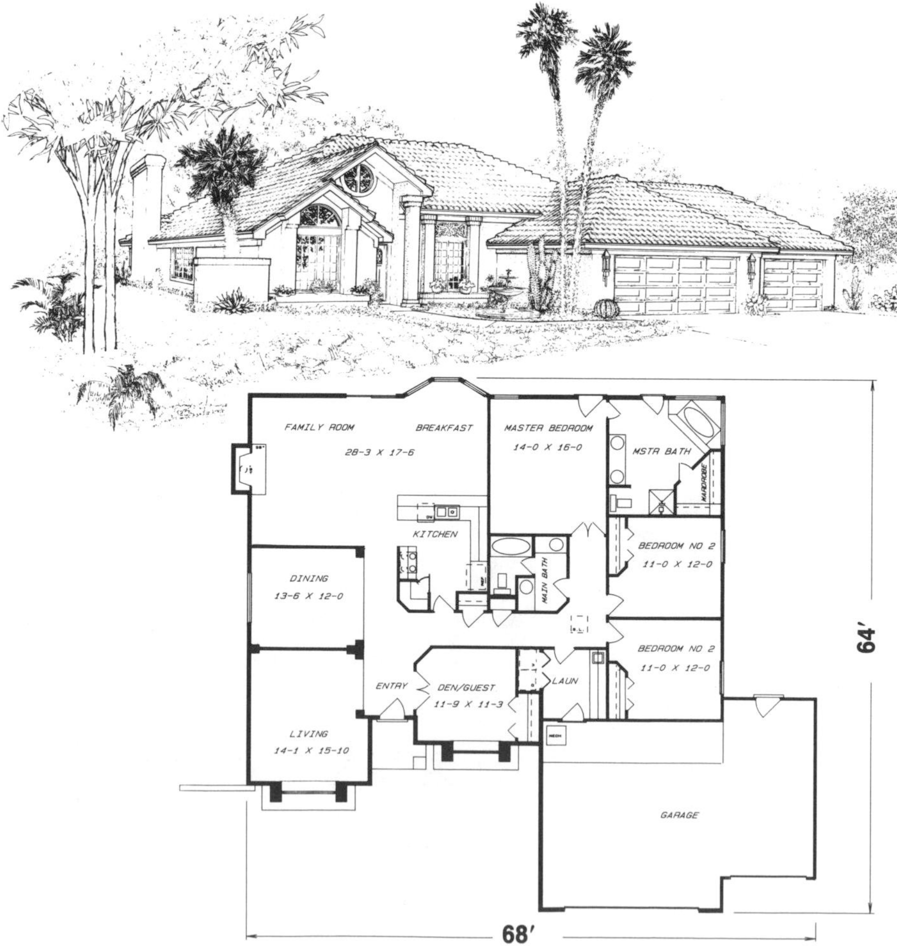

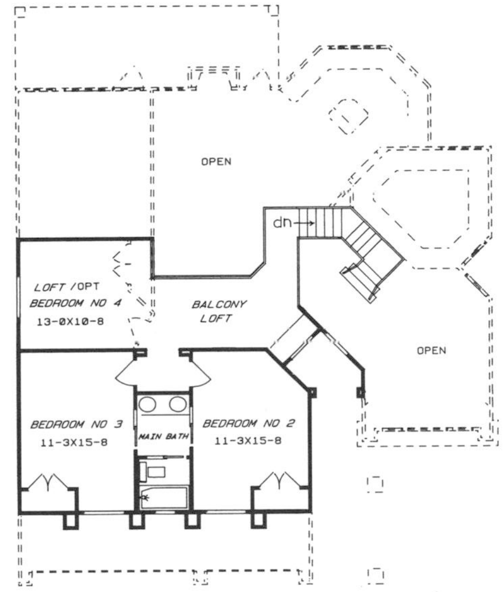

Second Floor

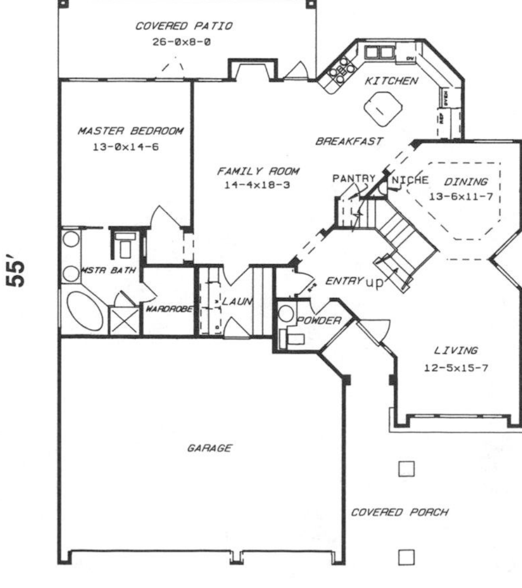

First Floor

Interior Arches Create Impressive Room Transitions

First floor—1325 sq. ft.
Second floor—753 sq. ft.
Total living space—2078 sq. ft.
3-4 bedrooms, 2½ baths
Shown with concrete slab construction

- Archways highlight the entry to the master bedroom, the family room and the dining room.
- Distinctive dining room features a dropped soffit ceiling.
- Well-planned kitchen has generous counter and cabinet space.
- Loft may be converted to a fourth bedroom.
- Main-floor location of the master suite gives it extra privacy.

Plan number DPI-2351-SW93. The plan price is $311.70. You may choose either five sets of bluelines or a reproducible mylar. Plan by Design Profile, Inc.

The diagrams presented here constitute only floor plans and elevations. Purchasers are advised to consult their state and local building regulations and a state-certified architect prior to any construction related to these plans.

Four-Bedroom Two Story Offers Optional Laundry Room Extension

First floor—1170 sq. ft.
Second floor—1065 sq. ft.
Total living space—2235 sq. ft.
4 bedrooms, 2 full baths
1-2 powder rooms
Shown with a basement

- Living and family rooms share a handy, walk-through wet bar.
- Formal dining room overlooks the covered front porch.
- Master bedroom and family room enjoy the warmth of fireplaces.
- Order each elevation separately.

The plan price is $335.25. You may choose either five sets of bluelines or a reproducible mylar. Plan by Design Profile, Inc.

The diagrams presented here constitute only floor plans and elevations. Purchasers are advised to consult their state and local building regulations and a state-certified architect prior to any construction related to these plans.

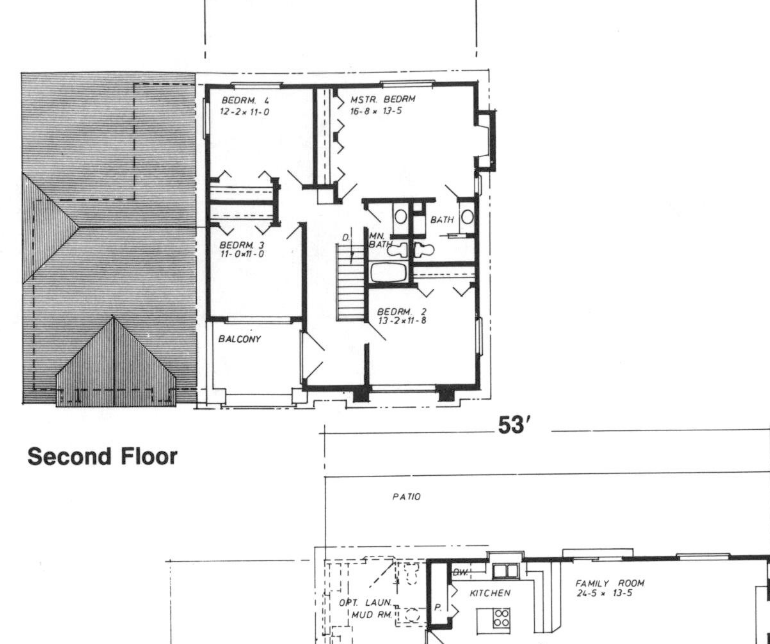

Second Floor

First Floor

Plan number DPI-2347-SW93

Plan number DPI-2348-SW93

Plan number DPI-2363-SW93

Plan number DPI-2364-SW93

Plan number DPI-2365-SW93

Dramatic Second-Floor Bridge Delivers High Excitement Inside

First floor—930 sq. ft.
Second floor—850 sq. ft.
Total living space—1780 sq. ft.
3 bedrooms, 2½ baths
Shown with concrete slab construction

- Soaring ceilings, divided by the bridge above, make the living and dining rooms unforgettable.
- Master suite occupies its own, very private section of the second floor.
- Family area is created by the combined space of the family room, breakfast nook and kitchen.
- Order each elevation separately.

The plan price is $300.00. You may choose either five sets of bluelines or a reproducible mylar. Plan by Design Profile, Inc.

The diagrams presented here constitute only floor plans and elevations. Purchasers are advised to consult their state and local building regulations and a state-certified architect prior to any construction related to these plans.

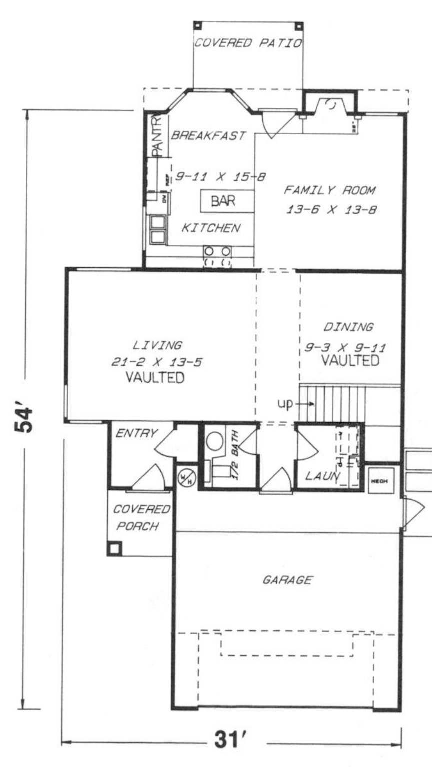

Second Floor

First Floor

Spacious Family Zone Boasts Of Cozy Corner Fireplace

Total living space—2260 sq. ft.
3 bedrooms, 2½ baths
Shown with a basement

- Formal living and dining rooms provide the right environment for entertaining.
- Family room includes a built-in bookcase.
- Walk-in pantry and a snack bar are included in the kitchen.
- Compartmented master bath includes a walk-in closet.
- Extra-large laundry/mud room features a handy coat closet and a powder room.

Plan number DPI-M2391-9002-SW93. The plan price is $339.00. You may choose either five sets of bluelines or a reproducible mylar. Plan by Design Profile, Inc.

The diagrams presented here constitute only floor plans and elevations. Purchasers are advised to consult their state and local building regulations and a state-certified architect prior to any construction related to these plans.

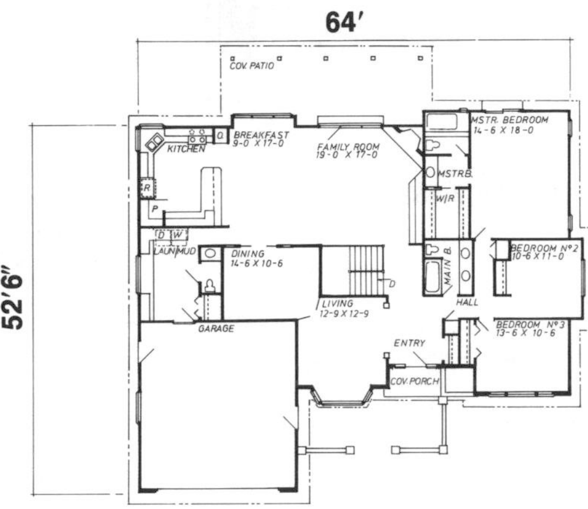

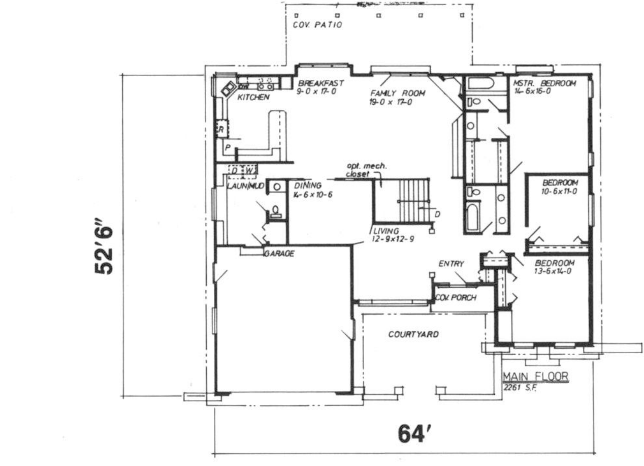

Formal, Informal Living Areas Give Ranch Plenty Of Versatility

Total living space—2261 sq. ft.
3 bedrooms, 2½ baths
Shown with a basement

- Living and dining rooms are distinctly separate areas for entertaining.
- Open arrangement of the kitchen, breakfast area and family room allow them to share visual space.
- Family room includes a fireplace and built-in bookshelves.
- Dual sink vanity is included in the main bath.

Plan number DPI-2335-SW93. The plan price is $339.15. You may choose either five sets of bluelines or a reproducible mylar. Plan by Design Profile, Inc.

The diagrams presented here constitute only floor plans and elevations. Purchasers are advised to consult their state and local building regulations and a state-certified architect prior to any construction related to these plans.

Plan number DPI-2394-AJ92-SW93

Volume Ceilings, Open Interior Expands Living Areas

Total living space—1440 sq. ft.
Unfinished basement—732 sq. ft.
3-4 bedrooms, 2-3 baths
Shown with a basement

- Attractive plant shelf accents the entry.
- Sliding glass doors in the dining room lead to a patio.
- Angled wall incorporates the living room bookcase on one side, kitchen pantry on the other.
- Master bath includes two sinks at its large vanity.
- Order each elevation separately.

The plan price is $300.00. You may choose either five sets of bluelines or a reproducible mylar. Plan by Design Profile, Inc.

The diagrams presented here constitute only floor plans and elevations. Purchasers are advised to consult their state and local building regulations and a state-certified architect prior to any construction related to these plans.

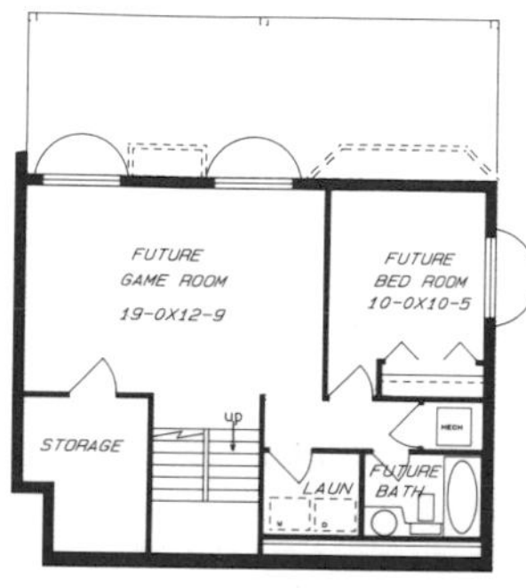

Basement

First Floor

Plan number DPI-2395-AJ92-SW93

Plan number DPI-2332-SW93

Wonderful Master Suite Occupies Its Own Floor

First Floor—1212 sq. ft.
Second floor—474 sq. ft.
Lower floor—901 sq. ft.
Total living space—2587 sq. ft.
3 bedrooms, 2½ baths
Shown with a basement

- Large bay window gives the living room extra appeal.
- Kitchen serves formal dining room or breakfast area with equal ease.
- French doors in the breakfast area open onto a deck.
- Master suite includes a compartmented bath, wall-length closet and a loft.
- Secondary bedrooms share the lower floor with a large game room.

Plan number DPI-2334-SW93. The plan price is $388.05. You may choose either five sets of bluelines or a reproducible mylar. Plan by Design Profile, Inc.

The diagrams presented here constitute only floor plans and elevations. Purchasers are advised to consult their state and local building regulations and a state-certified architect prior to any construction related to these plans.

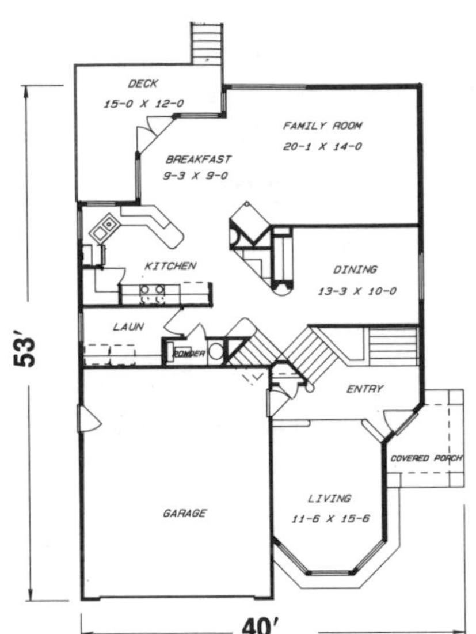

First Floor

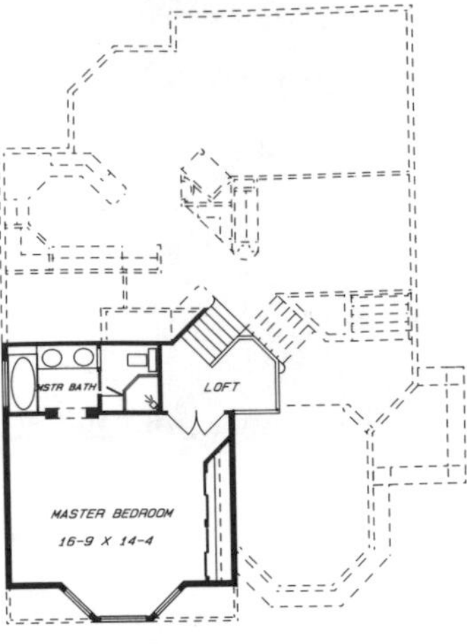

Second Floor

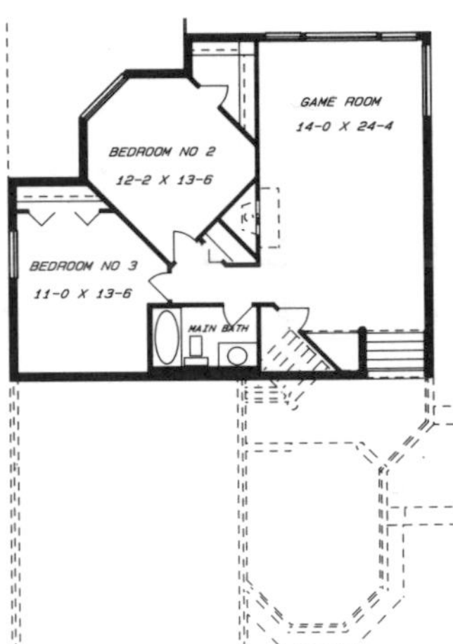

Basement

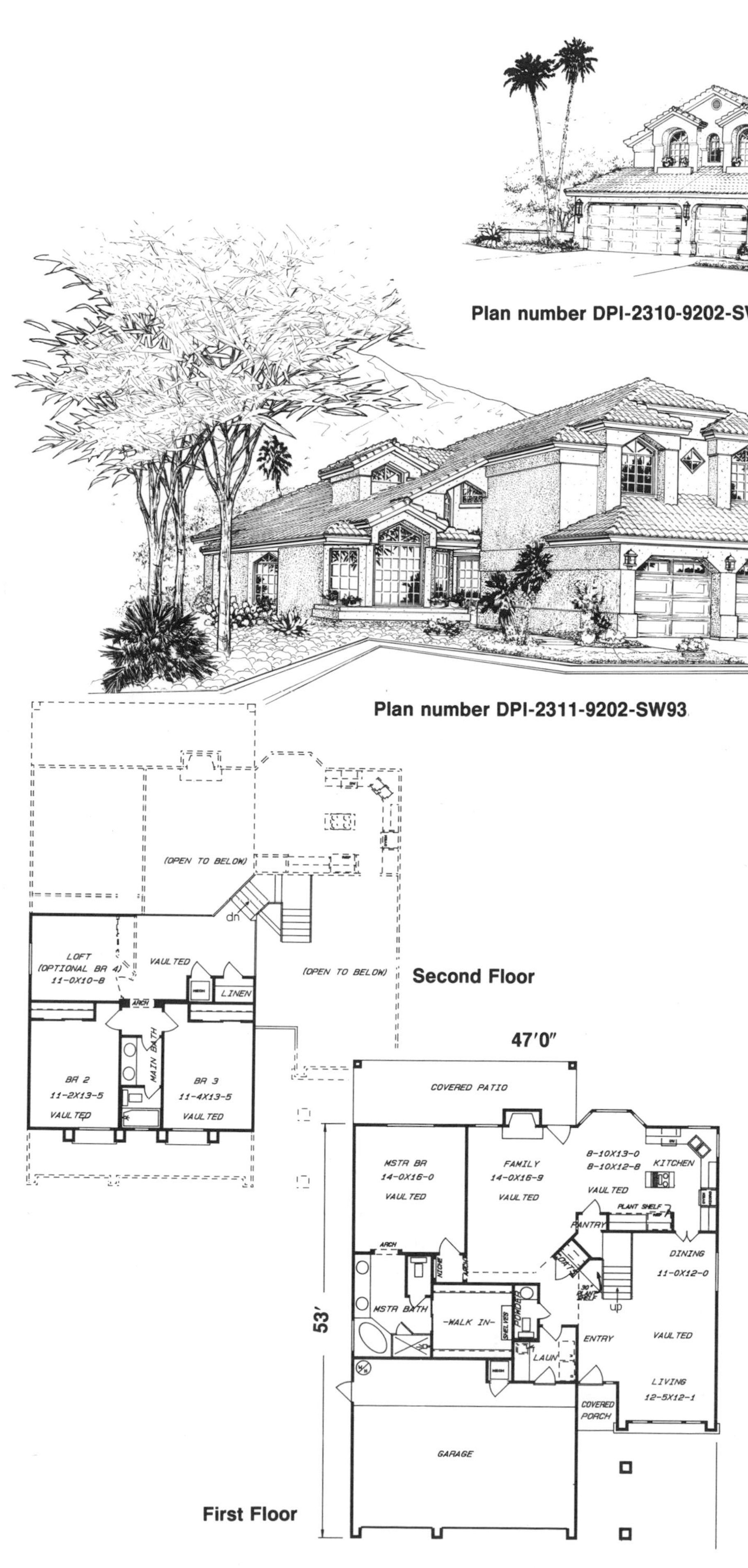

Plan number DPI-2310-9202-SW93

Plan number DPI-2311-9202-SW93

Second Floor

First Floor

Master Suite Exceptionally Private, Designed For Comfort

First floor—1589 sq. ft.
Second floor—794 sq. ft.
Total living space—2383 sq. ft.
3-4 bedrooms, 2½ baths
Shown with concrete slab construction

- Oversized master walk-in closet is accented by mirrored slide-by doors.
- Volume ceilings enhance virtually the entire interior.
- Enclosing the loft will turn it into a fourth bedroom.
- Kitchen amenities includes an adjoining breakfast bay, a cooktop island and a corner location for the sink.
- Order each elevation separately.

The plan price is $357.45. You may choose either five sets of bluelines or a reproducible mylar. Plan by Design Profile, Inc.

The diagrams presented here constitute only floor plans and elevations. Purchasers are advised to consult their state and local building regulations and a state-certified architect prior to any construction related to these plans.

Choice Of Exteriors Lets Two Story Suit Its Surroundings

First floor—1238 sq. ft.
Second floor—979 sq. ft.
Total living space—2217 sq. ft.
Unfinished basement—735 sq. ft.
3 bedrooms, 2½ baths
Shown with a basement

- Vaulted ceilings are used to increase visual appeal throughout the interior.
- Archways highlight the entry to the living and dining rooms.
- Bright corner window illuminates the kitchen sink.
- Master bath includes a separate tub and shower and a dual-basin vanity.
- Order each elevation separately.

The plan price is $332.55. You may choose either five sets of bluelines or a reproducible mylar. Plan by Design Profile, Inc.

The diagrams presented here constitute only floor plans and elevations. Purchasers are advised to consult their state and local building regulations and a state-certified architect prior to any construction related to these plans.

Plan number DPI-L2385-AJ91-SW93

Plan number DPI-L2384-AJ91-SW93

Plan number DPI-L2386-AJ91-SW93

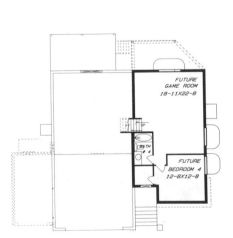

Plan number DPI-L2387-AJ91-SW93

FUTURE GAME ROOM 18-11X22-8
BATH # 4
FUTURE BEDROOM 4 12-8X12-8

Basement

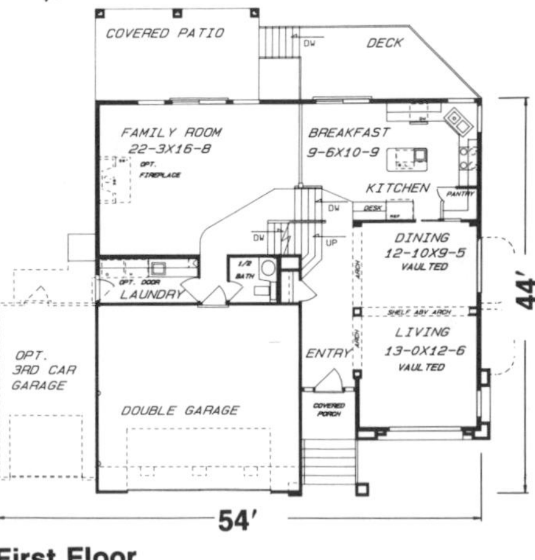

First Floor

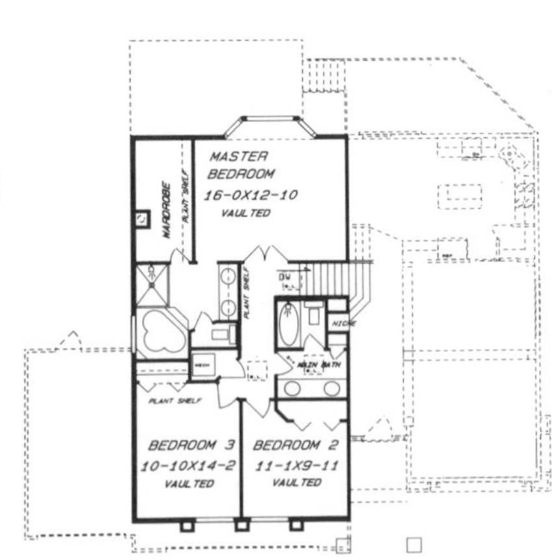

Second Floor

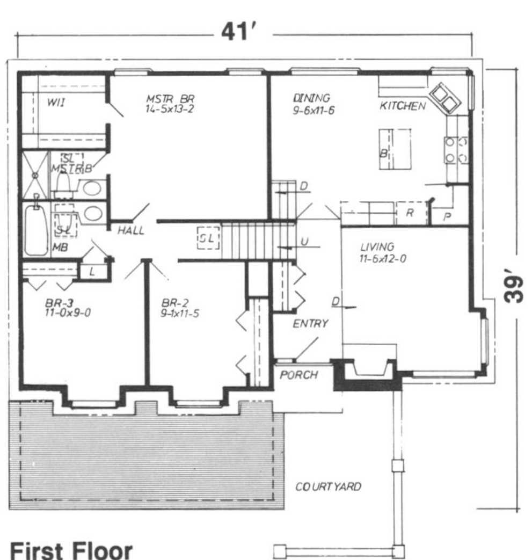

First Floor

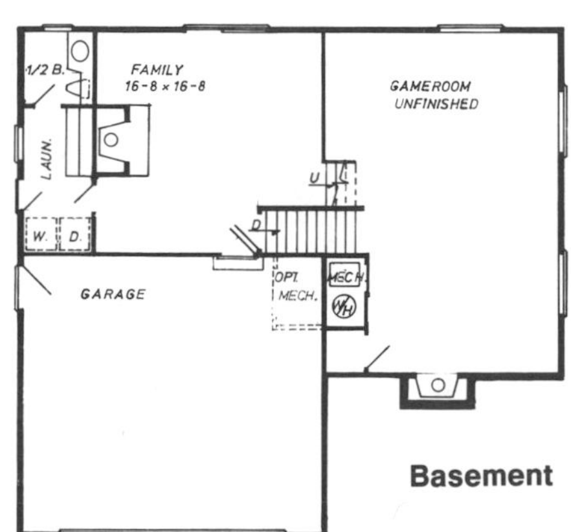

Basement

Split Level Has Cozy Family Room, Space For Future Game Room

Upper floors—1170 sq. ft.
Family room level—397 sq. ft.
Total living space—1567 sq. ft.
3 bedrooms, 2½ baths
Shown with a basement

- Foyer includes a convenient coat closet.
- Sunken living room includes a bright corner window arrangement and a fireplace.
- Kitchen island serves as a snack bar and a divider between the kitchen and dining area.
- Master bedroom features a walk-in closet and a private bath.
- Skylights provide natural illumination in the full baths.

Plan number DPI-2383-9002-SW93. The plan price is $300.00. You may choose either five sets of bluelines or a reproducible mylar. Plan by Design Profile, Inc.

The diagrams presented here constitute only floor plans and elevations. Purchasers are advised to consult their state and local building regulations and a state-certified architect prior to any construction related to these plans.

...reas Highlight ...ble Ranch

...al living space—1931 sq. ft.
3-4 bedrooms, 2 baths
Shown with concrete slab construction

- Attractive planter separates the main foyer from the formal dining room.
- Double doors open into the first-class master suite.
- Angled counter island defines the boundaries of the kitchen within the open family area, without restricting views.
- Versatile den may be converted to a fourth bedroom.
- Volume ceilings enhance the spacious environment of the interior.

Plan number DPI-M2390-AJ91-SW93. The plan price is $300.00. You may choose either five sets of bluelines or a reproducible vellum. Plan by Design Profile, Inc.

The diagrams presented here constitute only floor plans and elevations. Purchasers are advised to consult their state and local building regulations and a state-certified architect prior to any construction related to these plans.

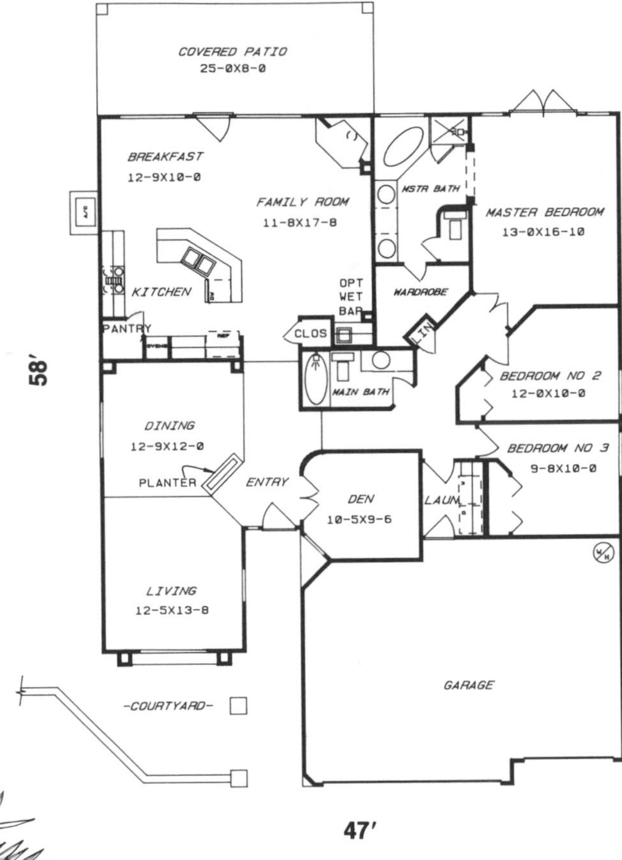

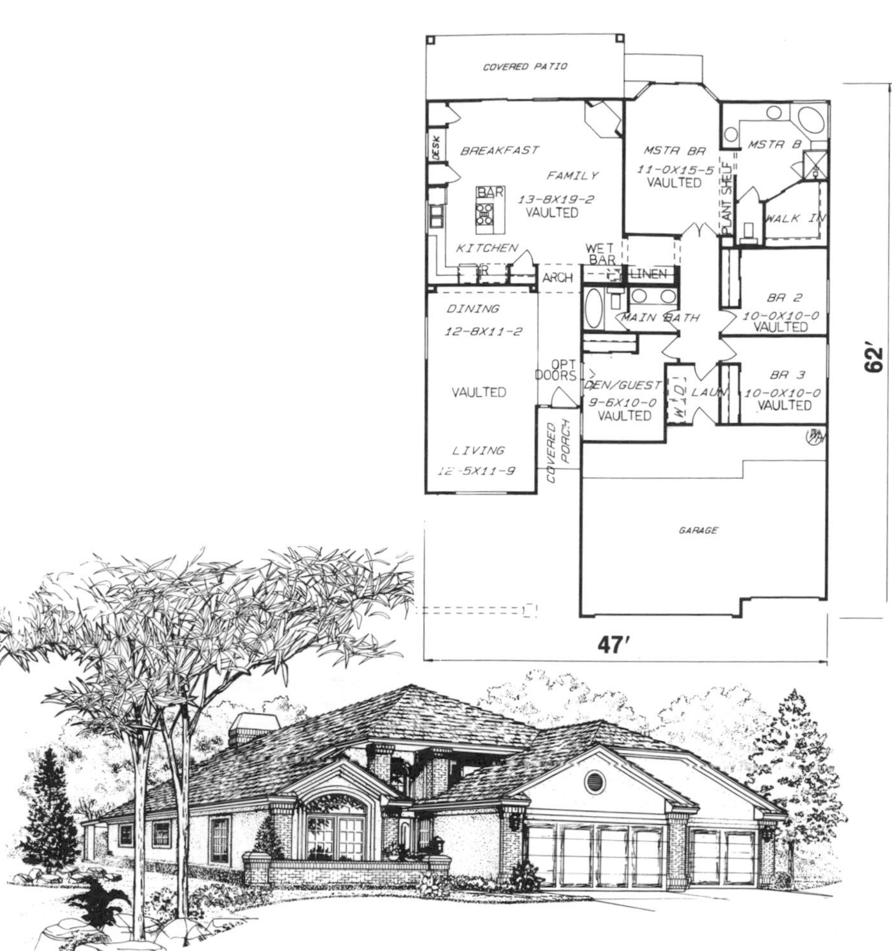

Interior Spaces Practically Explode Under Volume Ceilings

Total living space—1915 sq. ft.
3-4 bedrooms, 2 baths
Shown with concrete slab construction

- Archways and plant shelves customize room transitions.
- Kitchen/family area includes a built-in desk, a fireplace and a wet bar.
- Sliding glass doors are incorporated into the master suite's sitting bay.
- Compartmented design of the main bath facilitates multi-use situations.

Plan number DPI-M2389-AJ91-SW93. The plan price is $300.00. You may choose either five sets of bluelines or a reproducible mylar. Plan by Design Profile, Inc.

The diagrams presented here constitute only floor plans and elevations. Purchasers are advised to consult their state and local building regulations and a state-certified architect prior to any construction related to these plans.

Combined Spaces Expand Living Areas In Adaptable Ranch

Total living space—2339 sq. ft.
3-4 bedrooms, 2½ baths
Shown with concrete slab construction

- Formal entry offers a dramatic view into the living room.
- Windows provide a spectacular corner setting for the spa tub in the master bathroom.
- Open family area creates a comfortable zone for everyday living.
- Large laundry room includes generous storage space and a powder room.

Plan number DPI-M2300-8905-SW93. The plan price is $350.85. You may choose either five sets of bluelines or a reproducible mylar. Plan by Design Profile, Inc.

The diagrams presented here constitute only floor plans and elevations. Purchasers are advised to consult their state and local building regulations and a state-certified architect prior to any construction related to these plans.

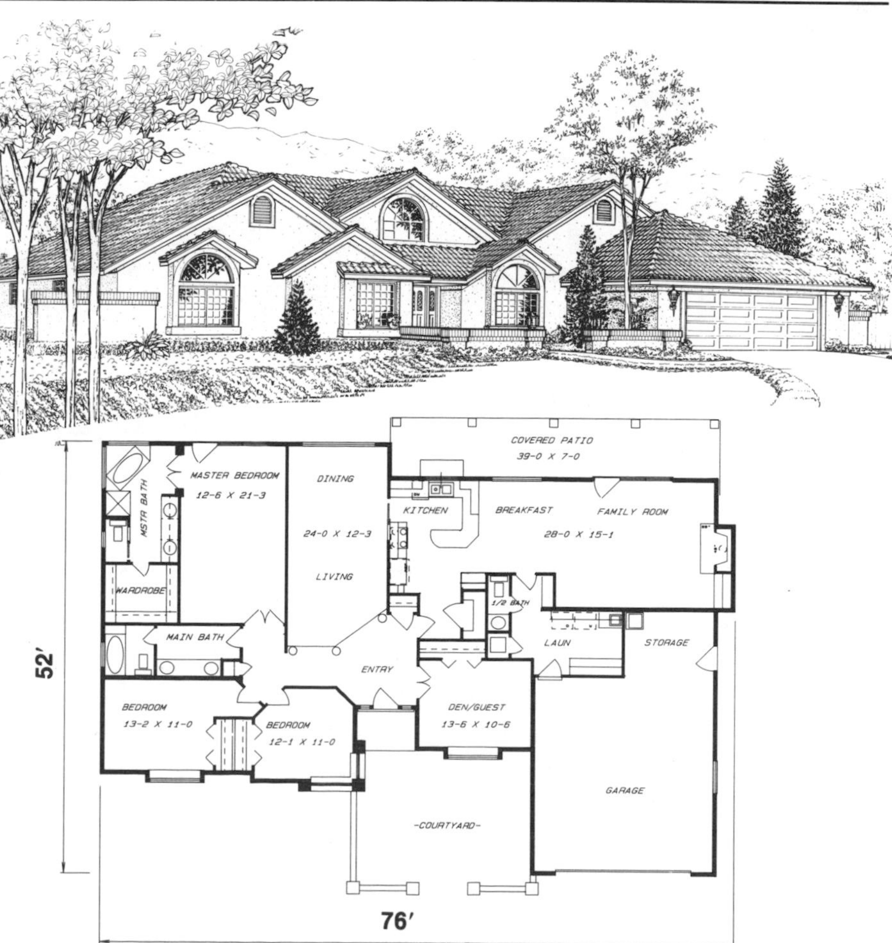

Custom Ranch Is Packed With Luxurious Features

Total living space—2165 sq. ft.
2-3 bedrooms, 2 baths
Shown with concrete slab construction

- Bay windows create two attractive 'towers' on the front elevation.
- Floor-to-ceiling columns define the boundaries of the formal dining room.
- First-class master bath includes sit down space at the double vanity.
- Den/bedroom includes an eye-catching curved glass block wall.

Plan number DPI-M2318-9009-SW93. The plan price is $324.75. You may choose either five sets of bluelines or a reproducible mylar. Plan by Design Profile, Inc.

The diagrams presented here constitute only floor plans and elevations. Purchasers are advised to consult their state and local building regulations and a state-certified architect prior to any construction related to these plans.

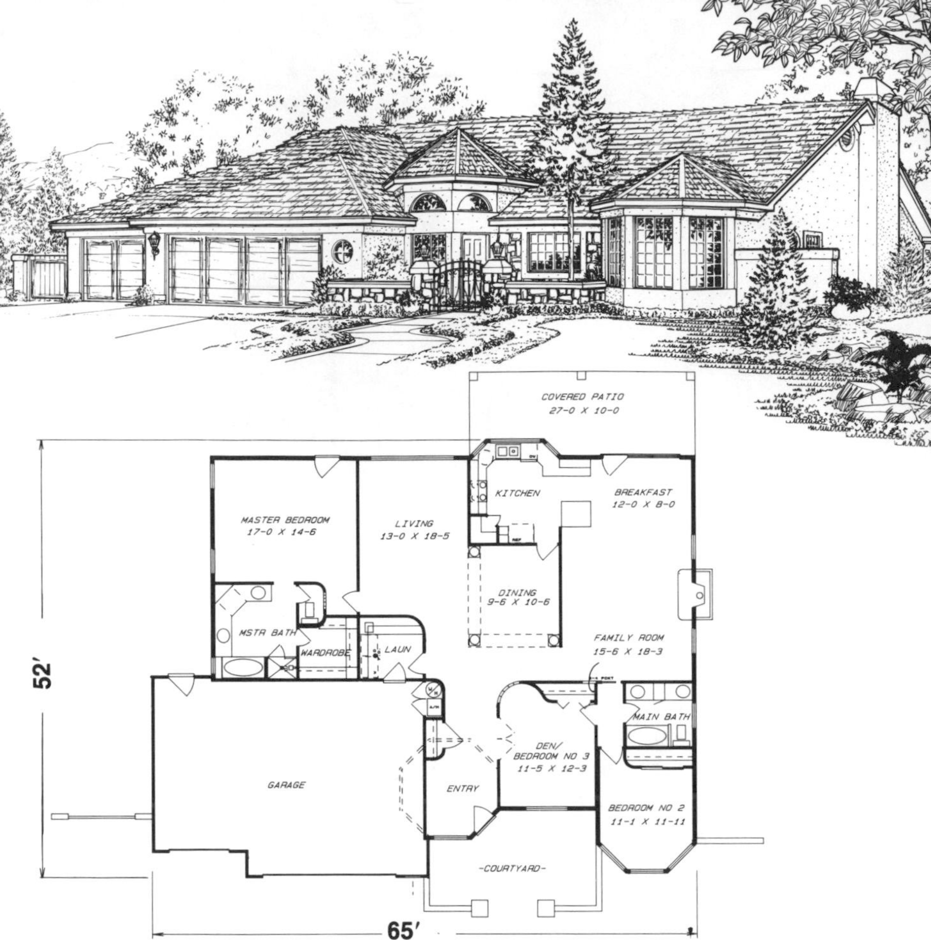

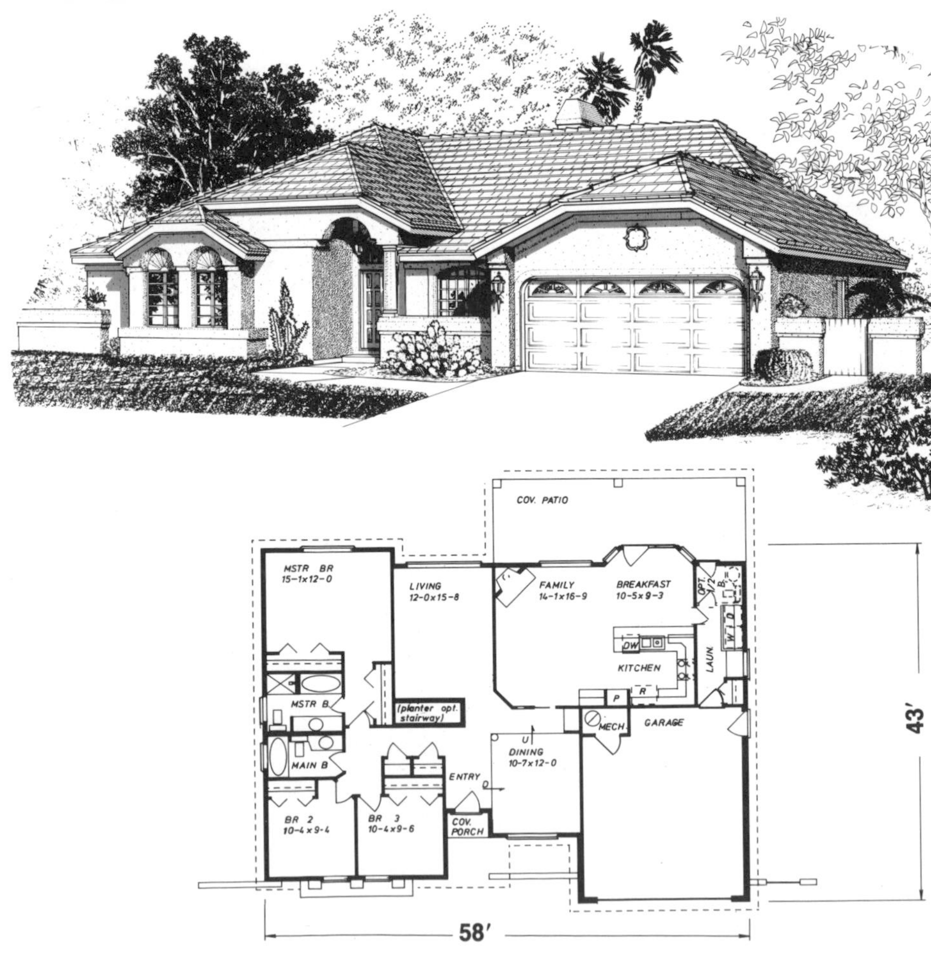

Downsized Ranch Is Packed With Luxury Features

Total living space—1694 ft.
3 bedrooms, 2-2½ baths
Shown with concrete slab construction

- High-impact, sunken dining room is surrounded by the entry gallery.
- Corner fireplace shares its appeal with the entire family area.
- Kitchen counter overlooks the breakfast area, serves as a snack bar.
- Master suite includes individual closets and a tub and shower in its private bath.
- Part of the laundry/mud room may be finished as a powder room.

Plan number DPI-2387-9002-SW93. The plan price is $300.00. You may choose either five sets of bluelines or a reproducible mylar. Plan by Design Profile, Inc.

The diagrams presented here constitute only floor plans and elevations. Purchasers are advised to consult their state and local building regulations and a state-certified architect prior to any construction related to these plans.

Plan number DPI-2305-9005-SW93

Plan number DPI-2306-9005-SW93

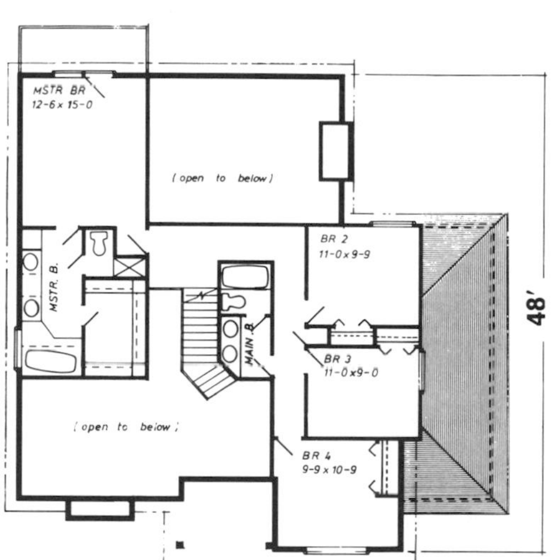

Second Floor

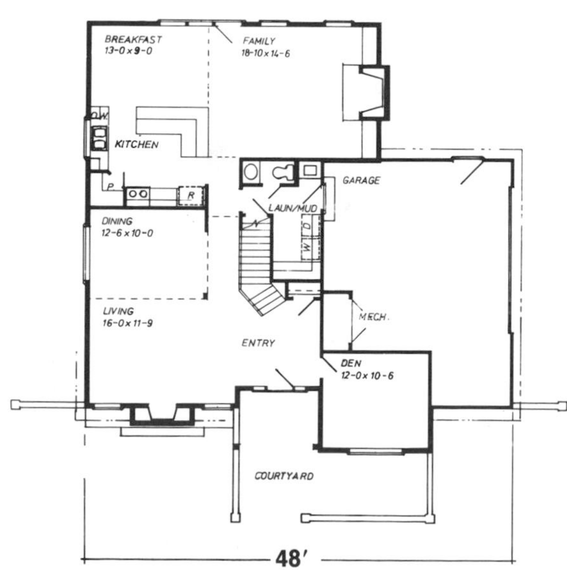

First Floor

Attractive Fireplace Highlights Two Story Inside And Out

First floor—1250 sq. ft.
Second floor—1015 sq. ft.
Total living space—2265 sq. ft.
4-5 bedrooms, 2½ baths
Shown with a basement

- Volume ceilings are featured in the living and family rooms.
- Master suite has its own private deck.
- Three additional bedrooms share a compartmented bath.
- Bonus storage space is provided in the garage which is reached through the laundry/mud room.
- Order each elevation separately.

The plan price is $339.75. You may choose either five sets of bluelines or a reproducible mylar. Plan by Design Profile, Inc.

The diagrams presented here constitute only floor plans and elevations. Purchasers are advised to consult their state and local building regulations and a state-certified architect prior to any construction related to these plans.

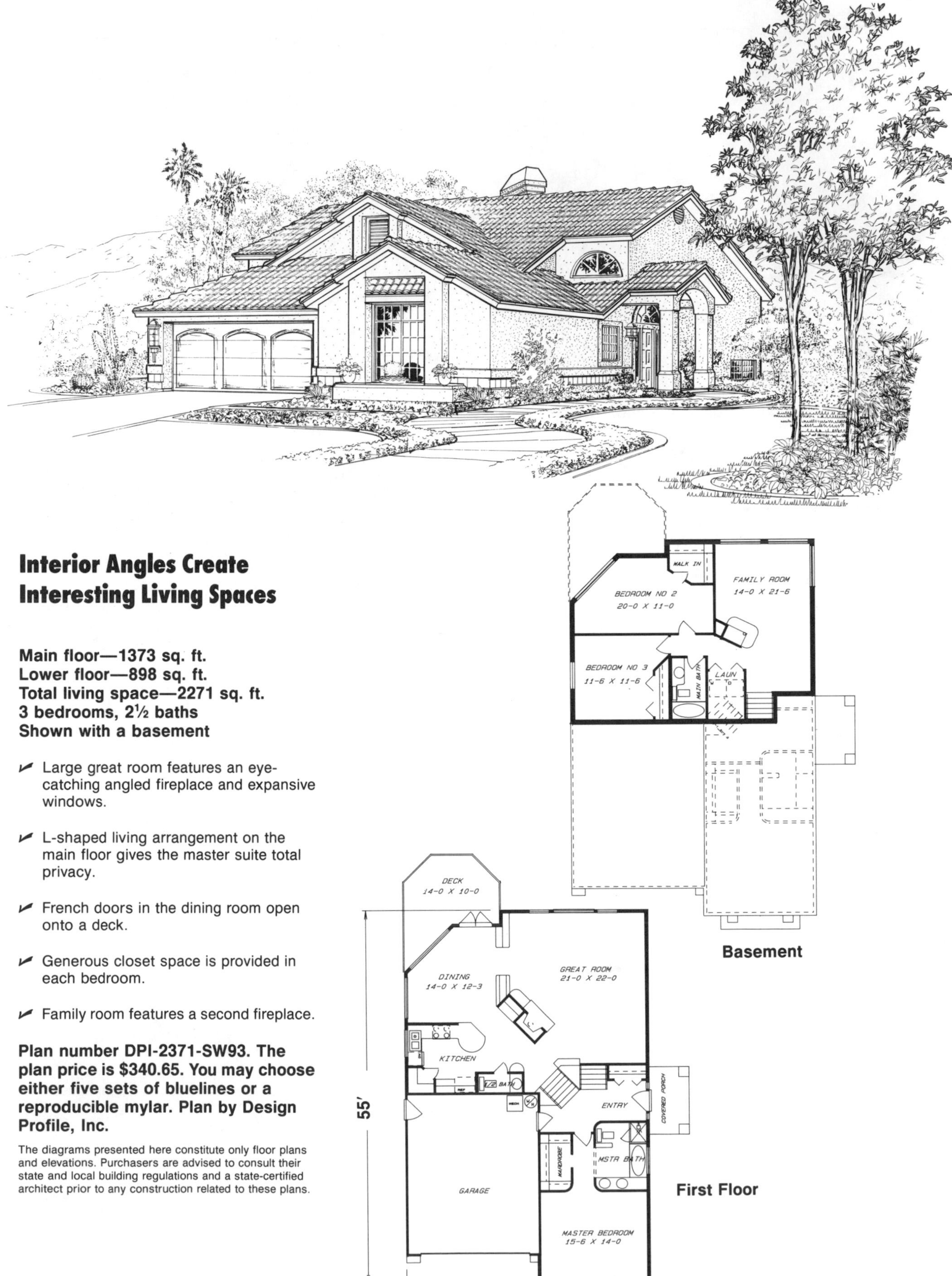

Interior Angles Create Interesting Living Spaces

Main floor—1373 sq. ft.
Lower floor—898 sq. ft.
Total living space—2271 sq. ft.
3 bedrooms, 2½ baths
Shown with a basement

- Large great room features an eye-catching angled fireplace and expansive windows.
- L-shaped living arrangement on the main floor gives the master suite total privacy.
- French doors in the dining room open onto a deck.
- Generous closet space is provided in each bedroom.
- Family room features a second fireplace.

Plan number DPI-2371-SW93. The plan price is $340.65. You may choose either five sets of bluelines or a reproducible mylar. Plan by Design Profile, Inc.

The diagrams presented here constitute only floor plans and elevations. Purchasers are advised to consult their state and local building regulations and a state-certified architect prior to any construction related to these plans.

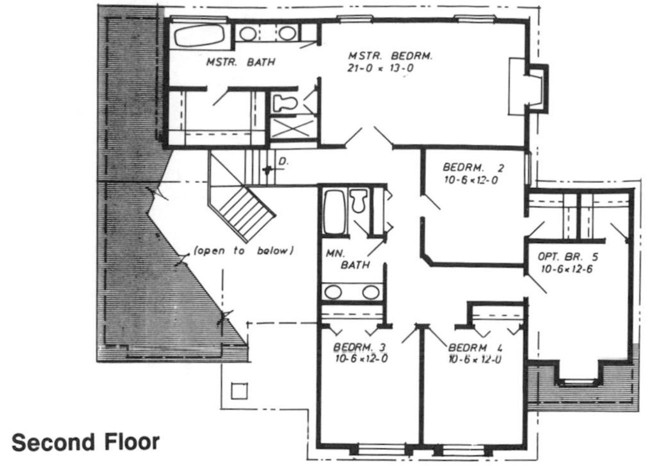

Second Floor

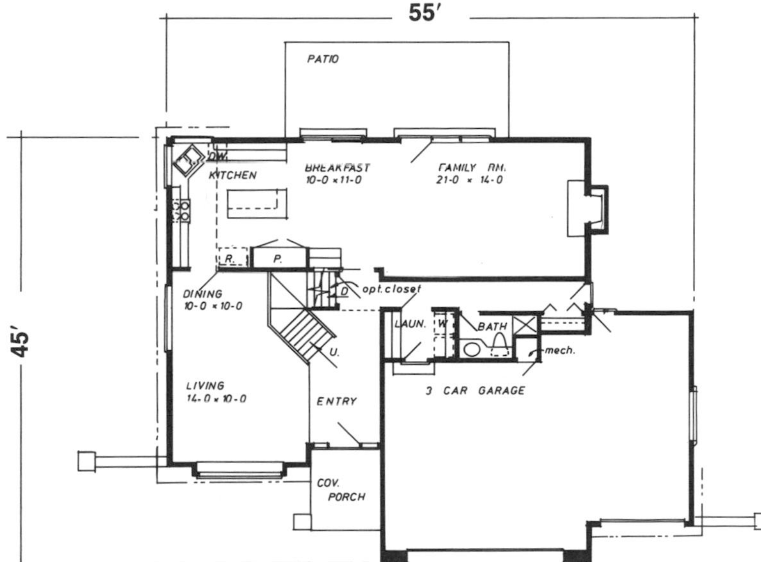

First Floor

Fireplace Beckons As Exciting Feature Of Master Suite

First floor—1225 sq. ft.
Second floor—1230 sq. ft.
Total living space—2455 sq. ft.
4-5 bedrooms, 3 baths
Shown with a basement

- Amenity-packed master suite includes a fireplace, large bath and a walk-in closet.
- Volume ceilings highlight the living and dining rooms and part of the kitchen.
- Large kitchen island doubles as a snack bar.
- Main bath has a handy, compartmented layout which separates the tub/toilet area from the dual-sink vanity.
- Utility room serves as a mud room entry from the garage.

Plan number DPI-2372-SW93. The plan price is $368.25. You may choose either five sets of bluelines or a reproducible mylar. Plan by Design Profile, Inc.

The diagrams presented here constitute only floor plans and elevations. Purchasers are advised to consult their state and local building regulations and a state-certified architect prior to any construction related to these plans.

Vaulted Ceilings Generate Entry Excitement In Expandable Split Level

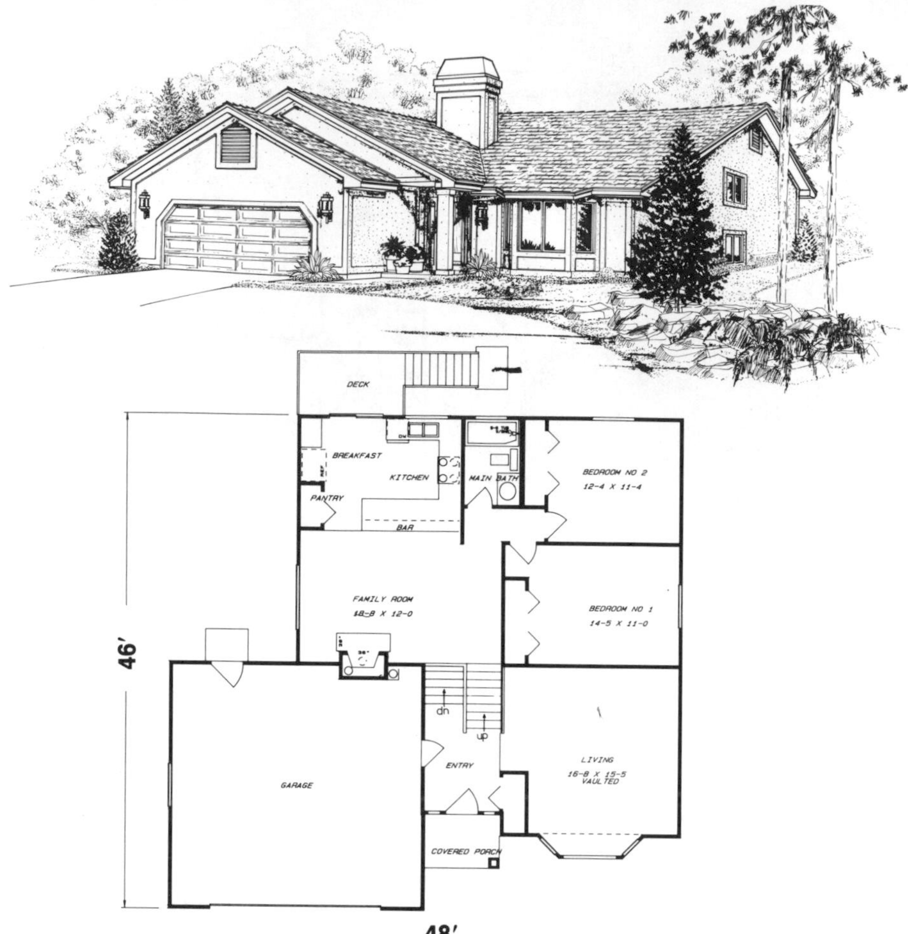

Total living space—1204 sq. ft.
Unfinished lower level—837 sq. ft.
2 bedrooms, 1 bath
Shown with a basement

- Foyer includes a handy coat closet.
- Eat-in kitchen includes a pantry, a snack bar and deck access.
- Fireplace is a charming focal point in the family room.
- Lower level may be finished to include a game room, an extra bedroom, a full bath and the laundry room.

Plan number DPI-2383-AJ91-SW93. The plan price is $300.00. You may choose either five sets of bluelines or a reproducible mylar. Plan by Design Profile, Inc.

The diagrams presented here constitute only floor plans and elevations. Purchasers are advised to consult their state and local building regulations and a state-certified architect prior to any construction related to these plans.

Elevated Foyer, Vaulted Ceilings Make A Dramatic Entry Statement

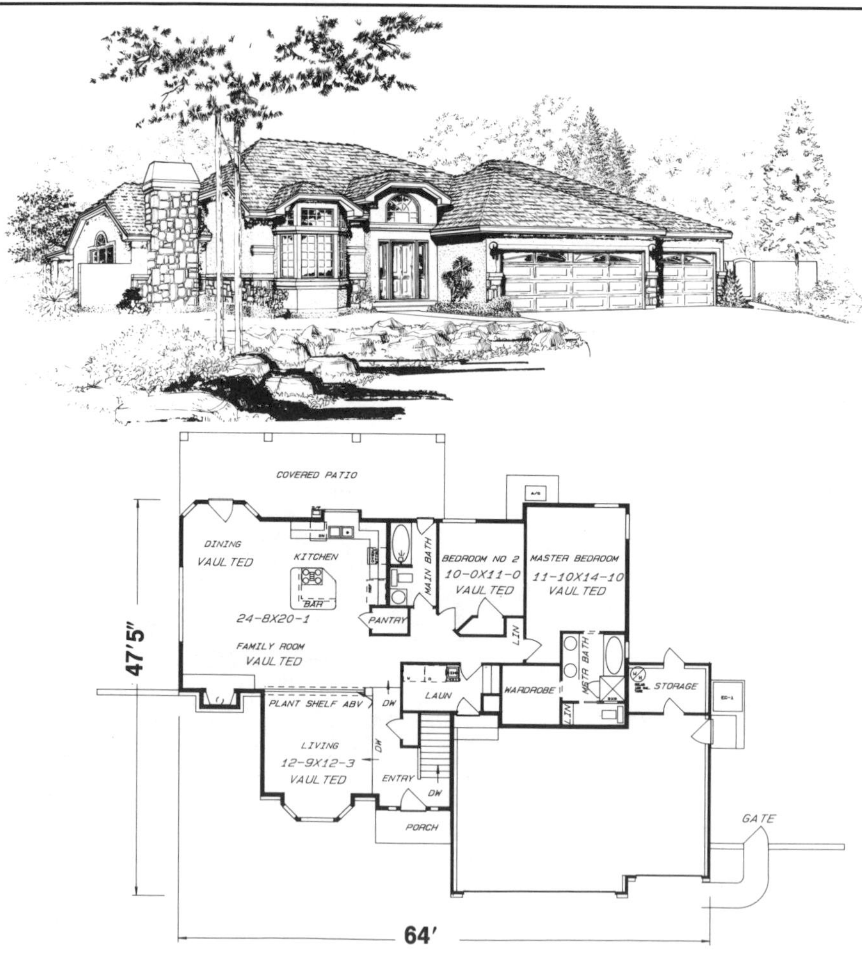

Total living space—1599 sq. ft.
Unfinished basement—1237 sq. ft.
3-5 bedrooms, 2-3 baths
Shown with a basement

- Open interior maximizes the impact of the volume ceilings.
- Kitchen island provides space for the stovetop, plus wrap-around seating.
- Bonus storage room is included in the three-car garage.
- Completion of the unfinished basement will add a game room, two bedrooms and a mechanical room.

Plan number DPI-M2304-9102-SW93. The plan price is $300.00. You may choose either five sets of bluelines or a reproducible mylar. Plan by Design Profile, Inc.

The diagrams presented here constitute only floor plans and elevations. Purchasers are advised to consult their state and local building regulations and a state-certified architect prior to any construction related to these plans.

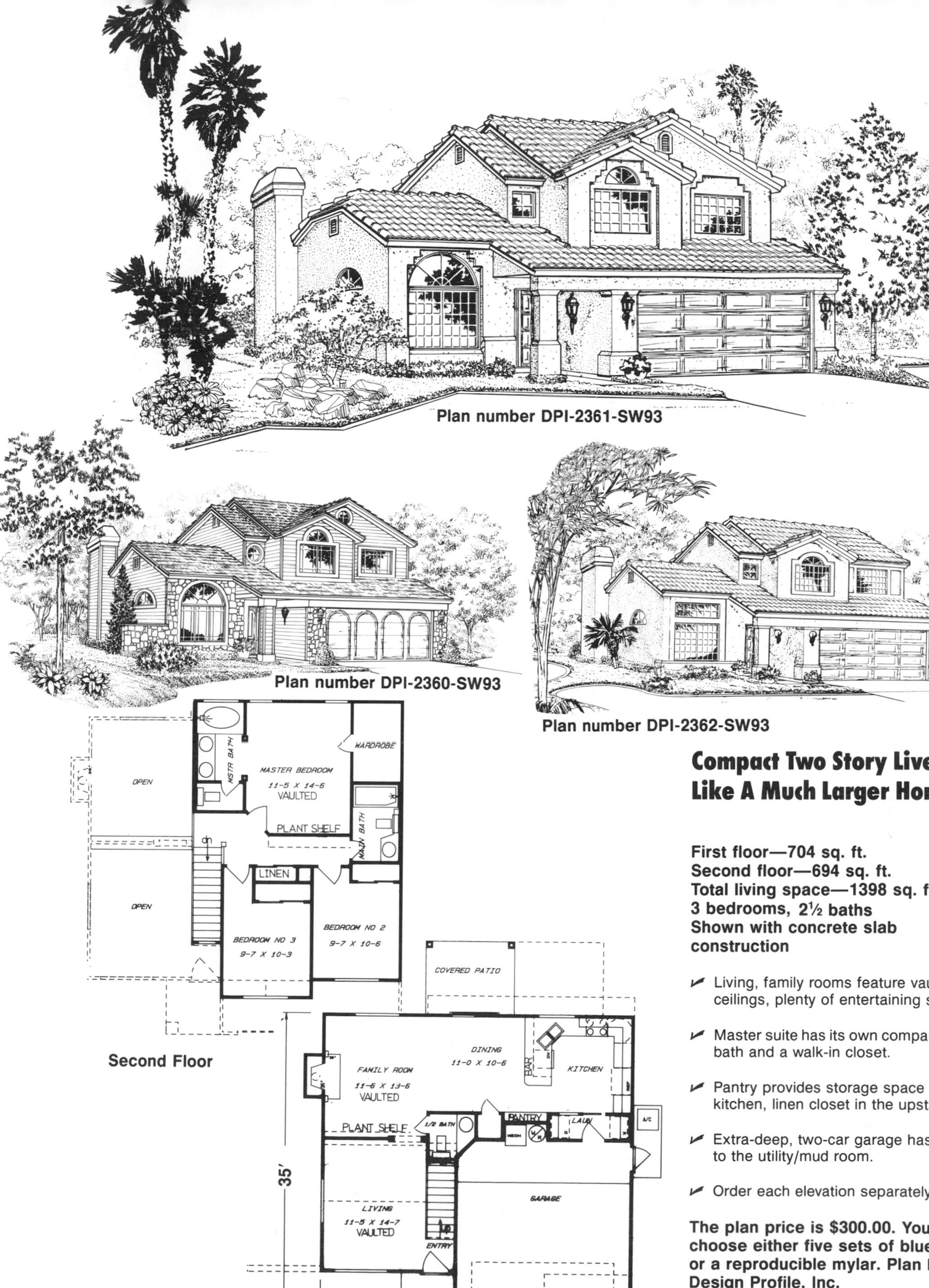

Plan number DPI-2361-SW93

Plan number DPI-2360-SW93

Plan number DPI-2362-SW93

Second Floor

First Floor

Compact Two Story Lives Like A Much Larger Home

First floor—704 sq. ft.
Second floor—694 sq. ft.
Total living space—1398 sq. ft.
3 bedrooms, 2½ baths
Shown with concrete slab construction

- Living, family rooms feature vaulted ceilings, plenty of entertaining space.
- Master suite has its own compartmented bath and a walk-in closet.
- Pantry provides storage space in the kitchen, linen closet in the upstairs hall.
- Extra-deep, two-car garage has access to the utility/mud room.
- Order each elevation separately.

The plan price is $300.00. You may choose either five sets of bluelines or a reproducible mylar. Plan by Design Profile, Inc.

The diagrams presented here constitute only floor plans and elevations. Purchasers are advised to consult their state and local building regulations and a state-certified architect prior to any construction related to these plans.

Smooth Flowing Floor Plan Ensures A Perfect Fit For Family Living

First floor—1190 sq. ft.
Second floor—976 sq. ft.
Total living space—2166 sq. ft.
4 bedrooms, 3 baths
Shown with a basement

- L-shaped room arrangement gives the kitchen easy access to both the formal and informal entertainment areas.
- Attractive, angled staircase features a landing.
- Compartmented master bath includes a dual-sink vanity and a walk-in closet.
- Bonus storage space is available in the three-car garage.
- Extra-long utility/mud room adjoins a full bath and has access to the garage or the back yard.

Plan number DPI-2355-SW93. The plan price is $324.90. You may choose either five sets of bluelines or a reproducible mylar. Plan by Design Profile, Inc.

The diagrams presented here constitute only floor plans and elevations. Purchasers are advised to consult their state and local building regulations and a state-certified architect prior to any construction related to these plans.

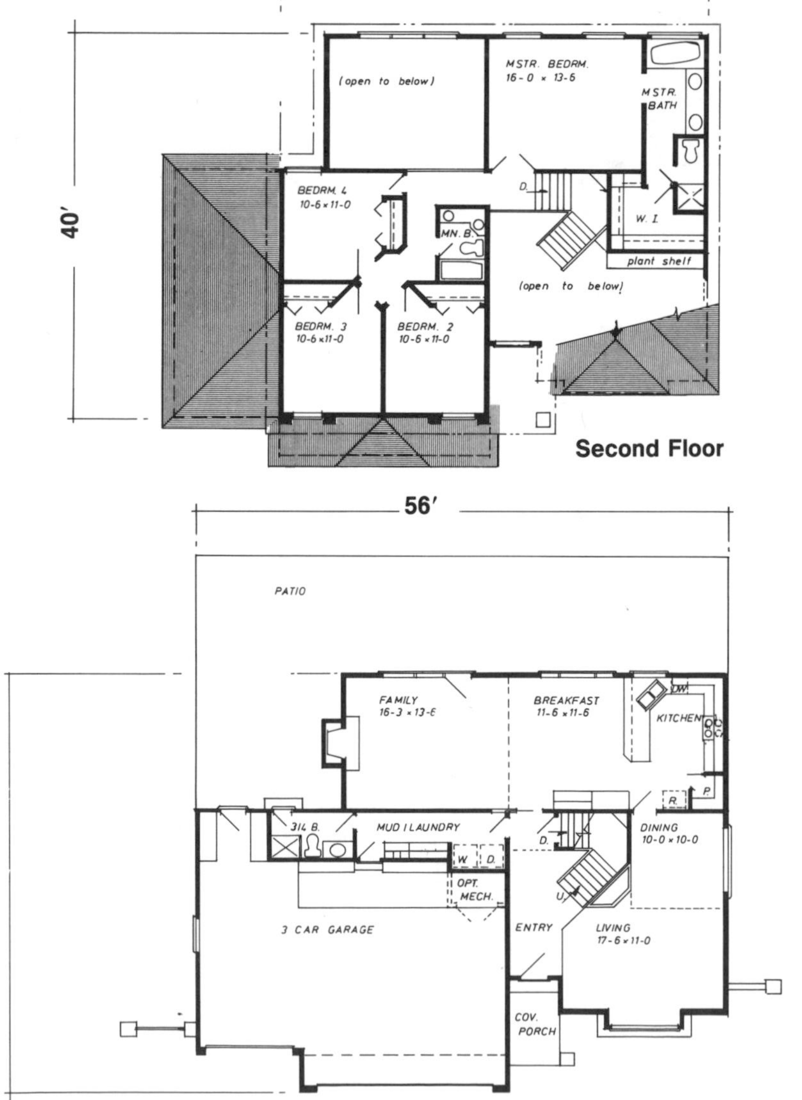

First Floor

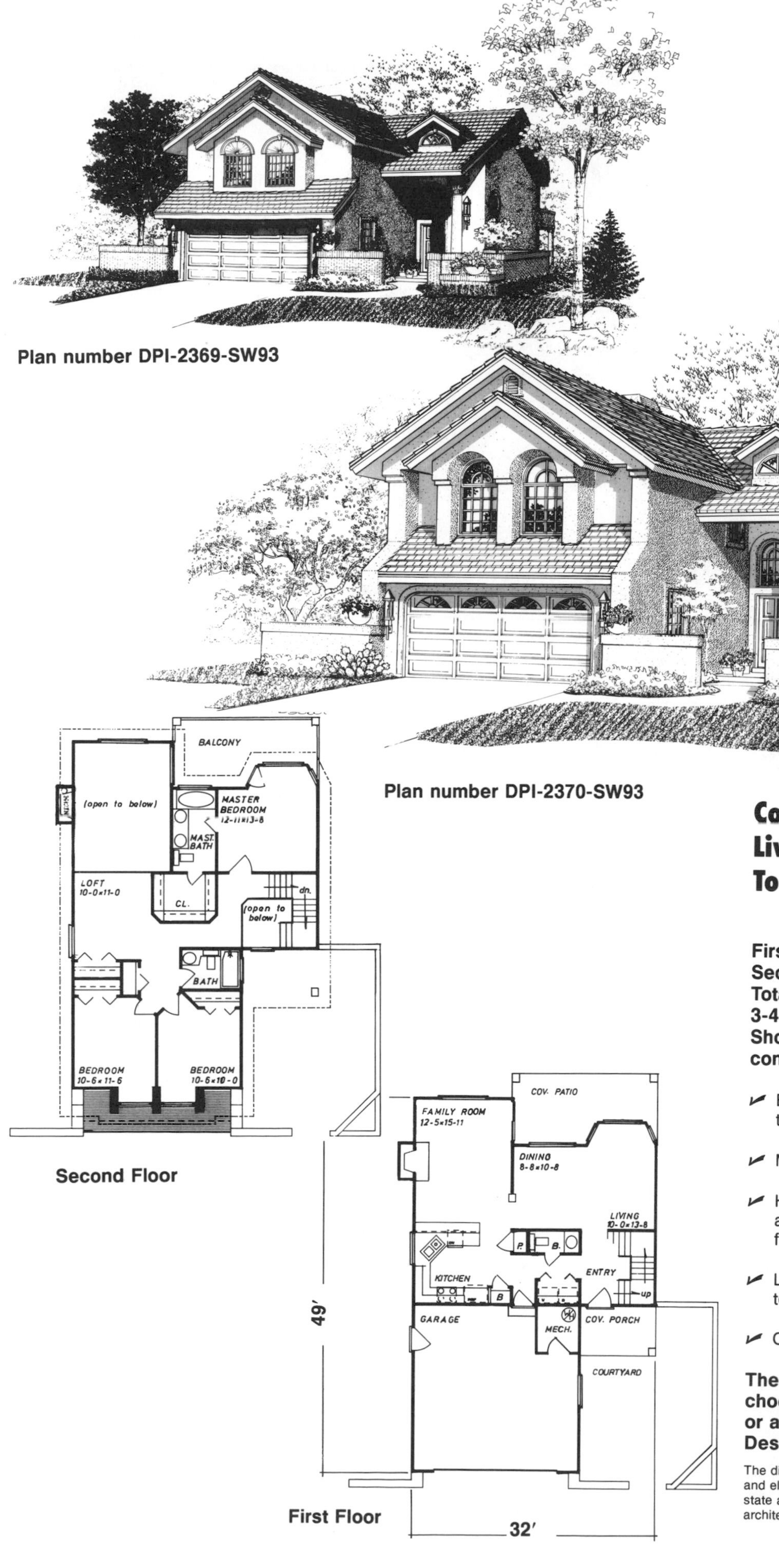

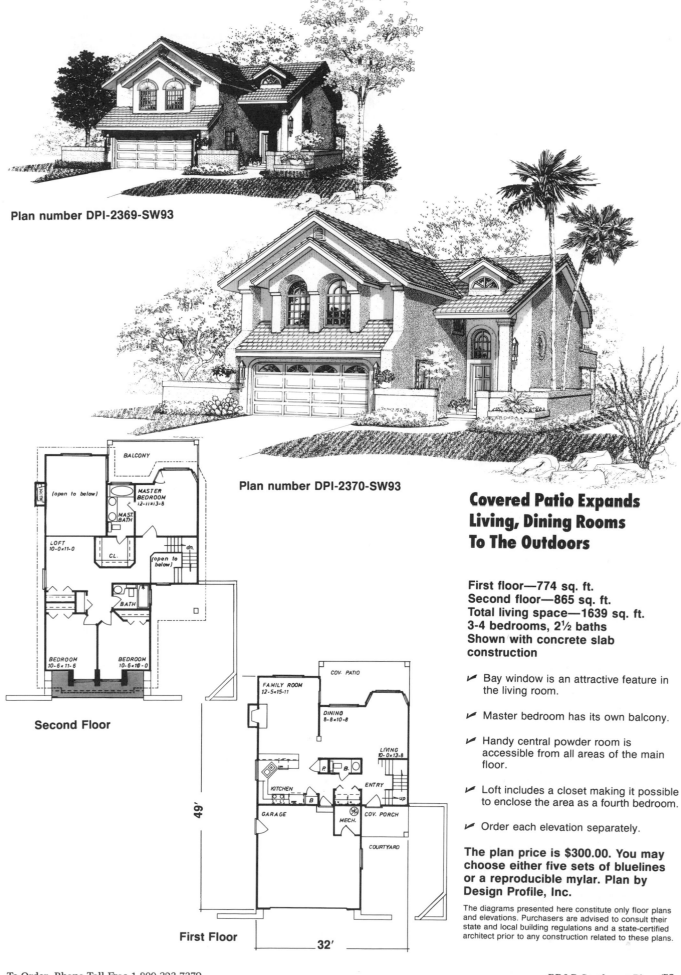

Plan number DPI-2369-SW93

Plan number DPI-2370-SW93

Second Floor

First Floor

Covered Patio Expands Living, Dining Rooms To The Outdoors

First floor—774 sq. ft.
Second floor—865 sq. ft.
Total living space—1639 sq. ft.
3-4 bedrooms, 2½ baths
Shown with concrete slab construction

- Bay window is an attractive feature in the living room.
- Master bedroom has its own balcony.
- Handy central powder room is accessible from all areas of the main floor.
- Loft includes a closet making it possible to enclose the area as a fourth bedroom.
- Order each elevation separately.

The plan price is $300.00. You may choose either five sets of bluelines or a reproducible mylar. Plan by Design Profile, Inc.

The diagrams presented here constitute only floor plans and elevations. Purchasers are advised to consult their state and local building regulations and a state-certified architect prior to any construction related to these plans.

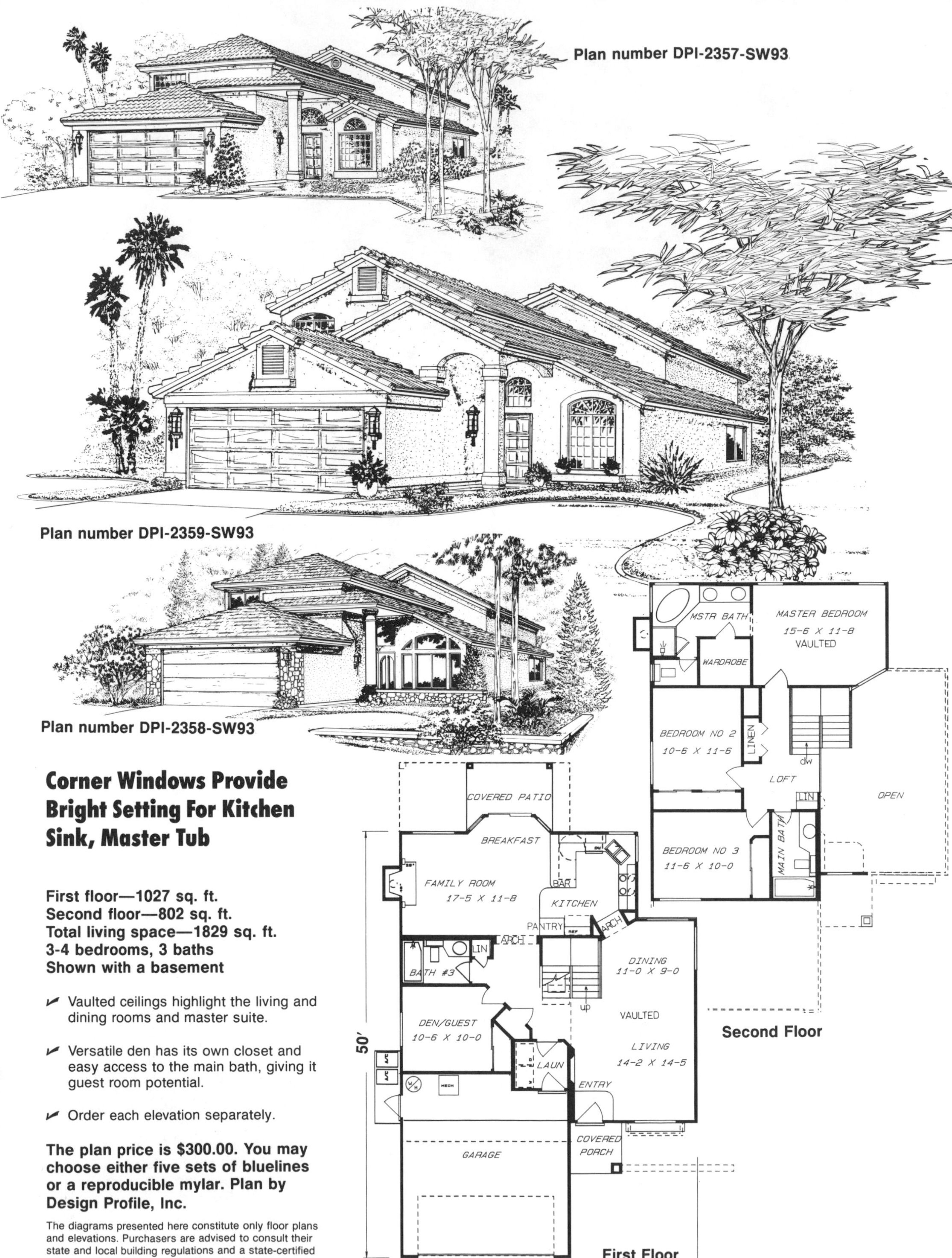

Corner Windows Provide Bright Setting For Kitchen Sink, Master Tub

First floor—1027 sq. ft.
Second floor—802 sq. ft.
Total living space—1829 sq. ft.
3-4 bedrooms, 3 baths
Shown with a basement

- Vaulted ceilings highlight the living and dining rooms and master suite.
- Versatile den has its own closet and easy access to the main bath, giving it guest room potential.
- Order each elevation separately.

The plan price is $300.00. You may choose either five sets of bluelines or a reproducible mylar. Plan by Design Profile, Inc.

The diagrams presented here constitute only floor plans and elevations. Purchasers are advised to consult their state and local building regulations and a state-certified architect prior to any construction related to these plans.

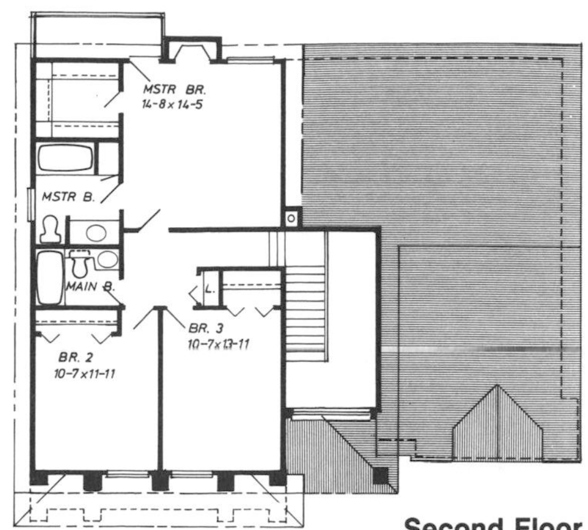

Second Floor

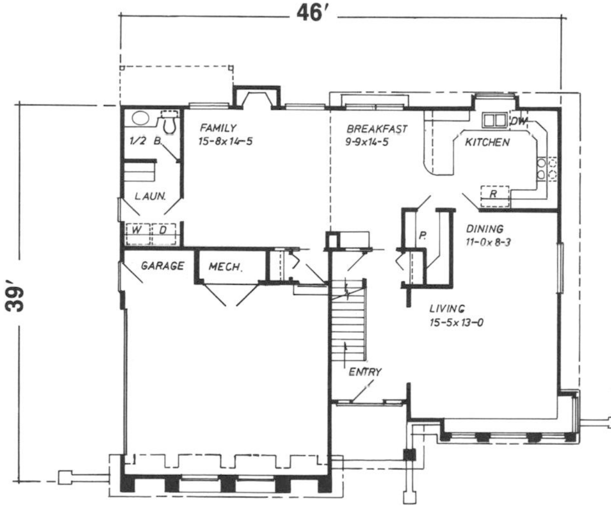

First Floor

Custom Windows Make Two Story Special Inside And Out

First floor—1058 sq. ft.
Second floor—771 sq. ft.
Total living space—1829 sq. ft.
3 bedrooms, 2½ baths
Shown with a basement

- Window seat provides the ideal spot to take in the views offered from the living room.
- Oversized walk-in pantry is included in the kitchen.
- Family room and master suite each have a fireplace.
- Sliding glass doors in the breakfast area offer access to the back yard.
- Laundry room serves as a practical mud room entry from the outside.

Plan number DPI-2356-SW93. The plan price is $300.00. You may choose either five sets of bluelines or a reproducible mylar. Plan by Design Profile, Inc.

The diagrams presented here constitute only floor plans and elevations. Purchasers are advised to consult their state and local building regulations and a state-certified architect prior to any construction related to these plans.

Fireplace Creates A Spark In Master Bedroom

First floor—1239 sq. ft.
Second floor—1221 sq. ft.
Total living space—2460 sq. ft.
4 bedrooms, 3 baths
Shown with a basement

- Open interior design creates a roomy atmosphere in the formal, informal living areas.
- Generous counter space in the kitchen makes meal preparation a pleasure.
- Attractive French doors open into the amenity-packed master suite.
- Staircase leading to the second-floor bedrooms has an attractive, turned landing.
- Three-car garage expands storage possibilities.

Plan number DPI-M2303-9003-SW93. The plan price is $369.00. You may choose either five sets of bluelines or a reproducible mylar. Plan by Design Profile, Inc.

The diagrams presented here constitute only floor plans and elevations. Purchasers are advised to consult their state and local building regulations and a state-certified architect prior to any construction related to these plans.

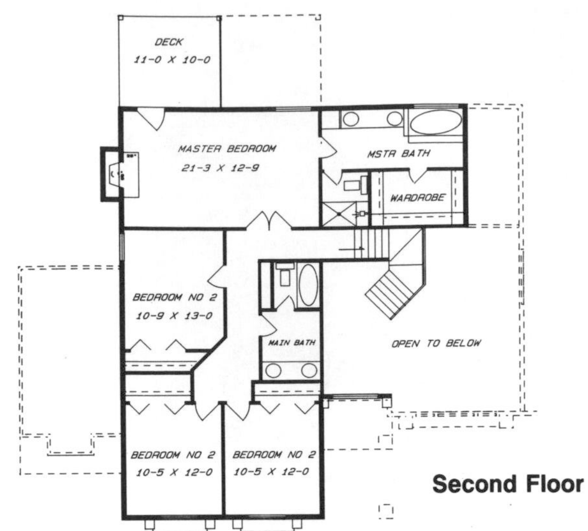

Second Floor

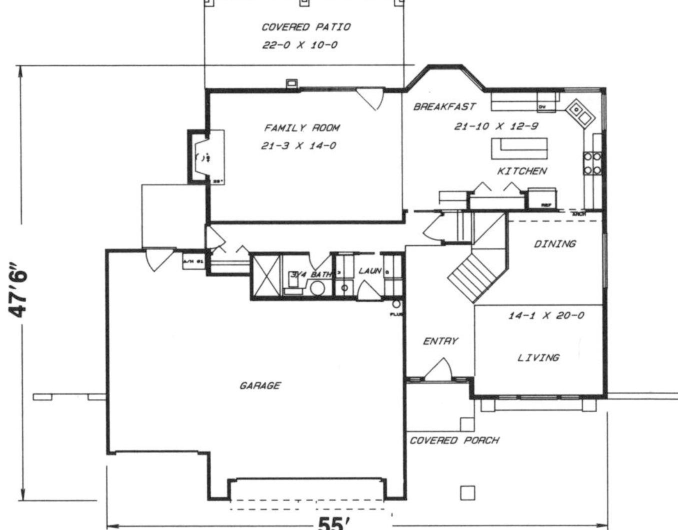

First Floor

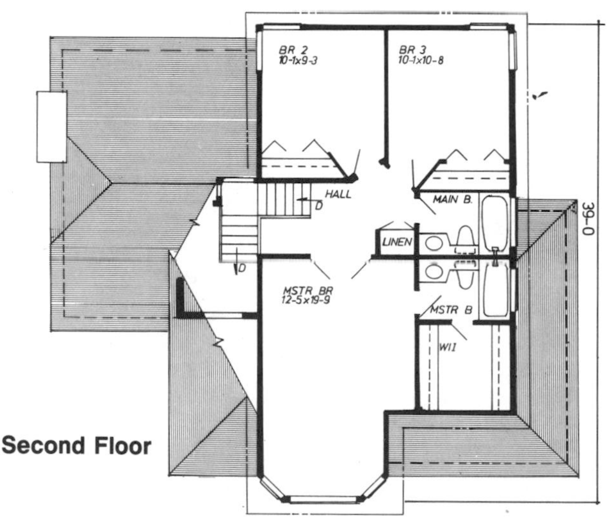

Second Floor

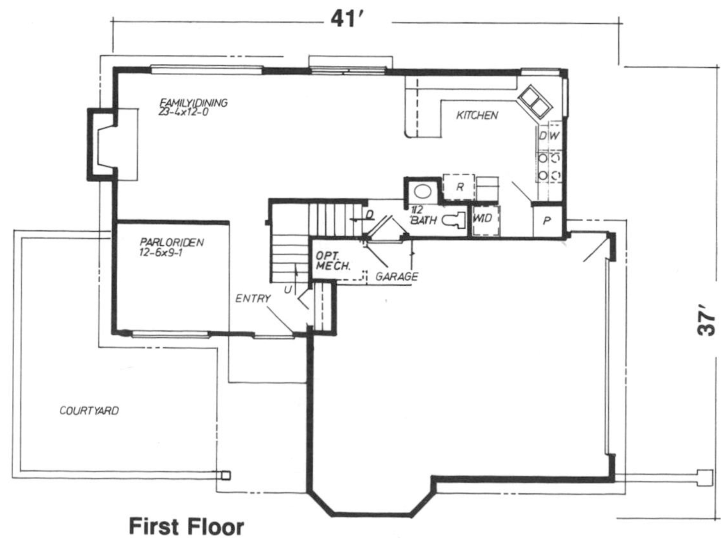

First Floor

Compact Two Story Is Versatile, Comfortable

First floor—668 sq. ft.
Second floor—728 sq. ft.
Total living space—1396 sq. ft.
3 bedrooms, 2½ baths
Shown with a basement

- Foyer includes a practical coat closet.
- Front room may be used as a conversation parlor, or enclosed as a private den.
- Open design of the family room/dining area creates a casual atmosphere.
- Projecting bay serves as shop zone in the garage, a sitting area in the master suite above.
- Walk-in closet provides generous storage space adjoining the master bath.

Plan number DPI-2313-9007-SW93. The plan price is $300.00. You may choose either five sets of bluelines or a reproducible mylar. Plan by Design Profile, Inc.

The diagrams presented here constitute only floor plans and elevations. Purchasers are advised to consult their state and local building regulations and a state-certified architect prior to any construction related to these plans.

Three-Bedroom Home Puts A Premium On Privacy

First floor—1860 sq. ft.
Second floor—676 sq. ft.
Total living space—2536 sq. ft.
3 bedrooms, 3 baths
Shown with a basement

- Master suite, and its adjoining study, occupies the entire second floor.
- Hidden courtyard serves as the ideal setting for a hot tub.
- Pass-through which connects the kitchen and family room can be used as a snack bar.
- Secondary bedrooms each have access to a full bath.
- Laundry room doubles as a mud room entry from the garage.

Plan number DPI-M2305-91MF-SW93. The plan price is $380.40. You may choose either five sets of bluelines or a reproducible mylar. Plan by Design Profile, Inc.

The diagrams presented here constitute only floor plans and elevations. Purchasers are advised to consult their state and local building regulations and a state-certified architect prior to any construction related to these plans.

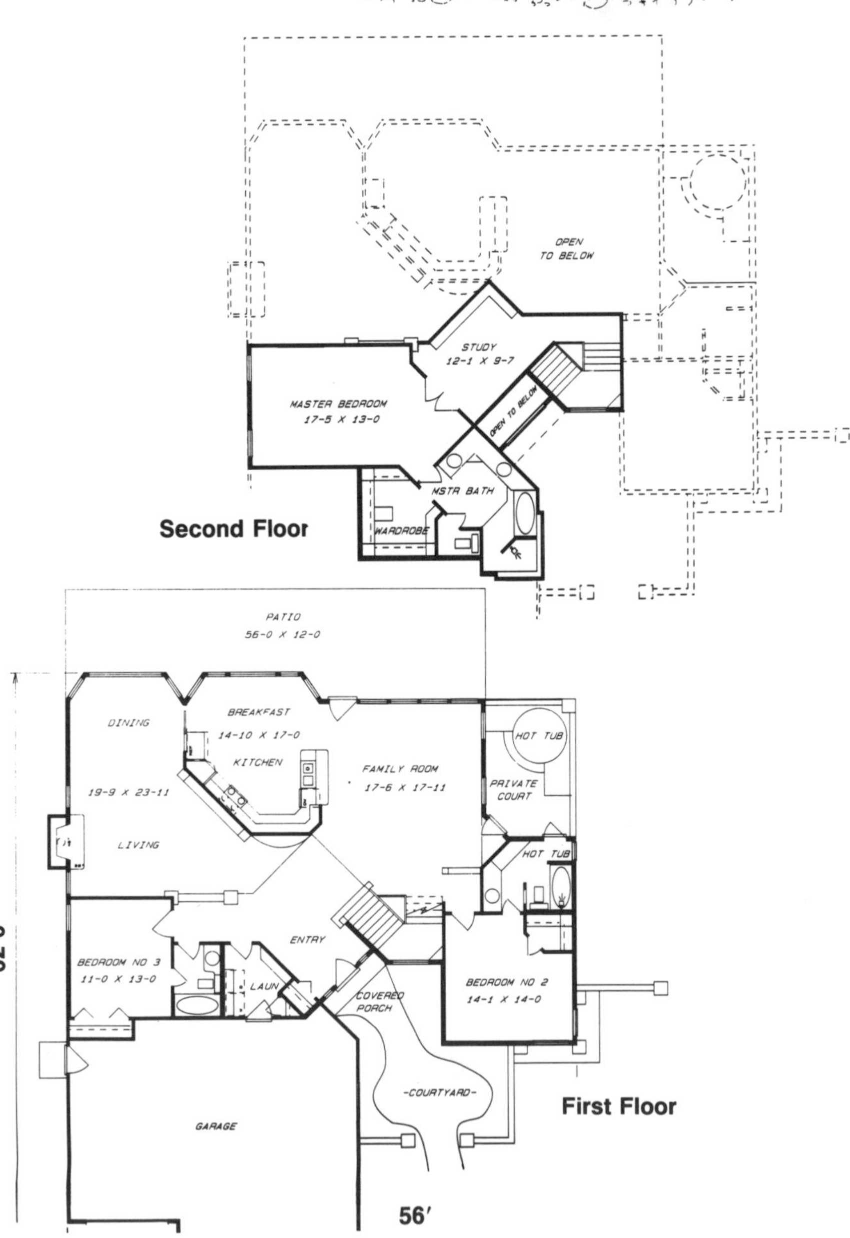

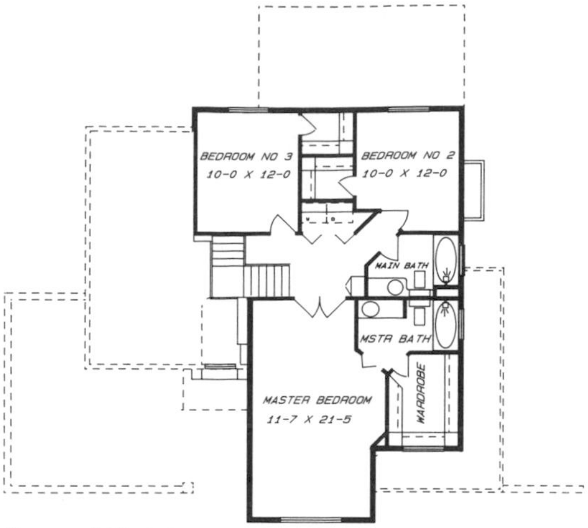

Well-Planned Two Story Has It All

First floor—777 sq. ft.
Second floor—855 sq. ft.
Total living space—1632 sq. ft.
3 bedrooms, 2½ baths
Shown with a basement

- Attractive exterior courtyard customizes the front elevation.
- Floor plan separates formal and informal living areas.
- Pantry and snack bar are included in the kitchen.
- Walk-in closets provide abundant storage space each bedroom.
- Washer and dryer feature a handy, second-floor location.

Plan number DPI-2386-9002-SW93. The plan price is $300.00. You may choose either five sets of bluelines or a reproducible mylar. Plan by Design Profile, Inc.

The diagrams presented here constitute only floor plans and elevations. Purchasers are advised to consult their state and local building regulations and a state-certified architect prior to any construction related to these plans.

Second Floor

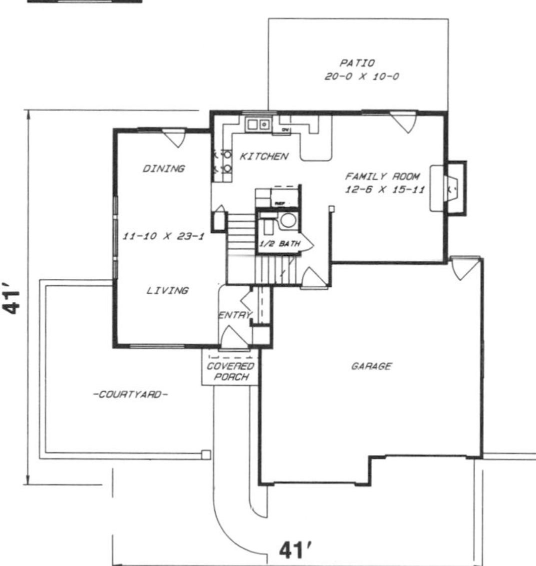

First Floor

Comfortable Family Living Characterizes Five-Bedroom Two Story

First floor—2490 ft.
Second floor—1751 ft.
Total living space—4241 ft.
5 bedrooms, 3½ baths
Shown with a basement

- French doors on either side of the high-ceilinged foyer offer access to the den or living room.
- Built-in bookcases frame the lovely fireplace in the family room.
- Master suite boasts of its own fireplace and a first-class bath.
- Main-floor mother's room is well suited for use as a hobby area or at-home office.
- Plentiful storage space is provided throughout the interior and garage.

Plan number DPI-2304-9004-SW93. The plan price is $636.15. You may choose either five sets of bluelines or a reproducible mylar. Plan by Design Profile, Inc.

The diagrams presented here constitute only floor plans and elevations. Purchasers are advised to consult their state and local building regulations and a state-certified architect prior to any construction related to these plans.

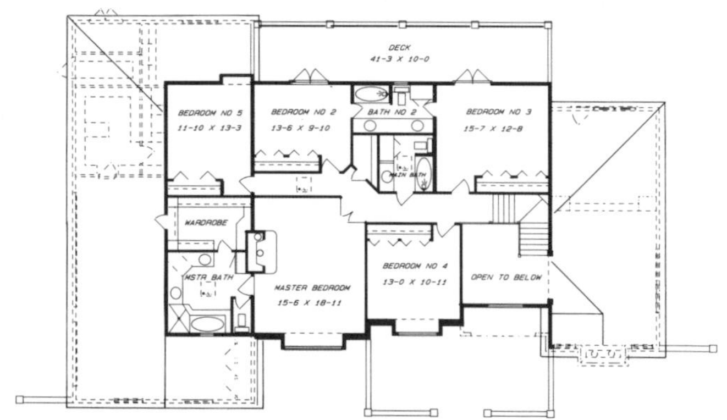

Second Floor

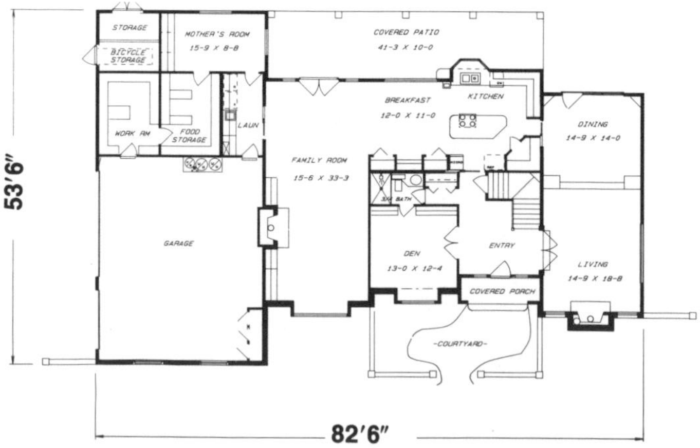

First Floor

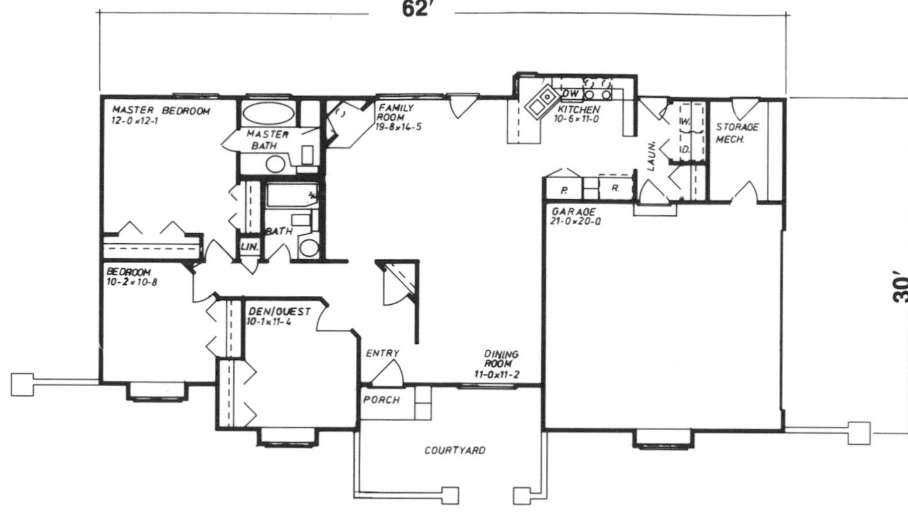

Appealing Corner Fireplace Accents Family Room

Total living space—1253 sq. ft.
2-3 bedrooms, 2 baths
Shown with concrete slab construction

- Separate entry foyer features a convenient coat closet.
- Closet space is provided in the den, making it suitable for use as a third bedroom.
- Dining room overlooks the private front courtyard.
- Master bedroom has its own bath which includes a separate tub and shower.
- Order each elevation separately.

The plan price is $300.00. You may choose either five sets of bluelines or a reproducible mylar. Plan by Design Profile, Inc.

The diagrams presented here constitute only floor plans and elevations. Purchasers are advised to consult their state and local building regulations and a state-certified architect prior to any construction related to these plans.

Plan number DPI-2381-9002-SW93

Plan number DPI-2382-9002-SW93

Kitchen Location Makes It Practical, Efficient

First floor—1417 sq. ft.
Second floor—1410 sq. ft.
Total living space—2827 sq. ft.
4 bedrooms, 2½ baths
Shown with a basement

- Functional snack bar separates the kitchen and family room without obstructing the view.
- Skylights illuminate the second floor hallway, master bedroom and its walk-in closet.
- Fireplaces are included in the living and family rooms.
- French doors in the den open onto the private, front courtyard.
- Extra garage space may be used for a vehicle or additional storage.

Plan number DPI-L2407-89MJ-SW93. The plan price is $424.05. You may choose either five sets of bluelines or a reproducible mylar. Plan by Design Profile, Inc.

The diagrams presented here constitute only floor plans and elevations. Purchasers are advised to consult their state and local building regulations and a state-certified architect prior to any construction related to these plans.

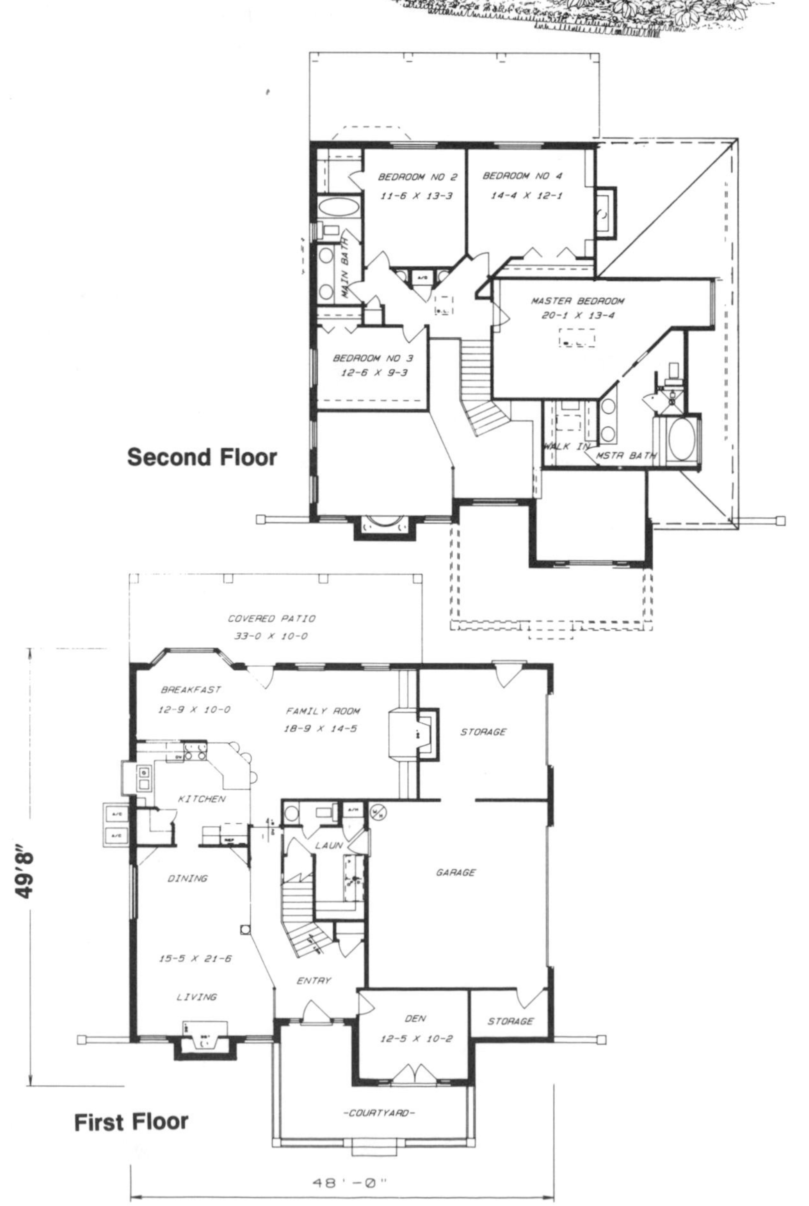

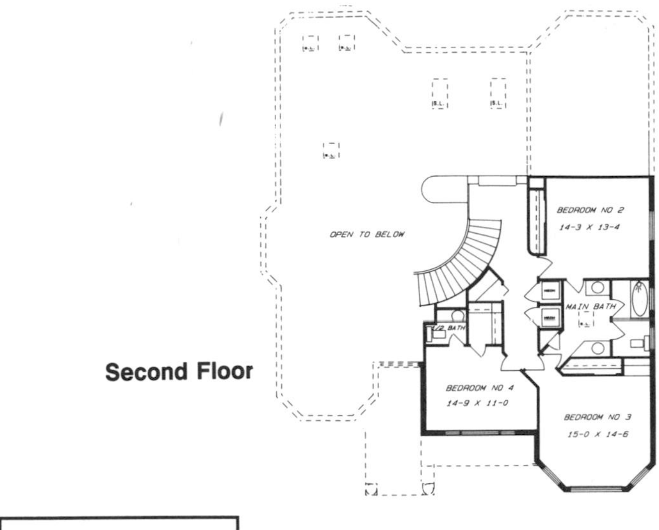

Second Floor

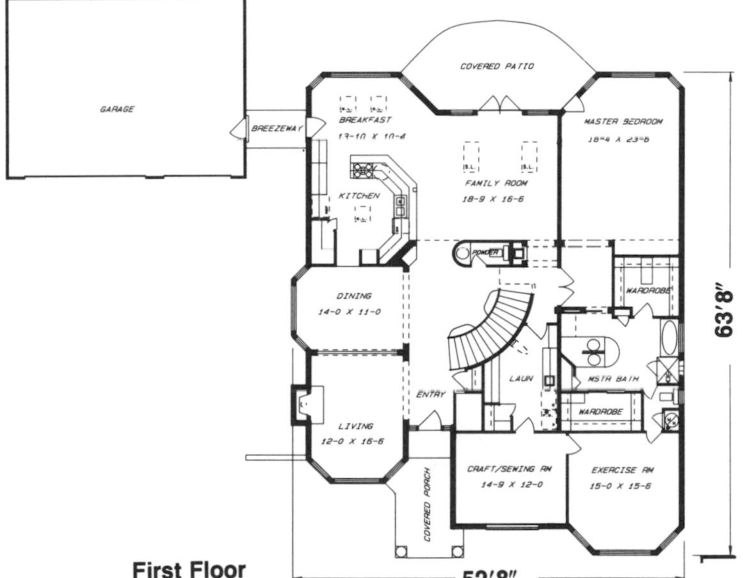

First Floor

Skylights Flood The Family Area With Sunshine

First floor—2835 sq. ft.
Second floor—995 sq. ft.
Total living space—3830 sq. ft.
4 bedrooms, 2 full baths
2 powder rooms
Shown with concrete slab construction

- French doors in the family room open out to a covered patio.
- Volume ceilings add extra impact to the entire living area.
- Top-of-the-line master suite includes a spacious bath/dressing area and private access to an exercise room.
- Craft/sewing room is also ideally suited as an at-home office.
- Very accessible central laundry room includes generous storage space and a built-in ironing board.

Plan number DPI-2405-89MJ-SW93. The plan price is $574.50. You may choose either five sets of bluelines or a reproducible mylar. Plan by Design Profile, Inc.

The diagrams presented here constitute only floor plans and elevations. Purchasers are advised to consult their state and local building regulations and a state-certified architect prior to any construction related to these plans.

Sunken Living, Family Rooms Afford Plenty Of Entertaining Space

First floor—1286 sq. ft.
Second floor—972 sq. ft.
Total living space—2258 sq. ft.
4 bedrooms, 2½ baths
Shown with a basement

- Formal entry is flanked by the living and dining rooms.
- Kitchen/breakfast area includes a convenient built-in desk.
- Generous closet space is provided in all of the bedrooms.
- Utility room serves as a mud room with access to the back yard.
- Order each elevation separately.

The plan price is $338.70. You may choose either five sets of bluelines or a reproducible mylar. Plan by Design Profile, Inc.

The diagrams presented here constitute only floor plans and elevations. Purchasers are advised to consult their state and local building regulations and a state-certified architect prior to any construction related to these plans.

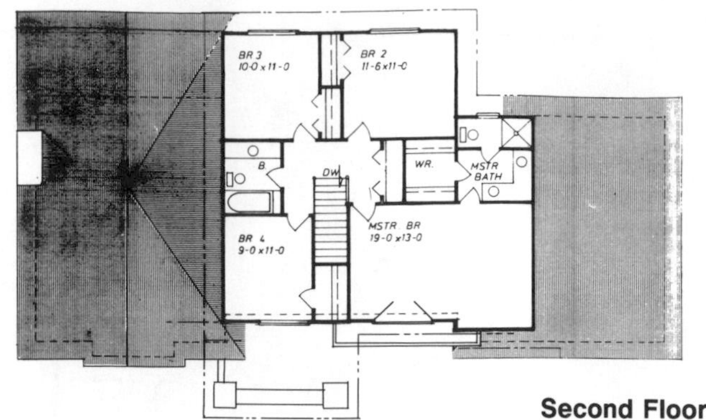

Second Floor

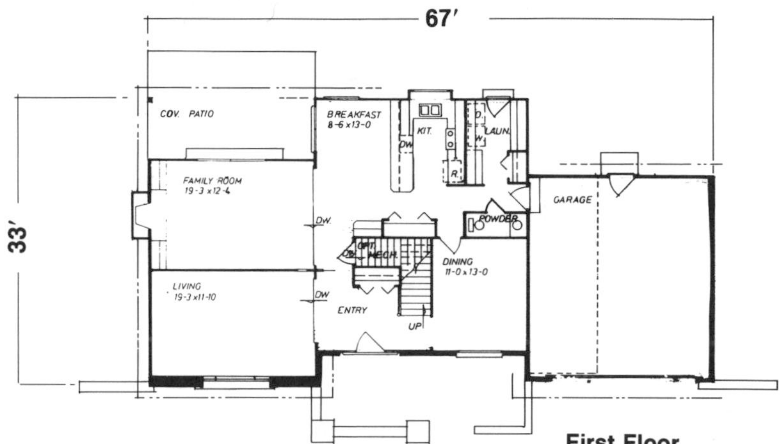

First Floor

Plan number DPI-M2315A-9008-SW93

Plan number DPI-M2315-9008-SW93

Lots Of Windows Ensure Sun-Filled Living Areas

Total living space—2352 sq. ft.
4 bedrooms, 2½ baths
Shown with concrete slab construction

- Volume ceilings enhance the sense of space throughout the living areas.
- Skylight in the kitchen provides natural illumination.
- Windows surround the breakfast area which overlooks the covered rear patio.
- Unusual spa tub is a distinctive feature in the plush master bath.

Plan number DPI-M2300-90MF-SW93. The plan price is $352.80. You may choose either five sets of bluelines or a reproducible mylar. Plan by Design Profile, Inc.

The diagrams presented here constitute only floor plans and elevations. Purchasers are advised to consult their state and local building regulations and a state-certified architect prior to any construction related to these plans.

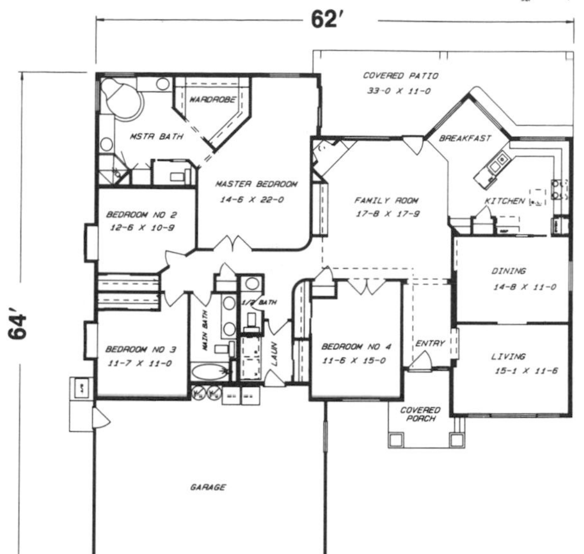

Courtyard Creates Totally Private Vestibule

Total living space—1520 sq. ft.
3 bedrooms, 2 baths
Shown with concrete slab construction

- Living space may be totally open, or choose to separate the living and family rooms with an optional low wall.
- Large, corner pantry is a desirable amenity in the kitchen.
- Master bedroom has a compartmented, walk-through bath which leads to a large walk-in closet.
- Fireplace can be enjoyed from anywhere in the open family zone.

Plan number DPI-2388-AJ92-SW93. The plan price is $300.00. You may choose either five sets of bluelines or a reproducible mylar. Plan by Design Profile, Inc.

The diagrams presented here constitute only floor plans and elevations. Purchasers are advised to consult their state and local building regulations and a state-certified architect prior to any construction related to these plans.

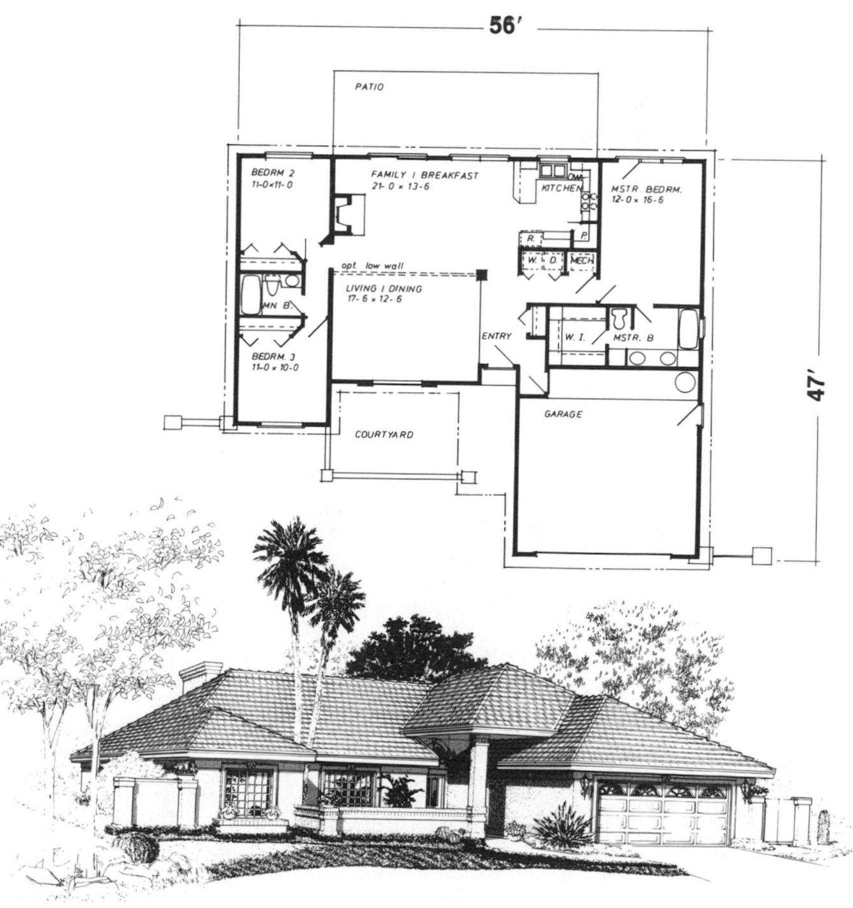

Plan number DPI-M2312-9006-SW93

Plan number DPI-M2311-9006-SW93

Four Bedrooms, Separate Living, Family Rooms In Versatile Ranch

Total living space—2076 sq. ft.
4 bedrooms, 2½ baths
Shown with concrete slab construction

- Kitchen's central location simplifies serving either the formal or informal entertainment areas.
- Dining room and breakfast nook each have access to a covered patio.
- Family room features a fireplace and built-in bookshelves.
- Compartmented master bath includes a dual-sink vanity.
- Order each elevation separately.

The plan price is $311.40. You may choose either five sets of bluelines or a reproducible mylar. Plan by Design Profile, Inc.

The diagrams presented here constitute only floor plans and elevations. Purchasers are advised to consult their state and local building regulations and a state-certified architect prior to any construction related to these plans.

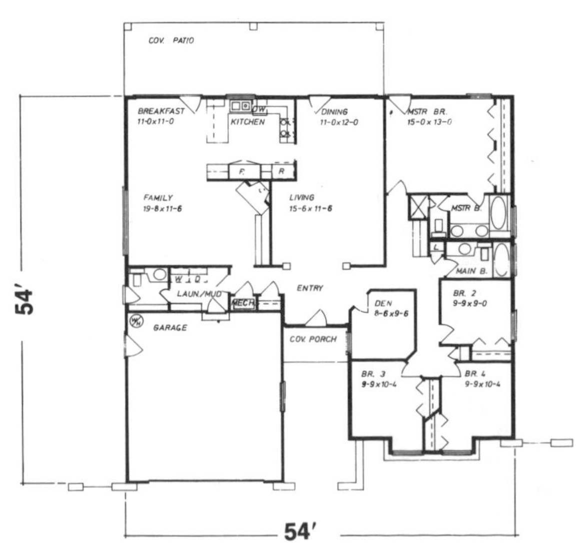

Rambling Ranch With Luxury Amenities

Total living space—4093 sq. ft.
3-4 bedrooms, 4½ baths
Shown with concrete slab construction

- Dramatic volume ceiling treatments are used throughout the interior.
- Each bedroom has access to its own bath.
- Master suite is exceptionally plush and includes a private lounge.
- Living room features a hidden wet bar, a fireplace and leaded glass windows at its entry.
- Two-car garage is extra deep to accommodate a golf cart.

Plan number DPI-2321-90MO-SW93. The plan price is $613.95. You may choose either five sets of bluelines or a reproducible mylar. Plan by Design Profile, Inc.

The diagrams presented here constitute only floor plans and elevations. Purchasers are advised to consult their state and local building regulations and a state-certified architect prior to any construction related to these plans.

PLANTER
BATH
WARDROBE
TERRACE
BREAKFAST 13-1X14-6
COVERED PATIO
BEDROOM NO 4 13-7X12-0
FAMILY ROOM 22-10X23-2
KITCHEN
LIVING 18-0X19-8
MASTER BEDROOM 18-3X16-1
3/4 BATH
BATH #3
MASTERS LOUNGE 10-7X10-6
BEDROOM NO 3 13-7X14-0
STORAGE
LAUN
DINING 13-6X18-0
ENTRY
1/2 BATH
GARAGE
COVERED PORCH
DEN/GUEST 16-1X13-6
-COURTYARD-
89'6"
83'1"

en/Guest Room Leaves The Choice To You

Total living space—2302 sq. ft.
3-4 bedrooms, 2 baths
Shown with concrete slab construction

- Spacious living/dining area is defined by attractive columns.
- Kitchen includes generous counter space and a walk-in pantry.
- Closet space is provided in the den.
- Skylights illuminate bedroom hallway and main bath.
- Dual-sink vanities are included in both bathrooms.

Plan number DPI-M2380-AJ91-SW93. The plan price is $345.30. You may choose either five sets of bluelines or a reproducible mylar. Plan by Design Profile, Inc.

The diagrams presented here constitute only floor plans and elevations. Purchasers are advised to consult their state and local building regulations and a state-certified architect prior to any construction related to these plans.

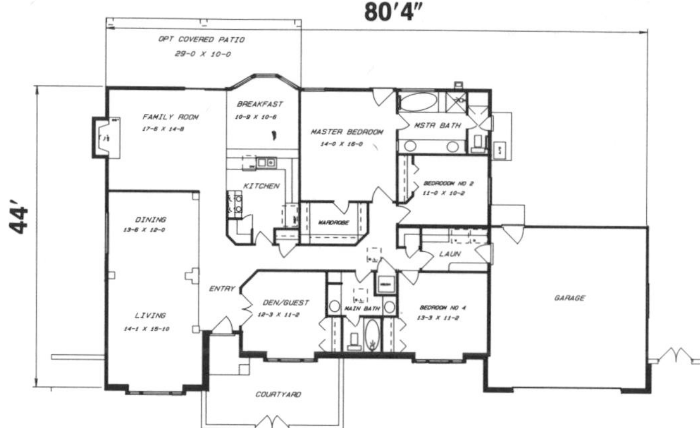

Arches Add Impact To Entryways

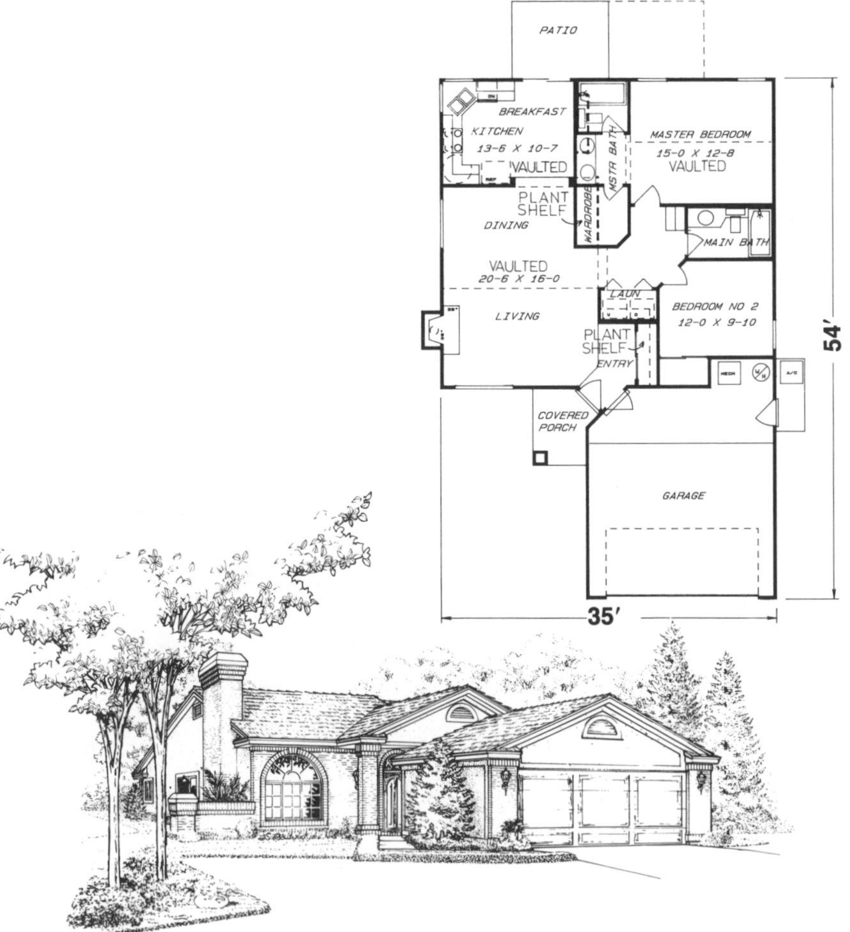

Total living space—1107 sq. ft.
2 bedrooms, 2 baths
Shown with concrete slab construction

- Archways highlight the entry to the breakfast nook, master bath and main hallway.
- Vaulted ceilings visually expand interior space.
- Plant shelves provide an accent over the entry and master closets.
- Sliding glass doors in the breakfast nook open onto a patio.
- Living room features a fireplace as its focal point.

Plan number DPI-2344-SW93. The plan price is $300.00. You may choose either five sets of bluelines or a reproducible mylar. Plan by Design Profile, Inc.

The diagrams presented here constitute only floor plans and elevations. Purchasers are advised to consult their state and local building regulations and a state-certified architect prior to any construction related to these plans.

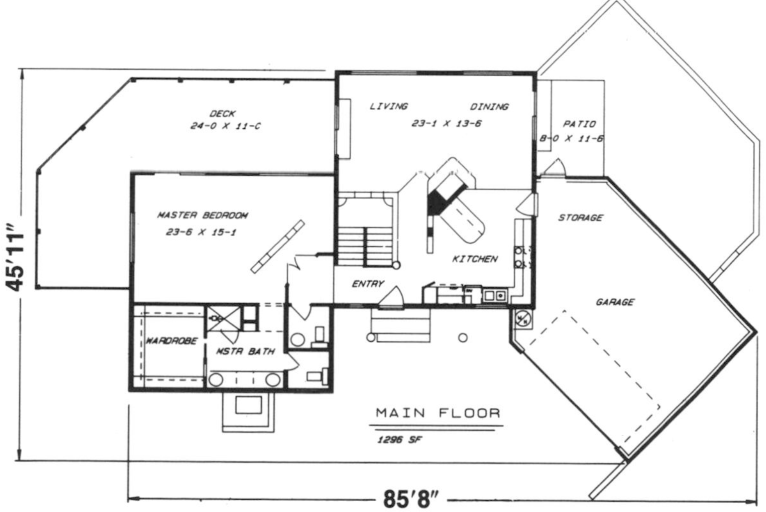

Basement

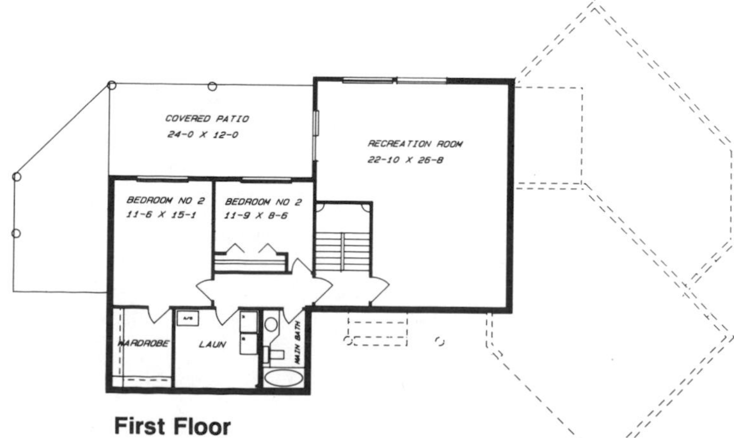

First Floor

Team Walk-Out Lower Level With Sloped Site For Winning Combination

Main floor—1296 sq. ft.
Lower floor—1250 sq. ft.
Total living space—2546 sq. ft.
3 bedrooms, 2½ baths
Shown with a basement

- Sliding glass doors in the living room, master bedroom open onto a deck.
- Lovely corner fireplace accents both the living and dining rooms.
- Angled snack bar is included in the kitchen.
- Spacious L-shaped rec room offers informal space on the lower level.
- Generous closet space is included in the bedrooms.

Plan number DPI-2331-SW93. The plan price is $381.90. You may choose either five sets of bluelines or a reproducible mylar. Plan by Design Profile, Inc.

The diagrams presented here constitute only floor plans and elevations. Purchasers are advised to consult their state and local building regulations and a state-certified architect prior to any construction related to these plans.

Casual, Open Interior Adapts Well To Formal Entertaining, Too

First floor—1078 sq. ft.
Second floor—737 sq. ft.
Total living space—1815 sq. ft.
3 bedrooms, 2½ baths
Shown with a basement

- Separate living room creates a formal environment when entertaining guests.
- Unrestricted views connect the family room, dining area and kitchen.
- Bi-fold doors hide a large pantry in the kitchen.
- Master bedroom has its own bathroom and walk-in closet.
- Garage entry opens into a mud room.

Plan number DPI-M2388-9002-SW93. The plan price is $300.00. You may choose either five sets of bluelines or a reproducible mylar. Plan by Design Profile, Inc.

The diagrams presented here constitute only floor plans and elevations. Purchasers are advised to consult their state and local building regulations and a state-certified architect prior to any construction related to these plans.

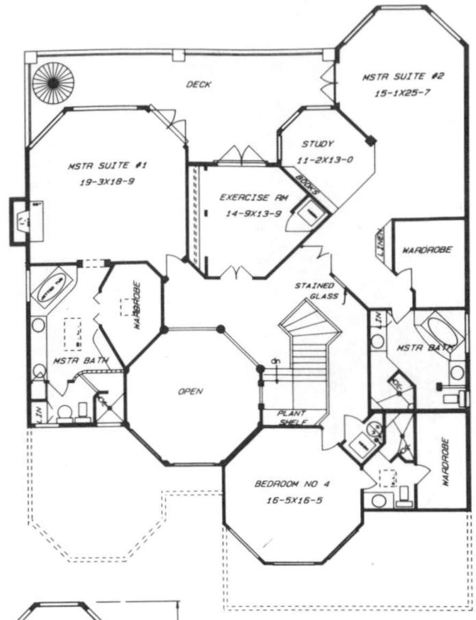

DECK
MSTR SUITE #2 15-1X25-7
MSTR SUITE #1 19-3X18-9
STUDY 11-2X13-0
EXERCISE RM 14-9X13-9
WARDROBE
STAINED GLASS
MSTR BATH
OPEN
PLANT SHELF
BEDROOM NO 4 16-5X16-5

Second Floor

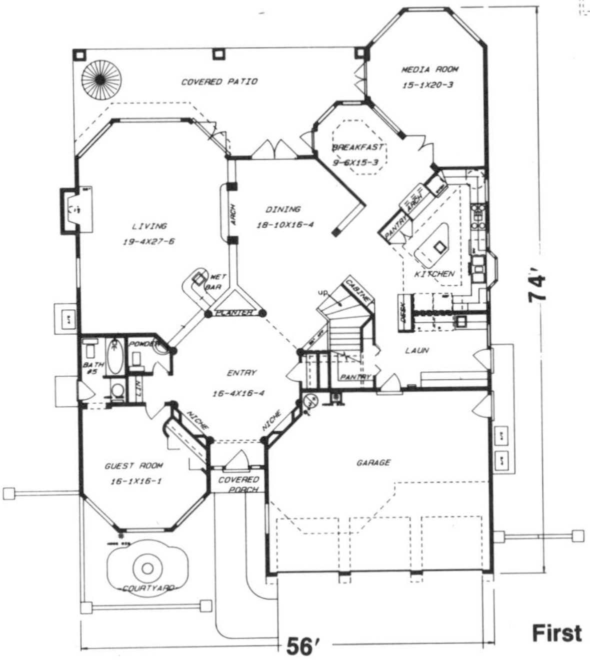

COVERED PATIO
MEDIA ROOM 15-1X20-3
BREAKFAST 9-6X15-3
LIVING 19-4X27-6
DINING 18-10X16-4
KITCHEN
WET BAR
PLANTER
POWDER
BATH #5
ENTRY 16-4X16-4
LAUN
PANTRY
GUEST ROOM 16-1X16-1
COVERED PORCH
GARAGE
COURTYARD
74′
56′

First Floor

Rambling Ranch Gives Its Owners Room To Roam

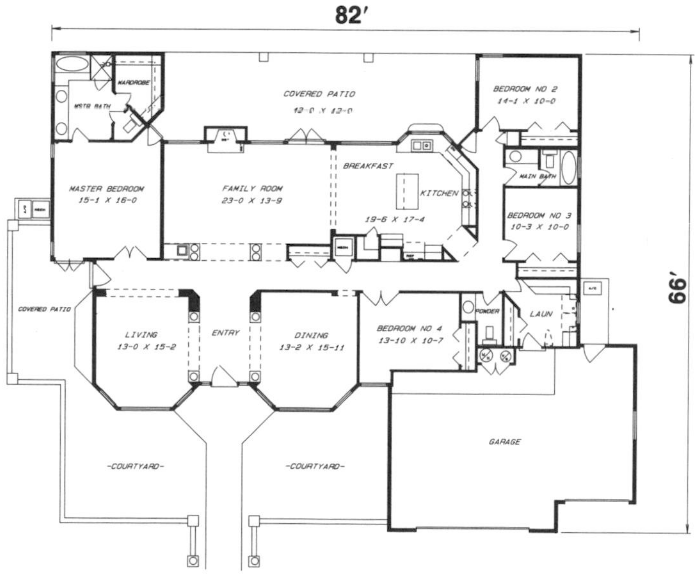

Total living space—2773 sq. ft.
4 bedrooms, 2½ baths
Shown with concrete slab construction

- Dramatic columns highlight the division of space between the foyer and living and dining areas, and the entry to the family room.
- Family room features a wet bar, a fireplace and French doors leading to a covered patio.
- Spacious kitchen includes a large center island a built-in desk and a pantry.
- First-class master bath highlights the master suite which also has outdoor access.

Plan number DPI-2380-AJ92-SW93. The plan price is $415.95. You may choose either five sets of bluelines or a reproducible mylar. Plan by Design Profile, Inc.

The diagrams presented here constitute only floor plans and elevations. Purchasers are advised to consult their state and local building regulations and a state-certified architect prior to any construction related to these plans.

Plan number DPI-L2322-90MO-SW93

Plan number DPI-L2323-90MO-SW93

Glamorous Master Bath, Efficient Kitchen, Expansion Space Add Up To A Winning Package

First floor—1099 sq. ft.
Second floor—944 sq. ft.
Total living space—2043 sq. ft.
Unfinished basement—1042 sq. ft.
3-5 bedrooms, 2-3½ baths
Shown with a basement

- Foyer, living and dining rooms feature vaulted ceilings.
- Family room has space for an optional fireplace.
- Finishing the basement level will add two bedrooms, a full bath and a large game room.
- Large master bath includes a separate tub and shower.
- Order each elevation separately.

The plan price is $306.45. You may choose either five sets of bluelines or a reproducible mylar. Plan by Design Profile, Inc.

The diagrams presented here constitute only floor plans and elevations. Purchasers are advised to consult their state and local building regulations and a state-certified architect prior to any construction related to these plans.

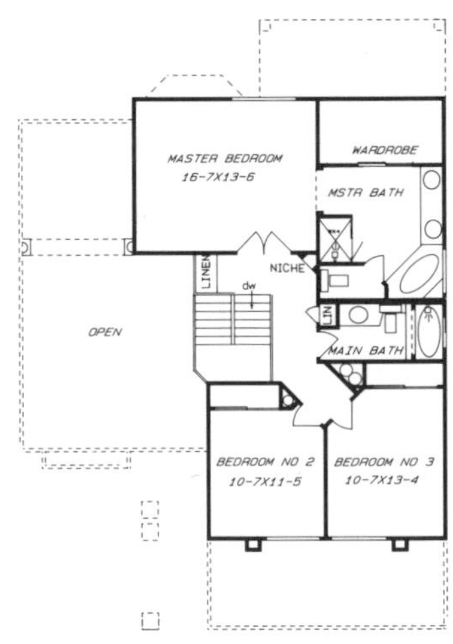

Second Floor

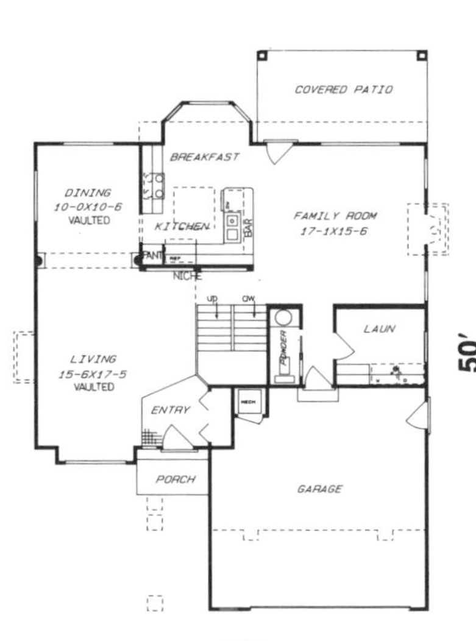

39′

First Floor

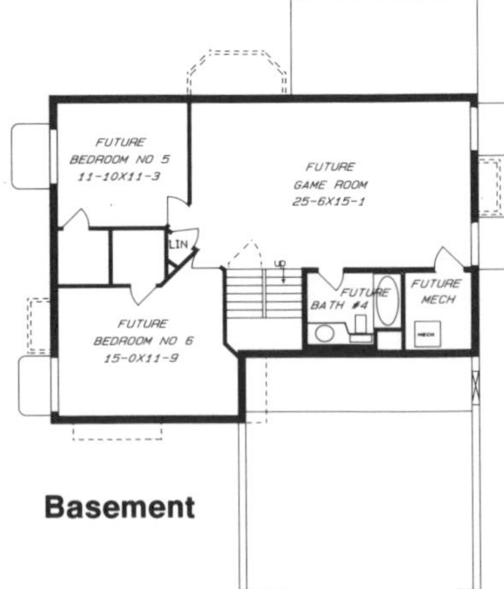

Basement

INDEX

Plans are available in standard blueline prints, mylar sepia or vellum prints. Plan prices are subject to change one month after date of publication.
To charge on American Express, MasterCard or Visa, call Toll Free 1-800-323-7379 (outside the United States call 708-635-8800) or send check to:

Professional Builder & Remodeler
1350 E. Touhy Avenue,
P.O. Box 5080
Des Plaines, IL 60017-5080

A house plan order will include the following:
- General specification design notes.
- Foundation and floor plans; basement plans included only where applicable.
- Exterior elevations of all four views.
- Building sections and details as required to construct individual design.
- Interior elevation of cabinets and walls with unique conditions.
- Schematic electrical plans with suggested switch, outlet and light fixture conditions.
- Some, but not all, plans have a list of building materials. (List is not recommended for use to order materials, but is generally helpful in acquiring an estimated construction price.)

Mechanical and plumbing drawings are not included. Mechanical and plumbing codes and regulations vary widely across the country; therefore, this portion of the design is left to the contractor.
Allow three weeks for processing and mailing. Plans are non-returnable. **Express mail delivery is available for an extra charge of $15. Canada express service at a cost of $20. One day overnight service is available for an extra charge of $40. Canada overnight service at a cost of $50. This charge is per each architect. Handling charge payable on all orders at a cost of $5.**

□ Check □ Bill American Express □ Bill MasterCard □ Bill Visa

I understand I will receive either 5 sets of bluelines, or a reproducible mylar or vellum. (Please refer to plan page to see which is available, mylar or vellum.) I would like to order the following plan numbers (homes under 2000 sq. ft. are a flat fee of $300.00).

________ ________ × $0.15 = $________
Plan Number Total sq. ft.
□ 5 bluelines □ mylars □ vellums

________ ________ × $0.15 = $________
Plan Number Total sq. ft.
□ 5 bluelines □ mylars □ vellums

________ ________ × $0.15 = $________
Plan Number Total sq. ft.
□ 5 bluelines □ mylars □ vellums

Special mailing charges (per each architect): = $________
Handling charges payable on all orders = $ 5.00
Total of order $________

Name________

Company name________

Address________
(cannot be delivered to a Post Office Box)

City/State/Zip Code________

Daytime phone with area code________

Credit card number________

Expiration date________

Plans are available in standard blueline prints, mylar sepia or vellum prints. Plan prices are subject to change one month after date of publication.
To charge on American Express, MasterCard or Visa, call Toll Free 1-800-323-7379 (outside the United States call 708-635-8800) or send check to:

Professional Builder & Remodeler
1350 E. Touhy Avenue,
P.O. Box 5080
Des Plaines, IL 60017-5080

A house plan order will include the following:
- General specification design notes.
- Foundation and floor plans; basement plans included only where applicable.
- Exterior elevations of all four views.
- Building sections and details as required to construct individual design.
- Interior elevation of cabinets and walls with unique conditions.
- Schematic electrical plans with suggested switch, outlet and light fixture conditions.
- Some, but not all, plans have a list of building materials. (List is not recommended for use to order materials, but is generally helpful in acquiring an estimated construction price.)

Mechanical and plumbing drawings are not included. Mechanical and plumbing codes and regulations vary widely across the country; therefore, this portion of the design is left to the contractor.
Allow three weeks for processing and mailing. Plans are non-returnable. **Express mail delivery is available for an extra charge of $15. Canada express service at a cost of $20. One day overnight service is available for an extra charge of $40. Canada overnight service at a cost of $50. This charge is per each architect. Handling charge payable on all orders at a cost of $5.**

□ Check □ Bill American Express □ Bill MasterCard □ Bill Visa

I understand I will receive either 5 sets of bluelines, or a reproducible mylar or vellum. (Please refer to plan page to see which is available, mylar or vellum.) I would like to order the following plan numbers (homes under 2000 sq. ft. are a flat fee of $300.00).

________ ________ × $0.15 = $________
Plan Number Total sq. ft.
□ 5 bluelines □ mylars □ vellums

________ ________ × $0.15 = $________
Plan Number Total sq. ft.
□ 5 bluelines □ mylars □ vellums

________ ________ × $0.15 = $________
Plan Number Total sq. ft.
□ 5 bluelines □ mylars □ vellums

Special mailing charges (per each architect): = $________
Handling charges payable on all orders = $ 5.00
Total of order $________

Name________

Company name________

Address________
(cannot be delivered to a Post Office Box)

City/State/Zip Code________

Daytime phone with area code________

Credit card number________

Expiration date________

INDEX

Plans are available in standard blueline prints, mylar sepia or vellum prints. Plan prices are subject to change one month after date of publication.
To charge on American Express, MasterCard or Visa, call Toll Free 1-800-323-7379 (outside the United States call 708-635-8800) or send check to:

Professional Builder & Remodeler
1350 E. Touhy Avenue,
P.O. Box 5080
Des Plaines, IL 60017-5080

A house plan order will include the following:

- General specification design notes.
- Foundation and floor plans; basement plans included only where applicable.
- Exterior elevations of all four views.
- Building sections and details as required to construct individual design.
- Interior elevation of cabinets and walls with unique conditions.
- Schematic electrical plans with suggested switch, outlet and light fixture conditions.
- Some, but not all, plans have a list of building materials. (List is not recommended for use to order materials, but is generally helpful in acquiring an estimated construction price.)

Mechanical and plumbing drawings are not included. Mechanical and plumbing codes and regulations vary widely across the country; therefore, this portion of the design is left to the contractor.
Allow three weeks for processing and mailing. Plans are non-returnable. **Express mail delivery is available for an extra charge of $15. Canada express service at a cost of $20. One day overnight service is available for an extra charge of $40. Canada overnight service at a cost of $50. This charge is per each architect. Handling charge payable on all orders at a cost of $5.**

□ Check □ Bill American Express □ Bill MasterCard □ Bill Visa

I understand I will receive either 5 sets of bluelines, or a reproducible mylar or vellum. (Please refer to plan page to see which is available, mylar or vellum.) I would like to order the following plan numbers (homes under 2000 sq. ft. are a flat fee of $300.00).

__________ __________ × $0.15 = $__________
Plan Number Total sq. ft.

□ 5 bluelines □ mylars □ vellums

__________ __________ × $0.15 = $__________
Plan Number Total sq. ft.

□ 5 bluelines □ mylars □ vellums

__________ __________ × $0.15 = $__________
Plan Number Total sq. ft.

□ 5 bluelines □ mylars □ vellums

Special mailing charges (per each architect): = $__________
Handling charges payable on all orders = $ 5.00

Total of order $__________

Name__________

Company name__________

Address__________
(cannot be delivered to a Post Office Box)

City/State/Zip Code__________

Daytime phone with area code__________

Credit card number__________

Expiration date__________

- - - - - - - - - - - - - - - - - - - -

Plans are available in standard blueline prints, mylar sepia or vellum prints. Plan prices are subject to change one month after date of publication.
To charge on American Express, MasterCard or Visa, call Toll Free 1-800-323-7379 (outside the United States call 708-635-8800) or send check to:

Professional Builder & Remodeler
1350 E. Touhy Avenue,
P.O. Box 5080
Des Plaines, IL 60017-5080

A house plan order will include the following:

- General specification design notes.
- Foundation and floor plans; basement plans included only where applicable.
- Exterior elevations of all four views.
- Building sections and details as required to construct individual design.
- Interior elevation of cabinets and walls with unique conditions.
- Schematic electrical plans with suggested switch, outlet and light fixture conditions.
- Some, but not all, plans have a list of building materials. (List is not recommended for use to order materials, but is generally helpful in acquiring an estimated construction price.)

Mechanical and plumbing drawings are not included. Mechanical and plumbing codes and regulations vary widely across the country; therefore, this portion of the design is left to the contractor.
Allow three weeks for processing and mailing. Plans are non-returnable. **Express mail delivery is available for an extra charge of $15. Canada express service at a cost of $20. One day overnight service is available for an extra charge of $40. Canada overnight service at a cost of $50. This charge is per each architect. Handling charge payable on all orders at a cost of $5.**

□ Check □ Bill American Express □ Bill MasterCard □ Bill Visa

I understand I will receive either 5 sets of bluelines, or a reproducible mylar or vellum. (Please refer to plan page to see which is available, mylar or vellum.) I would like to order the following plan numbers (homes under 2000 sq. ft. are a flat fee of $300.00).

__________ __________ × $0.15 = $__________
Plan Number Total sq. ft.

□ 5 bluelines □ mylars □ vellums

__________ __________ × $0.15 = $__________
Plan Number Total sq. ft.

□ 5 bluelines □ mylars □ vellums

__________ __________ × $0.15 = $__________
Plan Number Total sq. ft.

□ 5 bluelines □ mylars □ vellums

Special mailing charges (per each architect): = $__________
Handling charges payable on all orders = $ 5.00

Total of order $__________

Name__________

Company name__________

Address__________
(cannot be delivered to a Post Office Box)

City/State/Zip Code__________

Daytime phone with area code__________

Credit card number__________

Expiration date__________

BNi Building News™

Costbook

Los Angeles • Boston

Preface

For the past 47 years, *Building News* has been dedicated to providing construction professionals with timely and reliable information. Based on this experience, our staff has researched and compiled thousands of up-to-the minute costs for the second annual editions of *Building News Costbooks.*
This book is an essential reference for contractors, engineers, architects, facilities managers-any construction professional who must provide an estimate on any type of building project.

Whether working up a preliminary estimate or submitting a formal bid, the costs listed here can quickly and easily be tailored to your needs. All costs are based on national averages, while a table of modifiers is provided for regional adjustments. Overhead and profit are included in all costs.

All data is categorized according to the MASTERFORMAT of the Construction Specifications Institute (CSI). This industry standard provides an all-inclusive checklist to ensure that no element of a project is overlooked. In addition, to make specific items even easier to locate, there is a complete alphabetical index.

The "Features in this Book" section presents a clear overview of the many features of this book. Included is an explanation of the data, sample page layout and discussion of how to best use the information in the book.

Of course, all buildings and construction projects are unique. The costs provided in this book are based on averages from well-managed projects with good labor productivity under normal working conditions (eight hours a day). Other circumstances affecting costs such as overtime, unusual or hidden costs must be factored in as they arise.

The data provided in this book is for estimating purposes only. Check all applicable federal, state and local codes and regulations for specific requirements.

Editor-In-Chief
William D. Mahoney

Contributing Editors
Kenneth M. Randall
Edward B. Wetherill

Technical Services
Anthony Jackson
Ramon Lopez
Rita Wong

Design
Robert O. Wright

BNI Publications, Inc.

3055 Overland Avenue
Los Angeles, CA 90034
(310) 202-7775

77 Wexford Street
Needham Heights, MA 02194
(617) 455-1466

Geographic Cost Modifiers

The costs as presented in this book attempt to represent national averages. Costs, however, vary among regions, states and even between adjacent localities.

In order to more closely approximate the probable costs for specific locations throughout the U.S., this table of Geographic Cost Modifiers is provided. These adjustment factors are used to modify costs obtained from this book to help account for regional variations of construction costs and to provide a more accurate estimate for specific areas. The factors are formulated by comparing costs in a specific area to the costs as presented in the Costbook pages. An example of how to use these factors is shown below. Whenever local current costs are known, whether material prices or labor rates, they should be used when more accuracy is required.

Cost obtained from Costbook pages × Location Cost Adjustment Factor = Adjusted Cost

For example, a project estimated to cost \$125,000 using the Costbook pages can be adjusted to more closely approximate the cost in Los Angeles: \$125,000 × 1.07 = \$133,750.

Location	Factor
Alabama	0.78
Alaska	1.35
Arizona	0.88
Arkansas	0.72
California	
Los Angeles	1.07
San Francisco	1.21
Other	1.01
Colorado	0.87
Connecticut	1.02
Delaware	0.90
Florida	0.80
Georgia	
Atlanta	0.81
Other	0.73
Hawaii	1.20
Idaho	0.86
Illinois	
Chicago	0.99
Other	0.93
Indiana	0.88
Iowa	0.86
Kansas	0.80
Kentucky	0.83
Louisiana	0.84
Maine	0.87
Maryland	0.89
Massachusetts	
Boston	1.05
Other	0.98
Michigan	0.90
Minnesota	0.91
Missouri	0.84
Montana	0.85
Nebraska	0.81
Nevada	0.93
New Hampshire	0.88
New Jersey	0.98
New Mexico	0.82
New York	
New York City	1.24
Other	0.93
North Carolina	0.73
North Dakota	0.85
Ohio	0.86
Oklahoma	0.77
Oregon	0.89
Pennsylvania	
Philadelphia	1.03
Other	0.89
Rhode Island	0.99
South Carolina	0.75
South Dakota	0.75
Tennessee	0.78
Texas	0.80
Utah	0.81
Vermont	0.86
Virginia	0.81
Washington	1.00
Washington D.C.	0.93
West Virginia	0.86
Wisconsin	0.91
Wyoming	0.86

Features In This Book

Sample pages with graphic explanations are included before the Costbook pages and Man-Hour Tables. These explanations along with the discussions below, will provide a good understanding of what is included in this book and how it can best be used in construction estimating.

Material Costs

The material costs used in this book represent national averages for prices that a contractor would expect to pay plus an allowance for freight (if applicable), handling and storage. These costs reflect neither the lowest or highest prices, but rather a typical average cost over time. Periodic fluctuations in availability and in certain commodities (eg. cooper, lumber) can significantly affect local material pricing. In the final estimating and bidding stages of a project when the highest degree of accuracy is required, it is best to check local, current prices.

Labor Costs

Labor costs include the basic wage, plus commonly applicable taxes, insurance and markups for overhead and profit. The labor rates used here to develop the costs are typical average prevailing wage rates. Rates for different trades are used where appropriate for each type of work.

Taxes and insurance which are most often applied to labor rates included employer-paid Social Security/Medicare taxes (FICA), Worker's Compensation insurance, state and federal unemployment taxes, and business insurance. Fixed government rates as well as average allowances are included in the labor costs. However, most of these items vary significantly from state to state and within states. For more specific data, local agencies and sources should be consulted.

Equipment Costs

Cost for various types and pieces of equipment are included in Division I—General Requirements and can be included in an estimate when required either as a total "Equipment" category or with specific appropriate trades. Costs for equipment are included when appropriate in the installation of costs in the Costbook pages.

Overhead And Profit

Included in the labor costs are allowances for overhead and profit for the contractor/employer whose workers are performing the specific tasks. No cost allowances or fees are included for management of subcontractors by the general contractor or construction manager. These cost, where appropriate, must be added to the costs as listed in the book.

The allowance for overhead is included to account for office overhead, the contractors' typical costs of doing business. These costs normally include in-house office staff salaries and benefits, office rent and operating expenses, professional fees, vehicle costs and other operating costs which are not directly applicable to specific jobs. It should be noted for this book that office overhead as included should be distinguished from project overhead, the General Requirements (CSI Division 1) which are specific to particular projects. Project overhead should be included on an item by item basis for each job.

Depending on the trade, an allowance of 10 to 15 percent is incorporated into the labor/installation costs to account for typical profit of the installing contractor. See Division 1, General Requirements, for a more detailed review of typical profit allowances.

Adjustments to Costs

The costs as presented in this book attempt to represent national averages. Costs, however, vary among regions, states and even between adjacent localities.

In order to more closely approximate the probable costs for specific locations throughout the U.S., a table of Geographic Cost Modifiers is provided. These adjustment factors are used to modify costs obtained from this book to help account for regional variations of construction costs. Whenever local current cost are known, whether material or equipment prices or labor rates, they should be used if more accuracy is required.

Editors' Note: *The Building News Costbooks* are intended to provide accurate, reliable, average costs and typical productivities for thousands of common construction components. The data is developed and compiled from various industry sources, including government, manufacturers, suppliers and working professionals. The intent of the information is to provide assistance and guidelines to construction professionals in estimating. The user should be aware that local conditions, material and labor availability and cost variations, economic considerations, weather, local codes and regulations, etc., all affect the actual cost of construction. These and other such factors must be considered and incorporated into any and all construction estimates.

Sample Costbook Page

In order to best use the information in this book, please review this sample page and read the "Features In This Book" section.

CSI MASTERFORMAT Division

CSI Broadscope Category

CSI Mediumscope Category (First 5 Digits)

Detailed Descriptions
Complete descriptions of items may include information listed above a particular line. Review of the whole category is recommended for a complete description.

03	CONCRETE			
PLACING CONCRETE	**UNIT**	**MAT.**	**INST.**	**TOTAL**
03380.05 BEAM CONCRETE				
By crane	C.Y.	65.00	38.50	103.50
By pump	"	65.00	35.00	100.00
By hand buggy	"	65.00	20.40	85.40
Bond beam, 3000# concrete				
By pump				
8" high				
4" wide	L.F.	0.15	0.77	0.92
6" wide	"	0.36	0.87	1.23
8" wide	"	0.47	0.96	1.43
10" wide	"	0.63	1.05	1.68
12" wide	"	0.84	1.20	2.04
16" high				
8" wide	L.F.	1.15	1.20	2.35
10" wide	"	1.55	1.35	2.90
12" wide	"	2.05	1.60	3.65
By crane				
8" high				
4" wide	L.F.	0.18	0.84	1.02
6" wide	"	0.36	0.92	1.28
8" wide	"	0.47	0.96	1.43
10" wide	"	0.63	1.05	1.68
12" wide	"	0.84	1.20	2.04
16" high				
8" wide	L.F.	1.15	1.20	2.35
10" wide	"	1.55	1.30	2.85
12" wide	"	2.05	1.50	3.55
03380.15 COLUMN CONCRETE				
Columns				
2500# or 3000# concrete				
By crane	C.Y.	56.50	35.00	91.50
By pump	"	56.50	32.10	88.60
3500# or 4000# concrete				
By crane	C.Y.	60.50	35.00	95.50
By pump	"	60.50	32.10	92.60
5000# concrete				
By crane	C.Y.	65.00	35.00	100.00
By pump	"	65.00	32.10	97.10
03380.20 ELEVATED SLAB CONCRETE				
Elevated slab				
2500# or 3000# concrete				
By crane	C.Y.	56.50	19.25	75.75
By pump	"	56.50	14.80	71.30
By hand buggy	"	56.50	20.40	76.90
3500# or 4000# concrete				
By crane	C.Y.	60.50	19.25	79.75
By pump	"	60.50	14.80	75.30
By hand buggy	"	60.50	20.40	80.90
5000# concrete				
By crane	C.Y.	65.00	19.25	84.25
By pump	"	65.00	14.80	79.80

Material Cost
Material costs represent average contractor prices plus an allowance for freight, handling and storage.

Installation Cost
Installation costs include basic wage rates, markups for taxes, insurance overhead and profit and also include equipment costs where appropriate.

Total Cost
The total cost is the sum of material and installation costs. This total represents typical contractors' costs including overhead and profit, but does not include markups for the general contractor or construction management fees.

Unit of Measurement
Each item (and cost) is defined in terms of the common estimating unit. All costs are listed in dollars per unit.

01 GENERAL

REQUIREMENTS	UNIT	MAT.	INST.	TOTAL
01500.10 TEMPORARY FACILITIES				
Trailers, general office type, per month				
Minimum	EA.			110.00
Average	"			220.00
Maximum	"			440.00
01525.10 CONSTRUCTION AIDS				
Scaffolding/staging, rent per month				
Measured by lineal feet of base				
10' high	L.F.			6.60
20' high	"			11.00
01600.10 EQUIPMENT				
Air compressor				
60 cfm				
By day	EA.			55.00
By week	"			165.00
By month	"			495.00
Generators, 5 kw				
By day	EA.			44.00
By week	"			132.00
By month	"			396.00
Heaters, salamander type, per week				
Minimum	EA.			55.00
Average	"			82.50
Maximum	"			110.00
Pumps, submersible				
50 gpm				
By day	EA.			44.00
By week	"			132.00
By month	"			396.00
Pickup truck				
By day	EA.			110.00
By week	"			330.00
By month	"			990.00
Dump truck				
6 cy truck				
By day	EA.			220.00
By week	"			660.00
By month	"			1,980
16 cy truck				
By day	EA.			275.00
By week	"			825.00
By month	"			2,420
Backhoe, track mounted				
1 cy capacity				
By day	EA.			660.00
By week	"			1,980
By month	"			5,940
3 cy capacity				
By day	EA.			1,650
By week	"			4,950
By month	"			14,850

01 GENERAL

REQUIREMENTS	UNIT	MAT.	INST.	TOTAL
01600.10 EQUIPMENT				
Bulldozer				
75 hp				
By day	EA.			440.00
By week	"			1,320
By month	"			3,960
200 hp				
By day	EA.			880.00
By week	"			2,640
By month	"			7,920
Cranes, crawler type				
15 ton capacity				
By day	EA.			440.00
By week	"			1,320
By month	"			3,960
Truck mounted, hydraulic				
15 ton capacity				
By day	EA.			440.00
By week	"			1,320
By month	"			3,960
Loader, rubber tired				
1 cy capacity				
By day	EA.			440.00
By week	"			1,320
By month	"			3,960
2 cy capacity				
By day	EA.			550.00
By week	"			1,650
By month	"			4,950
01740.10 BONDS				
Performance bonds				
Minimum	PCT			1.00
Average	"			2.00
Maximum	"			3.00

02 SITEWORK

DEMOLITION

DEMOLITION	UNIT	MAT.	INST.	TOTAL
02060.10 BUILDING DEMOLITION				
Building, complete with disposal				
Wood frame	C.F.	0.00	0.15	0.15
Concrete	"	0.00	0.23	0.23
Steel frame	"	0.00	0.30	0.30
Partition removal				
Brick masonry partitions				
8" thick	S.F.	0.00	1.25	1.25
Stud partitions				
Metal or wood, with drywall both sides	S.F.	0.00	1.00	1.00
Door and frame removal				
Single				
2'6"x6'8"	EA.	0.00	14.55	14.55
3'x6'8"	"	0.00	17.00	17.00
Double				
2'6"x6'8"	EA.	0.00	20.40	20.40
3'x6'8"	"	0.00	22.65	22.65
Floor removal				
Residential wood	S.F.	0.00	0.58	0.58
Resilient tile or linoleum	"	0.00	0.20	0.20
Ceiling removal				
Acoustical tile ceiling				
Adhesive fastened	S.F.	0.00	0.20	0.20
Suspended grid	"	0.00	0.13	0.13
Drywall ceiling				
Nailed to framing	S.F.	0.00	0.20	0.20
Plastered ceiling				
Furred on framing	S.F.	0.00	0.51	0.51
Roofing removal				
Built up roof on wood deck	S.F.	0.00	0.63	0.63
Roof shingles	"	0.00	0.34	0.34
Window removal				
Metal windows, trim included				
2'x3'	EA.	0.00	20.40	20.40
3'x4'	"	0.00	25.50	25.50
Wood windows, trim included				
2'x3'	EA.	0.00	20.40	20.40
3'x4'	"	0.00	13.60	13.60
02065.15 SAW CUTTING PAVEMENT				
Pavement, bituminous				
2" thick	L.F.	0.00	0.80	0.80
3" thick	"	0.00	1.00	1.00
Concrete pavement, with wire mesh				
4" thick	L.F.	0.00	1.55	1.55
6" thick	"	0.00	1.80	1.80
02080.15 PIPE INSULATION REMOVAL				
Removal, asbestos insulation				
2" thick, pipe				
1" to 3" dia.	L.F.	0.00	1.70	1.70
4" to 6" dia.	"	0.00	1.95	1.95

02 SITEWORK

DEMOLITION

DEMOLITION	UNIT	MAT.	INST.	TOTAL
02080.15 PIPE INSULATION REMOVAL				
3" thick				
7" to 8" dia.	L.F.	0.00	2.05	2.05
15" to 18" dia.	"	0.00	2.55	2.55

SITE DEMOLITION

SITE DEMOLITION	UNIT	MAT.	INST.	TOTAL
02105.20 FENCES				
Remove fencing				
Chain link, 8' high				
For disposal	L.F.	0.00	1.00	1.00
For reuse	"	0.00	2.55	2.55
Wood				
4' high	EA.	0.00	0.68	0.68
6' high	"	0.00	0.82	0.82
Masonry				
8" thick				
4' high	EA.	0.00	2.05	2.05
6' high	"	0.00	2.55	2.55
8' high	"	0.00	2.90	2.90
02105.42 DRAINAGE PIPING				
Remove drainage pipe, not including excavation				
12" dia.	L.F.	0.00	4.60	4.60
18" dia.	"	0.00	5.80	5.80
02105.43 GAS PIPING				
Remove welded steel pipe, not including excavation				
4" dia.	L.F.	0.00	6.85	6.85
6" dia.	"	0.00	13.75	13.75
02105.45 SANITARY PIPING				
Remove sewer pipe, not including excavation				
4" dia.	L.F.	0.00	4.40	4.40
8" dia.	"	0.00	5.50	5.50
02105.48 WATER PIPING				
Remove water pipe, not including excavation				
4" dia.	L.F.	0.00	5.50	5.50
8" dia.	"	0.00	6.10	6.10

02 SITEWORK

SITE DEMOLITION

SITE DEMOLITION	UNIT	MAT.	INST.	TOTAL
02105.60 UNDERGROUND TANKS				
Remove underground storage tank, and backfill				
1000 gals	EA.	0.00	275.00	275.00
02105.66 SEPTIC TANKS				
Remove septic tank				
1000 gals	EA.	0.00	91.50	91.50
02105.80 WALLS, EXTERIOR				
Concrete wall				
Medium reinforcing				
6" thick	S.F.	0.00	8.45	8.45
8" thick	"	0.00	9.15	9.15
Masonry				
8" thick	S.F.	0.00	3.15	3.15
12" thick	"	0.00	3.65	3.65
02110.50 TREE CUTTING & CLEARING				
Cut trees and clear out stumps				
9" to 12" dia.	EA.	0.00	220.00	220.00
To 24" dia.	"	0.00	275.00	275.00

EARTHWORK

EARTHWORK	UNIT	MAT.	INST.	TOTAL
02210.10 HAULING MATERIAL				
Haul material by 10 cy dump truck, round trip distance				
5 mile	C.Y.	0.00	3.35	3.35
Site grading, cut & fill, sandy clay, 200' haul, 75 hp dozer	"	0.00	1.60	1.60
Spread topsoil by equipment on site	"	0.00	1.80	1.80
Site grading (cut and fill to 6") less than 1 acre				
75 hp dozer	C.Y.	0.00	2.65	2.65
1.5 cy backhoe/loader	"	0.00	4.00	4.00
02210.30 BULK EXCAVATION				
Hydraulic excavator				
Medium material	C.Y.	0.00	2.20	2.20
Wheel mounted front-end loader				
Medium material	C.Y.	0.00	1.60	1.60
Track mounted front-end loader				
Medium material	C.Y.	0.00	1.00	1.00

02 SITEWORK

EARTHWORK	UNIT	MAT.	INST.	TOTAL
02220.40 BUILDING EXCAVATION				
Structural excavation, unclassified earth				
3/8 cy backhoe	C.Y.	0.00	7.40	7.40
1 cy backhoe	"	0.00	4.65	4.65
Foundation backfill and compaction by machine	"	0.00	11.10	11.10
02220.60 TRENCHING				
Trenching and continuous footing excavation				
By gradall				
Medium soil	C.Y.	0.00	1.70	1.70
By hydraulic excavator				
Medium soil	C.Y.	0.00	2.00	2.00
Hand excavation				
Normal soil	C.Y.	0.00	22.65	22.65
Sand or gravel	"	0.00	25.50	25.50
Backfill trenches				
With compaction				
By hand	C.Y.	0.00	17.00	17.00
By 60 hp tracked dozer	"	0.00	1.00	1.00
02220.90 HAND EXCAVATION				
Excavation				
To 2' deep				
Normal soil	C.Y.	0.00	22.65	22.65
To 6' deep				
Normal soil	C.Y.	0.00	29.10	29.10
Excavation around obstructions and services	"	0.00	68.00	68.00
02270.40 RIPRAP				
Riprap				
Stone quarry run, max size 300 lb. stones	TON	22.00	27.90	49.90
400 lb. stones	"	22.00	25.90	47.90
750 lb. stones	"	22.00	22.70	44.70
02280.20 SOIL TREATMENT				
Soil treatment, termite control pretreatment, under slabs	S.F.	0.07	0.11	0.18
By walls	"	0.07	0.14	0.21

PAVING AND SURFACING	UNIT	MAT.	INST.	TOTAL
02510.20 ASPHALT SURFACES				
Asphalt wearing surface, for flexible pavement				
1" thick	S.Y.	1.65	1.00	2.65
1-1/2" thick	"	2.50	1.20	3.70
Bituminous sidewalk, no base				

02 SITEWORK

PAVING AND SURFACING	UNIT	MAT.	INST.	TOTAL
02510.20 ASPHALT SURFACES				
2" thick	S.Y.	3.60	1.30	4.90
02520.10 CONCRETE PAVING				
Concrete paving, reinforced, 5000 psi concrete				
6" thick	S.Y.	14.45	9.55	24.00
8" thick	"	18.25	10.90	29.15
10" thick	"	21.95	12.70	34.65
02810.40 LAWN IRRIGATION				
Residential system, complete				
Minimum	ACRE			11,000
Maximum	"			16,500
02830.10 CHAIN LINK FENCE				
Chain link fence, 9 ga., galvanized, with posts 10' o.c.				
4' high	L.F.	3.85	1.45	5.30
6' high	"	5.80	2.55	8.35
Swing gates, galvanized, 4' high				
Single gate				
3' wide	EA.	116.00	51.00	167.00
4' wide	"	126.00	51.00	177.00
Double gate				
10' wide	EA.	297.00	81.50	378.50

03 CONCRETE

FORMWORK	UNIT	MAT.	INST.	TOTAL
03110.05 BEAM FORMWORK				
Beam forms, job built				
Beam bottoms				
1 use	S.F.	2.65	4.30	6.95
5 uses	"	0.86	3.65	4.51
Beam sides				
1 use	S.F.	1.85	2.85	4.70
5 uses	"	0.75	2.35	3.10
03110.15 COLUMN FORMWORK				
Column, square forms, job built				
8" x 8" columns				
1 use	S.F.	2.20	5.15	7.35
5 uses	"	0.77	4.45	5.22
12" x 12" columns				
1 use	S.F.	2.10	4.70	6.80
5 uses	"	0.66	4.10	4.76
03110.20 ELEVATED SLAB FORMWORK				
Elevated slab formwork				
1 use	S.F.	2.05	2.05	4.10
5 uses	"	0.74	1.75	2.49
03110.25 EQUIPMENT PAD FORMWORK				
Equipment pad, job built				
1 use	S.F.	2.10	3.20	5.30
3 uses	"	0.99	2.85	3.84
03110.35 FOOTING FORMWORK				
Wall footings, job built, continuous				
1 use	S.F.	0.80	2.55	3.35
5 uses	"	0.30	2.15	2.45
Column footings, spread				
1 use	S.F.	0.96	3.20	4.16
5 uses	"	0.30	2.55	2.85
03110.50 GRADE BEAM FORMWORK				
Grade beams, job built				
1 use	S.F.	1.65	2.55	4.20
5 uses	"	0.50	2.15	2.65
03110.55 SLAB/MAT FORMWORK				
Mat foundations, job built				
1 use	S.F.	1.55	3.20	4.75
5 uses	"	0.44	2.55	2.99

03 CONCRETE

FORMWORK

FORMWORK	UNIT	MAT.	INST.	TOTAL
03110.65 WALL FORMWORK				
Wall forms, exterior, job built				
Up to 8' high wall				
1 use	S.F.	1.75	2.55	4.30
5 uses	"	0.63	2.15	2.78

REINFORCEMENT

REINFORCEMENT	UNIT	MAT.	INST.	TOTAL
03210.05 BEAM REINFORCING				
Beam-girders				
#3 - #4	TON	638.00	731.00	1,369
#5 - #6	"	578.00	585.00	1,163
03210.15 COLUMN REINFORCING				
Columns				
#3 - #4	TON	638.00	835.00	1,473
#5 - #6	"	578.00	650.00	1,228
03210.20 ELEVATED SLAB REINFORCING				
Elevated slab				
#3 - #4	TON	638.00	366.00	1,004
#5 - #6	"	578.00	325.00	903.00
03210.25 EQUIP. PAD REINFORCING				
Equipment pad				
#3 - #4	TON	638.00	585.00	1,223
#5 - #6	"	578.00	532.00	1,110
03210.35 FOOTING REINFORCING				
Footings				
#3 - #4	TON	638.00	487.00	1,125
#5 - #6	"	578.00	418.00	996.00
03210.45 FOUNDATION REINFORCING				
Foundations				
#3 - #4	TON	638.00	487.00	1,125
#5 - #6	"	578.00	418.00	996.00

03 CONCRETE

REINFORCEMENT	UNIT	MAT.	INST.	TOTAL
03210.50 GRADE BEAM REINFORCING				
Grade beams				
#3 - #4	TON	638.00	450.00	1,088
#5 - #6	"	578.00	390.00	968.00
03210.55 SLAB/MAT REINFORCING				
Bars, slabs				
#3 - #4	TON	638.00	487.00	1,125
#5 - #6	"	578.00	418.00	996.00
Wire mesh, slabs				
Galvanized				
4x4				
W1.4xW1.4	S.F.	0.22	0.19	0.41
W4.0xW4.0	"	0.57	0.24	0.81
6x6				
W1.4xW1.4	S.F.	0.15	0.15	0.30
W4.0xW4.0	"	0.42	0.19	0.61
03210.65 WALL REINFORCING				
Walls				
#3 - #4	TON	638.00	418.00	1,056
#5 - #6	"	578.00	366.00	944.00

CAST-IN-PLACE CONCRETE	UNIT	MAT.	INST.	TOTAL
03300.10 CONCRETE ADMIXTURES				
Concrete admixtures				
Water reducing admixture	GAL			9.35
Set retarder	"			16.50
Floor finishes				
Broom	S.F.	0.00	0.29	0.29
Float	"	0.00	0.34	0.34

03 CONCRETE

PLACING CONCRETE	UNIT	MAT.	INST.	TOTAL
03380.05 BEAM CONCRETE				
2500# or 3000# concrete				
By crane	C.Y.	56.50	38.50	95.00
By pump	"	56.50	35.00	91.50
By hand buggy	"	56.50	20.40	76.90
03380.15 COLUMN CONCRETE				
2500# or 3000# concrete				
By crane	C.Y.	56.50	35.00	91.50
By pump	"	56.50	32.10	88.60
03380.25 EQUIPMENT PAD CONCRETE				
Equipment pad				
2500# or 3000# concrete				
By chute	C.Y.	56.50	6.80	63.30
By pump	"	56.50	27.50	84.00
By crane	"	56.50	32.10	88.60
03380.35 FOOTING CONCRETE				
Continuous footing				
2500# or 3000# concrete				
By chute	C.Y.	56.50	6.80	63.30
By pump	"	56.50	24.05	80.55
By crane	"	56.50	27.50	84.00
Spread footing				
2500# or 3000# concrete				
By chute	C.Y.	56.50	6.80	63.30
By pump	"	56.50	25.70	82.20
By crane	"	56.50	29.60	86.10
03380.50 GRADE BEAM CONCRETE				
Grade beam				
2500# or 3000# concrete				
By chute	C.Y.	56.50	6.80	63.30
By crane	"	56.50	27.50	84.00
By pump	"	56.50	24.05	80.55
By hand buggy	"	56.50	20.40	76.90
03380.55 SLAB/MAT CONCRETE				
Slab on grade				
2500# or 3000# concrete				
By chute	C.Y.	56.50	5.10	61.60
By crane	"	56.50	16.05	72.55
By pump	"	56.50	13.75	70.25
By hand buggy	"	56.50	13.60	70.10
03380.58 SIDEWALKS				
Walks, cast in place with wire mesh, base not incl.				
4" thick	S.F.	0.78	0.68	1.46
5" thick	"	1.05	0.82	1.87

03 CONCRETE

PLACING CONCRETE	UNIT	MAT.	INST.	TOTAL
03380.58 SIDEWALKS				
6" thick	S.F.	1.25	1.00	2.25
03380.65 WALL CONCRETE				
Walls				
2500# or 3000#				
To 4'				
By chute	C.Y.	56.50	5.85	62.35
By crane	"	56.50	32.10	88.60
By pump	"	56.50	29.60	86.10
To 8'				
By crane	C.Y.	56.50	35.00	91.50
By pump	"	56.50	32.10	88.60
Filled block (CMU)				
3000# concrete, by pump				
4" wide	S.F.	0.21	1.35	1.56
6" wide	"	0.47	1.60	2.07
8" wide	"	0.74	1.90	2.64

04 MASONRY

MORTAR AND GROUT

	UNIT	MAT.	INST.	TOTAL
04100.10 MASONRY GROUT				
Grout-filled concrete block (CMU)				
4" wide	S.F.	0.26	0.92	1.18
6" wide	"	0.56	1.00	1.56
8" wide	"	1.05	1.10	2.15
04150.10 MASONRY ACCESSORIES				
Rectangular wall ties				
3/16" dia., galvanized				
2" x 6"	EA.	0.13	0.42	0.55
2" x 8"	"	0.14	0.42	0.56
"Z" type wall ties, galvanized				
6" long				
1/8" dia.	EA.	0.13	0.42	0.55
8" long				
1/8" dia.	EA.	0.14	0.42	0.56
Brick anchors				
Corrugated, 3-1/2" long				
16 ga.	EA.	0.12	0.42	0.54

UNIT MASONRY

	UNIT	MAT.	INST.	TOTAL
04210.10 BRICK MASONRY				
Standard size brick, running bond				
Face brick, red (6.4/sf)				
Veneer	S.F.	1.80	4.20	6.00
9" solid wall	"	3.95	7.20	11.15
Select common for veneers	"	2.00	4.20	6.20
04210.60 PAVERS, MASONRY				
Brick walk laid on sand, sand joints				
Laid flat, (4.5 per sf)	S.F.	1.10	2.80	3.90
Laid on edge, (7.2 per sf)	"	1.65	4.20	5.85
Precast concrete patio blocks				
Natural	S.F.	0.83	0.84	1.67
Colors	"	1.05	0.84	1.89
Bluestone				
Irregular	S.F.	1.55	6.30	7.85
Snapped rectangular	"	2.70	5.05	7.75
Slate				
Irregular, 3/4" thick	S.F.	1.45	7.20	8.65
Crushed stone, white marble, 3" thick	"	0.55	0.41	0.96

04 MASONRY

UNIT MASONRY	UNIT	MAT.	INST.	TOTAL
04220.10 CONCRETE MASONRY UNITS				
Hollow, load bearing				
4"	S.F.	1.05	1.85	2.90
8"	"	1.85	2.10	3.95
12"	"	2.60	2.50	5.10
Solid, load bearing				
4"	S.F.	1.55	1.85	3.40
8"	"	2.10	2.10	4.20
12"	"	3.05	2.50	5.55
Back-up block, sand aggregate, 8" x 16"				
2"	S.F.	0.76	1.45	2.21
4"	"	1.10	1.50	2.60
6"	"	1.35	1.55	2.90
8"	"	1.60	1.70	3.30

STONE	UNIT	MAT.	INST.	TOTAL
04400.10 STONE				
Rubble stone				
Walls set in mortar				
8" thick	S.F.	8.25	6.30	14.55
24" thick	"	16.50	16.75	33.25
Dry set wall				
8" thick	S.F.	9.35	4.20	13.55
24" thick	"	17.60	10.05	27.65
Cut stone				
Facing panels				
3/4" thick	S.F.	22.00	10.05	32.05
1-1/2" thick	"	33.00	11.45	44.45
04550.10 REFRACTORIES				
Flue liners				
Rectangular				
8" x 12"	L.F.	4.05	4.20	8.25
12" x 12"	"	5.50	4.55	10.05

05 METALS

METAL FASTENING

05050.10 STRUCTURAL WELDING

METAL FASTENING	UNIT	MAT.	INST.	TOTAL
Welding				
Single pass				
1/8"	L.F.	0.34	1.45	1.79
3/16"	"	0.68	1.90	2.58
1/4"	"	0.91	2.40	3.31

05050.90 METAL ANCHORS

METAL FASTENING	UNIT	MAT.	INST.	TOTAL
Anchor bolts				
3/8" x				
8" long	EA.			2.75
10" long	"			2.95
12" long	"			3.20
1/2" x				
8" long	EA.			3.85
10" long	"			3.95
12" long	"			4.30
Expansion shield				
1/4"	EA.			0.44
3/8"	"			0.72
1/2"	"			1.15
Non-drilling anchor				
1/4"	EA.			0.33
3/8"	"			0.45
1/2"	"			0.70
Self-drilling anchor				
1/4"	EA.			0.44
3/8"	"			0.68
1/2"	"			1.00

COLD FORMED FRAMING

05410.10 METAL FRAMING

COLD FORMED FRAMING	UNIT	MAT.	INST.	TOTAL
Furring channel, galvanized				
Beams and columns, 3/4"				
12" o.c.	S.F.	0.33	2.85	3.18
16" o.c.	"	0.28	2.60	2.88
Walls, 3/4"				
12" o.c.	S.F.	0.33	1.45	1.78
16" o.c.	"	0.28	1.20	1.48
24" o.c.	"	0.22	0.95	1.17
Stud, load bearing				
16" o.c.				

05 METALS

COLD FORMED FRAMING

COLD FORMED FRAMING	UNIT	MAT.	INST.	TOTAL
05410.10 METAL FRAMING				
16 ga.				
2-1/2"	S.F.	0.92	1.25	2.17
3-5/8"	"	1.10	1.25	2.35
4"	"	1.15	1.25	2.40
24" o.c.				
16 ga.				
2-1/2"	S.F.	0.55	1.10	1.65
3-5/8"	"	0.64	1.10	1.74
4"	"	0.75	1.10	1.85
6"	"	0.89	1.20	2.09
05520.10 RAILINGS				
Railing, pipe				
1-1/4" diameter, welded steel				
2-rail				
Primed	L.F.	14.85	5.70	20.55
Galvanized	"	17.85	5.70	23.55
3-rail				
Primed	L.F.	19.50	7.15	26.65
Galvanized	"	23.55	7.15	30.70
1-1/2" diameter, welded steel				
2-rail				
Primed	L.F.	18.10	5.70	23.80
Galvanized	"	21.70	5.70	27.40
3-rail				
Primed	L.F.	23.75	7.15	30.90
Galvanized	"	28.50	7.15	35.65
05700.10 ORNAMENTAL METAL				
Railings, vertical square bars, 6" o.c., with shaped top rails				
Steel	L.F.	31.20	14.30	45.50
Aluminum	"	48.50	14.30	62.80
Bronze	"	89.00	19.05	108.05
Stainless steel	"	74.00	19.05	93.05

06 WOOD AND PLASTICS

FASTENERS AND ADHESIVES

FASTENERS AND ADHESIVES	UNIT	MAT.	INST.	TOTAL
06050.10 ACCESSORIES				
Column/post base, cast aluminum				
4" x 4"	EA.	1.65	6.45	8.10
6" x 6"	"	3.75	6.45	10.20
Anchors				
Bolts, threaded two ends, with nuts and washers				
1/2" dia.				
4" long	EA.	0.75	1.60	2.35
7-1/2" long	"	0.92	1.60	2.52
15" long	"	1.60	1.60	3.20
Bolts, carriage				
1/4 x 4	EA.	0.87	2.55	3.42
5/16 x 6	"	0.92	2.70	3.62
Joist and beam hangers				
18 ga.				
2 x 4	EA.	0.41	2.55	2.96
2 x 6	"	0.46	2.55	3.01
2 x 8	"	0.52	2.55	3.07
2 x 10	"	0.66	2.85	3.51
2 x 12	"	0.71	3.20	3.91
Sill anchors				
Embedded in concrete	EA.	5.30	2.55	7.85
Strap ties, 14 ga., 1-3/8" wide				
12" long	EA.	0.23	2.15	2.38
06110.30 FLOOR FRAMING				
Floor joists				
12" o.c.				
2x6	S.F.	0.50	0.51	1.01
2x8	"	0.69	0.52	1.21
2x10	"	1.00	0.54	1.54
2x12	"	1.30	0.56	1.86
3x6	"	1.20	0.55	1.75
3x8	"	1.55	0.56	2.11
3x10	"	1.95	0.58	2.53
16" o.c.				
2x6	S.F.	0.42	0.43	0.85
2x8	"	0.58	0.44	1.02
2x10	"	0.85	0.44	1.29
2x12	"	1.10	0.46	1.56
3x6	"	0.99	0.44	1.43
3x8	"	1.30	0.46	1.76
3x10	"	1.65	0.48	2.13
Sister joists for floors				
2x4	L.F.	0.28	1.60	1.88
2x6	"	0.38	1.85	2.23
2x8	"	0.58	2.15	2.73
2x10	"	0.85	2.55	3.40
2x12	"	1.10	3.20	4.30

06 WOOD AND PLASTICS

FASTENERS AND ADHESIVES	UNIT	MAT.	INST.	TOTAL
06110.40 FURRING				
Furring, wood strips				
On masonry or concrete walls				
12" o.c.	S.F.	0.14	0.80	0.94
16" o.c.	"	0.12	0.73	0.85
24" o.c.	"	0.09	0.68	0.77
On wood walls				
12" o.c.	S.F.	0.14	0.57	0.71
16" o.c.	"	0.12	0.51	0.63
24" o.c.	"	0.09	0.47	0.56
Ceilings				
On masonry or concrete ceilings				
12" o.c.	S.F.	0.14	1.45	1.59
16" o.c.	"	0.12	1.30	1.42
24" o.c.	"	0.09	1.15	1.24
On wood ceilings				
12" o.c.	S.F.	0.14	0.95	1.09
16" o.c.	"	0.12	0.86	0.98
24" o.c.	"	0.09	0.78	0.87
06110.50 ROOF FRAMING				
Roof framing				
Rafters, gable end				
12" o.c.				
2x4	S.F.	0.33	0.54	0.87
2x6	"	0.50	0.56	1.06
2x8	"	0.69	0.58	1.27
2x10	"	1.00	0.61	1.61
2x12	"	1.30	0.64	1.94
16" o.c.				
2x6	S.F.	0.42	0.46	0.88
2x8	"	0.58	0.48	1.06
2x10	"	0.85	0.49	1.34
2x12	"	1.10	0.51	1.61
24" o.c.				
2x6	S.F.	0.33	0.39	0.72
2x8	"	0.46	0.40	0.86
2x10	"	0.68	0.41	1.09
2x12	"	0.88	0.43	1.31
Ridge boards				
2x6	L.F.	0.42	1.30	1.72
2x8	"	0.58	1.45	2.03
2x10	"	0.85	1.60	2.45
2x12	"	1.10	1.85	2.95
Hip rafters				
2x6	L.F.	0.42	0.92	1.34
2x8	"	0.58	0.95	1.53
2x10	"	0.85	0.99	1.84
2x12	"	1.10	1.05	2.15
Fascia boards				
2x4	L.F.	0.28	1.30	1.58
2x6	"	0.42	1.30	1.72
2x8	"	0.58	1.45	2.03

06 WOOD AND PLASTICS

FASTENERS AND ADHESIVES	UNIT	MAT.	INST.	TOTAL
06110.50 ROOF FRAMING				
2x10	L.F.	0.85	1.45	2.30
2x12	"	1.10	1.60	2.70
Cant strips				
3x3	L.F.	0.18	0.73	0.91
4x4	"	0.23	0.78	1.01
06110.60 SLEEPERS				
Sleepers, over concrete				
12" o.c.				
1x2	S.F.	0.14	0.58	0.72
2x4	"	0.33	0.71	1.04
06110.65 SOFFITS				
Soffit framing				
2x3	L.F.	0.21	1.85	2.06
2x4	"	0.28	2.00	2.28
2x6	"	0.42	2.15	2.57
2x8	"	0.58	2.35	2.93
06110.70 WALL FRAMING				
Framing wall, studs				
12" o.c.				
2x3	S.F.	0.24	0.48	0.72
2x4	"	0.33	0.48	0.81
2x6	"	0.50	0.51	1.01
2x8	"	0.69	0.54	1.23
16" o.c.				
2x3	S.F.	0.21	0.40	0.61
2x4	"	0.28	0.40	0.68
2x6	"	0.42	0.43	0.85
2x8	"	0.58	0.44	1.02
24" o.c.				
2x4	S.F.	0.22	0.35	0.57
2x6	"	0.33	0.37	0.70
2x8	"	0.46	0.38	0.84
Plates, top or bottom				
2x3	L.F.	0.21	0.76	0.97
2x4	"	0.28	0.80	1.08
2x6	"	0.42	0.86	1.28
2x8	"	0.58	0.92	1.50
Headers, door or window				
2x6				
Single				
3' long	EA.	1.25	12.85	14.10
6' long	"	2.50	16.10	18.60
2x8				
Single				
4' long	EA.	2.30	16.10	18.40
8' long	"	4.60	19.80	24.40
2x10				

06 WOOD AND PLASTICS

FASTENERS AND ADHESIVES	UNIT	MAT.	INST.	TOTAL
06110.70 WALL FRAMING				
Single				
5' long	EA.	4.20	19.80	24.00
10' long	"	8.45	25.70	34.15
2x12				
Single				
6' long	EA.	6.50	19.80	26.30
12' long	"	13.00	25.70	38.70
06115.10 FLOOR SHEATHING				
Sub-flooring, plywood, CDX				
1/2" thick	S.F.	0.36	0.32	0.68
5/8" thick	"	0.44	0.37	0.81
3/4" thick	"	0.58	0.43	1.01
Underlayment				
Plywood				
3/8" thick	S.F.	0.32	0.32	0.64
1/2" thick	"	0.37	0.34	0.71
5/8" thick	"	0.44	0.37	0.81
3/4" thick	"	0.50	0.40	0.90
06115.20 ROOF SHEATHING				
Sheathing				
3/8" thick	S.F.	0.35	0.33	0.68
1/2" thick	"	0.36	0.34	0.70
5/8" thick	"	0.44	0.37	0.81
3/4" thick	"	0.58	0.40	0.98
06115.30 WALL SHEATHING				
Sheathing				
Plywood, CDX				
3/8" thick	S.F.	0.35	0.38	0.73
1/2" thick	"	0.36	0.40	0.76
5/8" thick	"	0.44	0.43	0.87
3/4" thick	"	0.58	0.47	1.05
06125.10 WOOD DECKING				
Decking, T&G solid				
Fir				
3" thick	S.F.	1.85	0.64	2.49
4" thick	"	2.00	0.69	2.69
Southern yellow pine				
3" thick	S.F.	1.90	0.73	2.63
4" thick	"	2.10	0.79	2.89
White pine				
3" thick	S.F.	2.50	0.64	3.14
4" thick	"	3.25	0.69	3.94

06 WOOD AND PLASTICS

FASTENERS AND ADHESIVES

FASTENERS AND ADHESIVES	UNIT	MAT.	INST.	TOTAL
06130.10 HEAVY TIMBER				
Mill framed structures				
Beams to 20' long				
Douglas fir				
6x8	L.F.	4.05	3.20	7.25
6x10	"	4.85	3.30	8.15
Southern yellow pine				
6x8	L.F.	3.80	3.20	7.00
6x10	"	4.75	3.30	8.05
Columns to 12' high				
6x6	L.F.	3.45	4.80	8.25
10x10	"	7.15	5.35	12.50
06190.20 WOOD TRUSSES				
Truss, fink, 2x4 members				
3-in-12 slope				
24' span	EA.	35.50	27.50	63.00
30' span	"	48.50	29.20	77.70

FINISH CARPENTRY

FINISH CARPENTRY	UNIT	MAT.	INST.	TOTAL
06200.10 FINISH CARPENTRY				
Casing				
11/16 x 2-1/2	L.F.	0.81	1.15	1.96
11/16 x 3-1/2	"	1.05	1.20	2.25
Half round				
1/2	L.F.	0.21	1.05	1.26
5/8	"	0.25	1.05	1.30
Railings, balusters				
1-1/4 x 2-1/4	L.F.	1.40	2.55	3.95
1-1/8 x 1-1/8	"	1.20	2.35	3.55
Stop				
5/8 x 1-5/8				
Colonial	L.F.	0.29	1.60	1.89
Ranch	"	0.26	1.60	1.86
Exterior trim, casing, select pine, 1x3	"	0.87	1.30	2.17
Cornices, white pine, #2 or better				
1x4	L.F.	0.44	1.30	1.74
1x8	"	0.81	1.50	2.31
Shelving, pine				
1x8	L.F.	0.81	2.00	2.81
1x12	"	1.45	2.15	3.60

06 WOOD AND PLASTICS

FINISH CARPENTRY

06220.10 MILLWORK	UNIT	MAT.	INST.	TOTAL
Countertop, laminated plastic				
25" x 7/8"				
Minimum	L.F.	8.80	6.45	15.25
Average	"	16.15	8.55	24.70
Maximum	"	25.40	10.30	35.70
Base cabinets, 34-1/2" high, 24" deep, hardwood, no tops				
Minimum	L.F.	40.40	10.30	50.70
Average	"	52.00	12.85	64.85
Maximum	"	81.00	17.15	98.15
Wall cabinets				
Minimum	L.F.	28.90	8.55	37.45
Average	"	40.40	10.30	50.70
Maximum	"	75.00	12.85	87.85

ARCHITECTURAL WOODWORK

06420.10 PANEL WORK	UNIT	MAT.	INST.	TOTAL
Plywood unfinished, 1/4" thick				
Birch				
Natural	S.F.	0.91	0.86	1.77
Select	"	1.20	0.86	2.06
Knotty pine	"	1.20	0.86	2.06
Plywood, prefinished, 1/4" thick, premium grade				
Birch veneer	S.F.	1.50	1.05	2.55
Cherry veneer	"	1.60	1.05	2.65
06430.10 STAIRWORK				
Risers, 1x8, 42" wide				
White oak	EA.	11.55	12.85	24.40
Pine	"	8.20	12.85	21.05
Treads, 1-1/16" x 9-1/2" x 42"				
White oak	EA.	15.00	16.10	31.10
06440.10 COLUMNS				
Column, hollow, round				
12" diameter				
10' high	EA.	346.00	36.70	382.70
12' high	"	416.00	39.30	455.30
24" diameter				
16' high	EA.	1,850	55.00	1,905
18' high	"	2,180	58.00	2,238

07 THERMAL AND MOISTURE

MOISTURE PROTECTION	UNIT	MAT.	INST.	TOTAL
07100.10 WATERPROOFING				
Membrane waterproofing, elastomeric				
Neoprene				
1/32" thick	S.F.	0.85	0.82	1.67
1/16" thick	"	1.35	0.85	2.20
Plastic vapor barrier (polyethylene)				1.90
4 mil	S.F.	0.01	0.08	0.09
6 mil	"	0.02	0.08	0.10
Bituminous membrane waterproofing, asphalt felt, 15 lb.				
One ply	S.F.	0.28	0.51	0.79
Two ply	"	0.33	0.62	0.95
Three ply	"	0.44	0.73	1.17
Bentonite waterproofing, panels				
3/16" thick	S.F.	0.15	0.51	0.66
1/4" thick	"	0.90	0.51	1.41
07160.10 BITUMINOUS DAMPPROOFING				
Building paper, asphalt felt				
15 lb	S.F.	0.07	0.82	0.89
30 lb	"	0.11	0.85	0.96
Asphalt dampproofing, troweled, cold, primer plus				
1 coat	S.F.	0.44	0.68	1.12
2 coats	"	0.68	1.00	1.68
3 coats	"	1.00	1.25	2.25
07190.10 VAPOR BARRIERS				
Vapor barrier, polyethylene				
2 mil	S.F.	0.01	0.10	0.11
6 mil	"	0.02	0.10	0.12
8 mil	"	0.03	0.11	0.14

INSULATION	UNIT	MAT.	INST.	TOTAL
07210.10 BATT INSULATION				
Ceiling, fiberglass, unfaced				
3-1/2" thick, R11	S.F.	0.24	0.24	0.48
6" thick, R19	"	0.41	0.27	0.68
9" thick, R30	"	0.63	0.31	0.94
Crawl space, unfaced				
3-1/2" thick, R11	S.F.	0.24	0.31	0.55
6" thick, R19	"	0.41	0.34	0.75
9" thick, R30	"	0.63	0.37	1.00
Wall, fiberglass				
Paper backed				

07 THERMAL AND MOISTURE

INSULATION	UNIT	MAT.	INST.	TOTAL
07210.10 BATT INSULATION				
2" thick, R7	S.F.	0.17	0.21	0.38
3" thick, R8	"	0.18	0.23	0.41
4" thick, R11	"	0.20	0.24	0.44
Foil backed, 1 side				
2" thick, R7	S.F.	0.35	0.21	0.56
3" thick, R11	"	0.37	0.23	0.60
4" thick, R14	"	0.42	0.24	0.66
Unfaced				
2" thick, R7	S.F.	0.15	0.21	0.36
3" thick, R9	"	0.18	0.23	0.41
4" thick, R11	"	0.22	0.24	0.46
6" thick, R19	"	0.25	0.25	0.50
07210.20 BOARD INSULATION				
Insulation, rigid				
0.75" thick, R2.78	S.F.	0.22	0.19	0.41
1.06" thick, R4.17	"	0.44	0.19	0.63
Perlite board, roof				
1.00" thick, R2.78	S.F.	0.44	0.17	0.61
Rigid urethane				
1" thick, R6.67	S.F.	0.53	0.17	0.70
1.20" thick, R8.33	"	0.67	0.17	0.84
Polystyrene				
1.0" thick, R4.17	S.F.	0.56	0.17	0.73
1.5" thick, R6.26	"	0.92	0.18	1.10
07210.60 LOOSE FILL INSULATION				
Blown-in type				
5" thick, R11	S.F.	0.18	0.17	0.35
6" thick, R13	"	0.21	0.20	0.41
Poured type				
1" thick, R4	S.F.	0.12	0.13	0.25
2" thick, R8	"	0.23	0.15	0.38
4" thick, R16	"	0.46	0.20	0.66
07210.70 SPRAYED INSULATION				
Foam, sprayed on				
Polystyrene				
1" thick, R4	S.F.	0.38	0.20	0.58
2" thick, R8	"	0.71	0.27	0.98
Urethane				
1" thick, R7.7	S.F.	0.44	0.20	0.64
2" thick, R15.4	"	0.77	0.27	1.04

07 THERMAL AND MOISTURE

SHINGLES AND TILES

SHINGLES AND TILES	UNIT	MAT.	INST.	TOTAL
07310.10 ASPHALT SHINGLES				
Standard asphalt shingles, strip shingles				
210 lb/square	SQ.	34.70	25.00	59.70
240 lb/square	"	38.10	31.30	69.40
Roll roofing, mineral surface				
90 lb	SQ.	18.50	17.90	36.40
140 lb	"	31.20	25.00	56.20
07310.30 METAL SHINGLES				
Aluminum, .020" thick				
Plain	SQ.	116.00	50.00	166.00
Steel, galvanized				
Plain	SQ.	154.00	50.00	204.00
07310.60 SLATE SHINGLES				
Slate shingles				
Ribbon	SQ.	346.00	125.00	471.00
Clear	"	462.00	125.00	587.00
07310.70 WOOD SHINGLES				
Wood shingles, on roofs				
White cedar, #1 shingles				
4" exposure	SQ.	154.00	83.50	237.50
5" exposure	"	138.00	62.50	200.50
#2 shingles				
4" exposure	SQ.	110.00	83.50	193.50
5" exposure	"	93.50	62.50	156.00
Resquared and rebutted				
4" exposure	SQ.	138.00	83.50	221.50
5" exposure	"	116.00	62.50	178.50
07310.80 WOOD SHAKES				
Shakes, hand split, 24" red cedar, on roofs				
5" exposure	SQ.	107.00	125.00	232.00
7" exposure	"	99.00	100.00	199.00
9" exposure	"	88.00	83.50	171.50

ROOFING AND SIDING

ROOFING AND SIDING	UNIT	MAT.	INST.	TOTAL
07410.10 MANUFACTURED ROOFS				
Aluminum roof panels, for structural steel framing				
Corrugated				
Natural finish				
.024"	S.F.	1.10	0.63	1.73

07 THERMAL AND MOISTURE

ROOFING AND SIDING	UNIT	MAT.	INST.	TOTAL
07410.10 MANUFACTURED ROOFS				
.030"	S.F.	1.35	0.63	1.98
Painted finish				
.024"	S.F.	1.55	0.63	2.18
.030"	"	1.75	0.63	2.38
Steel roof panels, for structural steel framing				
Corrugated, painted				
18 ga.	S.F.	3.35	0.63	3.98
20 ga.	"	3.10	0.63	3.73
07460.10 METAL SIDING PANELS				
Aluminum siding panels				
Corrugated				
Plain natural finish				
.024"	S.F.	1.00	1.15	2.15
.032"	"	1.20	1.15	2.35
Painted finish				
.024"	S.F.	1.25	1.15	2.40
.032"	"	1.45	1.15	2.60
Steel siding panels				
Corrugated				
22 ga.	S.F.	2.65	1.90	4.55
24 ga.	"	2.45	1.90	4.35
07460.50 PLASTIC SIDING				
Horizontal vinyl siding, solid				
8" wide				
Standard	S.F.	0.65	0.99	1.64
Insulated	"	0.95	0.99	1.94
10" wide				
Standard	S.F.	0.71	0.92	1.63
Insulated	"	1.05	0.92	1.97
07460.60 PLYWOOD SIDING				
Texture 1-11, 5/8" thick				
Cedar	S.F.	1.10	0.92	2.02
Fir	"	0.58	0.92	1.50
Redwood	"	1.10	0.89	1.99
Southern Yellow Pine	"	0.65	0.92	1.57
07460.70 STEEL SIDING				
Ribbed, sheets, galvanized				
22 ga.	S.F.	1.30	1.15	2.45
24 ga.	"	1.10	1.15	2.25
Primed				
24 ga.	S.F.	1.55	1.15	2.70
26 ga.	"	0.97	1.15	2.12

07 THERMAL AND MOISTURE

ROOFING AND SIDING

ROOFING AND SIDING	UNIT	MAT.	INST.	TOTAL
07460.80 WOOD SIDING				
Beveled siding, cedar				
A grade				
1/2 x 6	S.F.	1.70	1.30	3.00
1/2 x 8	"	2.00	1.05	3.05
3/4 x 10	"	1.80	0.86	2.66
Board and batten				
Cedar				
1x8	S.F.	1.85	1.05	2.90
1x12	"	1.45	0.83	2.28
Pine				
1x8	S.F.	0.55	1.05	1.60
1x12	"	0.47	0.83	1.30
Redwood				
1x8	S.F.	2.55	1.05	3.60
1x12	"	2.10	0.83	2.93
Tongue and groove				
Cedar				
1x6	S.F.	2.35	1.35	3.70
1x10	"	2.10	1.20	3.30
Pine				
1x6	S.F.	0.66	1.35	2.01
1x10	"	0.55	1.20	1.75
Redwood				
1x6	S.F.	2.45	1.35	3.80
1x10	"	2.20	1.20	3.40

MEMBRANE ROOFING

MEMBRANE ROOFING	UNIT	MAT.	INST.	TOTAL
07510.10 BUILT-UP ASPHALT ROOFING				
Built-up roofing, asphalt felt, including gravel				
2 ply	SQ.	25.40	62.50	87.90
3 ply	"	35.80	83.50	119.30
4 ply	"	47.40	100.00	147.40
Cant strip, 4" x 4"				
Treated wood	L.F.	1.15	0.72	1.87
Foamglass	"	0.32	0.63	0.95
New gravel for built-up roofing, 400 lb/sq	SQ.	17.35	50.00	67.35
07530.10 SINGLE-PLY ROOFING				
Elastic sheet roofing				
Neoprene, 1/16" thick	S.F.	0.89	0.31	1.20
PVC				
45 mil	S.F.	1.25	0.31	1.56

07 THERMAL AND MOISTURE

MEMBRANE ROOFING

07530.10 SINGLE-PLY ROOFING	UNIT	MAT.	INST.	TOTAL
Flashing				
Pipe flashing, 90 mil thick				
1" pipe	EA.	12.10	6.25	18.35
Neoprene flashing, 60 mil thick strip				
6" wide	L.F.	0.85	2.10	2.95
12" wide	"	1.65	3.15	4.80

FLASHING AND SHEET METAL

07620.10 FLASHING AND TRIM	UNIT	MAT.	INST.	TOTAL
Counter flashing				
Aluminum, .032"	S.F.	0.88	2.50	3.38
Stainless steel, .015"	"	2.65	2.50	5.15
Copper				
16 oz.	S.F.	2.40	2.50	4.90
Valley flashing				
Aluminum, .032"	S.F.	0.88	1.55	2.43
Stainless steel, .015	"	2.65	1.55	4.20
Copper				
16 oz.	S.F.	2.40	1.55	3.95
Base flashing				
Aluminum, .040"	S.F.	0.94	2.10	3.04
Stainless steel, .018"	"	2.65	2.10	4.75
Copper				
16 oz.	S.F.	2.40	2.10	4.50
Flashing and trim, aluminum				
.019" thick	S.F.	0.76	1.80	2.56
.032" thick	"	0.91	1.80	2.71

07620.20 GUTTERS AND DOWNSPOUTS	UNIT	MAT.	INST.	TOTAL
Aluminum gutter and downspout				
Downspouts				
2" x 3"	L.F.	0.63	1.65	2.28
3" x 4"	"	0.84	1.80	2.64
4" x 5"	"	0.94	1.95	2.89
Round				
3" dia.	L.F.	1.20	1.65	2.85
4" dia.	"	1.85	1.80	3.65
Gutters, stock units				
4" wide	L.F.	1.05	2.65	3.70
5" wide	"	1.15	2.80	3.95

07 THERMAL AND MOISTURE

FLASHING AND SHEET METAL

07700.10 ROOFING SPECIALTIES	UNIT	MAT.	INST.	TOTAL
Smoke vent, 48" x 48"				
Aluminum	EA.	431.00	62.50	493.50
Galvanized steel	"	417.00	62.50	479.50
Heat/smoke vent, 48" x 96"				
Aluminum	EA.	1,660	83.50	1,744
Galvanized steel	"	1,620	83.50	1,704
Ridge vent strips				
Mill finish	L.F.	2.30	1.65	3.95
Soffit vents				
Mill finish				
2-1/2" wide	L.F.	0.25	1.00	1.25
Roof hatches				
Steel, plain, primed				
2'6" x 3'0"	EA.	363.00	62.50	425.50
Galvanized steel				
2'6" x 3'0"	EA.	375.00	62.50	437.50
Aluminum				
2'6" x 3'0"	EA.	399.00	62.50	461.50
Gravity ventilators, with curb, base, damper and screen				
Wind driven spinner				
6" dia.	EA.	15.10	16.70	31.80
12" dia.	"	23.00	16.70	39.70

SKYLIGHTS

07810.10 PLASTIC SKYLIGHTS	UNIT	MAT.	INST.	TOTAL
Single thickness, not including mounting curb				
2' x 4'	EA.	145.00	31.30	176.30
4' x 4'	"	232.00	41.70	273.70
Double thickness, not including mounting curb				
2' x 4'	EA.	184.00	31.30	215.30
4' x 4'	"	290.00	41.70	331.70

08 DOORS AND WINDOWS

METAL

METAL	UNIT	MAT.	INST.	TOTAL
08110.10 METAL DOORS				
Flush hollow metal, standard duty, 20 ga., 1-3/8"				
2-6 x 6-8	EA.	133.00	28.60	161.60
2-8 x 6-8	"	136.00	28.60	164.60
3-0 x 6-8	"	150.00	28.60	178.60
1-3/4"				
2-6 x 6-8	EA.	158.00	28.60	186.60
2-8 x 6-8	"	167.00	28.60	195.60
3-0 x 6-8	"	179.00	28.60	207.60
Heavy duty, 20 ga., unrated, 1-3/4"				
2-8 x 6-8	EA.	139.00	28.60	167.60
3-0 x 6-8	"	150.00	28.60	178.60
08110.40 METAL DOOR FRAMES				
Hollow metal, stock, 18 ga., 4-3/4" x 1-3/4"				
2-0 x 7-0	EA.	56.50	32.20	88.70
2-4 x 7-0	"	56.50	32.20	88.70
2-6 x 7-0	"	58.00	32.20	90.20
3-0 x 7-0	"	59.00	32.20	91.20
08120.10 ALUMINUM DOORS				
Aluminum doors, commercial				
Narrow stile				
2-6 x 7-0	EA.	343.00	143.00	486.00
3-0 x 7-0	"	345.00	143.00	488.00
3-6 x 7-0	"	359.00	143.00	502.00
Wide stile				
2-6 x 7-0	EA.	808.00	143.00	951.00
3-0 x 7-0	"	808.00	143.00	951.00
3-6 x 7-0	"	832.00	143.00	975.00

WOOD AND PLASTIC

WOOD AND PLASTIC	UNIT	MAT.	INST.	TOTAL
08210.10 WOOD DOORS				
Solid core, 1-3/8" thick				
Birch faced				
2-4 x 6-8	EA.	99.00	32.20	131.20
2-6 x 6-8	"	105.00	32.20	137.20
2-8 x 6-8	"	110.00	32.20	142.20
3-0 x 6-8	"	114.00	32.20	146.20
Hollow core, 1-3/8" thick				
Lauan faced				

08 DOORS AND WINDOWS

WOOD AND PLASTIC	UNIT	MAT.	INST.	TOTAL
08210.10 WOOD DOORS				
2-4 x 6-8	EA.	32.60	32.20	64.80
2-6 x 6-8	"	35.00	32.20	67.20
2-8 x 6-8	"	37.30	32.20	69.50
3-0 x 6-8	"	39.60	32.20	71.80
Closet doors, 1-3/4" thick				
Bi-fold or bi-passing, includes frame and trim				
Paneled				
4-0 x 6-8	EA.	220.00	42.90	262.90
6-0 x 6-8	"	268.00	42.90	310.90
Louvered				
4-0 x 6-8	EA.	152.00	42.90	194.90
6-0 x 6-8	"	194.00	42.90	236.90
Flush				
4-0 x 6-8	EA.	134.00	42.90	176.90
6-0 x 6-8	"	163.00	42.90	205.90
Primed				
4-0 x 6-8	EA.	140.00	42.90	182.90
6-0 x 6-8	"	169.00	42.90	211.90
08210.90 WOOD FRAMES				
Frame, interior, pine				
2-6 x 6-8	EA	24.25	36.70	60.95
2-8 x 6-8	"	25.40	36.70	62.10
3-0 x 6-8	"	25.40	36.70	62.10
5-0 x 6-8	"	27.60	36.70	64.30
6-0 x 6-8	"	28.90	36.70	65.60
08300.10 SPECIAL DOORS				
Garage door, flush insulated metal, primed, 9-0 x 7-0	EA.	572.00	85.50	657.50
Roll-up doors				
13-0 high x 14-0 wide	EA.	700.00	367.00	1,067
12-0 high x 14-0 wide	"	898.00	367.00	1,265
Accordion folding doors, tracks and fittings included				
Vinyl covered, 2 layers	S.F.	7.35	10.30	17.65
Woven mahogany and vinyl	"	9.20	10.30	19.50
Economy vinyl	"	6.15	10.30	16.45
Rigid polyvinyl chloride	"	9.80	10.30	20.10
Sectional wood overhead doors, frames not included				
Commercial grade, heavy duty, 1-3/4" thick, manual				
8' x 8'	EA.	496.00	214.00	710.00
10' x 10'	"	770.00	234.00	1,004
12' x 12'	"	1,040	257.00	1,297
Sectional metal overhead doors, complete				
Residential grade, manual				
9' x 7'	EA.	280.00	103.00	383.00
16' x 7'	"	630.00	129.00	759.00
Sliding glass doors				
Tempered plate glass, 1/4" thick				
6' wide				
Economy grade	EA.	583.00	85.50	668.50
Premium grade	"	676.00	85.50	761.50
Insulating glass, 5/8" thick				

08 DOORS AND WINDOWS

WOOD AND PLASTIC	UNIT	MAT.	INST.	TOTAL
08300.10 SPECIAL DOORS				
6' wide				
Economy grade	EA.	816.00	85.50	901.50
Premium grade	"	1,520	85.50	1,606

STOREFRONTS	UNIT	MAT.	INST.	TOTAL
08410.10 STOREFRONTS				
Storefront, aluminum and glass				
Minimum	S.F.	13.85	3.55	17.40
Average	"	18.50	4.10	22.60
Maximum	"	25.40	4.75	30.15
08520.10 ALUMINUM WINDOWS				
Fixed window				
6 sf to 8 sf	S.F.	8.10	4.10	12.20
12 sf to 16 sf	"	7.50	3.15	10.65
Projecting window				
6 sf to 8 sf	S.F.	18.50	7.15	25.65
12 sf to 16 sf	"	16.15	4.75	20.90
Horizontal sliding				
6 sf to 8 sf	S.F.	12.70	3.55	16.25
12 sf to 16 sf	"	11.55	2.85	14.40
Double hung				
6 sf to 8 sf	S.F.	11.55	5.70	17.25
10 sf to 12 sf	"	11.00	4.75	15.75
Storm window, 0.5 cfm, up to				
60 u.i. (united inches)	EA.	41.60	14.30	55.90
70 u.i.	"	42.70	14.30	57.00
80 u.i.	"	46.20	14.30	60.50

WOOD AND PLASTIC	UNIT	MAT.	INST.	TOTAL
08600.10 WOOD WINDOWS				
Double hung				
24" x 36"				

08 DOORS AND WINDOWS

WOOD AND PLASTIC	UNIT	MAT.	INST.	TOTAL
08600.10 WOOD WINDOWS				
Minimum	EA.	131.00	25.70	156.70
Average	"	187.00	32.20	219.20
Maximum	"	233.00	42.90	275.90
30" x 48"				
Minimum	EA.	187.00	28.60	215.60
Average	"	233.00	36.70	269.70
Maximum	"	280.00	51.50	331.50
Casement				
1 leaf, 22" x 38" high				
Minimum	EA.	187.00	25.70	212.70
Average	"	210.00	32.20	242.20
Maximum	"	233.00	42.90	275.90
2 leaf, 50" x 50" high				
Minimum	EA.	466.00	32.20	498.20
Average	"	560.00	42.90	602.90
Maximum	"	606.00	64.50	670.50
Picture window, fixed glass, 54" x 54" high				
Minimum	EA.	350.00	32.20	382.20
Average	"	437.00	36.70	473.70
Maximum	"	595.00	42.90	637.90
Sliding, 40" x 31" high				
Minimum	EA.	163.00	25.70	188.70
Average	"	257.00	32.20	289.20
Maximum	"	303.00	42.90	345.90
Awning windows				
34" x 21" high				
Minimum	EA.	173.00	25.70	198.70
Average	"	198.00	32.20	230.20
Maximum	"	245.00	42.90	287.90
40" x 21" high				
Minimum	EA.	204.00	28.60	232.60
Average	"	222.00	36.70	258.70
Maximum	"	268.00	51.50	319.50

HARDWARE	UNIT	MAT.	INST.	TOTAL
08710.10 HINGES				
Hinges				
3 x 3 butts, steel, interior, plain bearing	PAIR			11.00
4 x 4 butts, steel, standard	"			16.50
5 x 4-1/2 butts, bronze/s. steel, heavy duty	"			44.00

08 DOORS AND WINDOWS

HARDWARE	UNIT	MAT.	INST.	TOTAL
08710.20 LOCKSETS				
Latchset, heavy duty				
Cylindrical	EA.	90.50	16.10	106.60
Mortise	"	81.50	25.70	107.20
Lockset, heavy duty				
Cylindrical	EA.	113.00	16.10	129.10
Mortise	"	131.00	25.70	156.70
08710.30 CLOSERS				
Door closers				
Standard	EA.	100.00	32.20	132.20
Heavy duty	"	111.00	32.20	143.20
08710.40 DOOR TRIM				
Panic device, unlabeled, rim type	EA.	373.00	64.50	437.50
Mortise	"	472.00	64.50	536.50
Vertical rod	"	548.00	64.50	612.50
Labeled, rim type	"	490.00	64.50	554.50
Mortise	"	589.00	64.50	653.50
Vertical rod	"	665.00	64.50	729.50
Door plates				
Kick plate, .050" aluminum, 3 beveled edges				
10" x 30"	EA.	11.65	12.85	24.50
10" x 34"	"	12.85	12.85	25.70
10" x 38"	"	14.00	12.85	26.85
Push plate, 4" x 16", .050"				
Aluminum	EA.	3.50	5.15	8.65
Bronze	"	7.00	5.15	12.15
Stainless steel	"	5.25	5.15	10.40
08710.60 WEATHERSTRIPPING				
Weatherstrip, head and jamb, metal strip, neoprene bulb				
Standard duty	L.F.	2.30	1.45	3.75
Heavy duty	"	3.00	1.60	4.60
Thresholds				
Bronze	L.F.	18.50	6.45	24.95
Aluminum				
Plain	L.F.	6.95	6.45	13.40
Vinyl insert	"	13.85	6.45	20.30
Aluminum with grit	"	12.15	6.45	18.60
Steel				
Plain	L.F.	9.25	6.45	15.70
Interlocking	"	14.45	21.45	35.90

08 DOORS AND WINDOWS

GLAZING	UNIT	MAT.	INST.	TOTAL
08810.10 GLAZING				
Sheet glass, 1/8" thick	S.F.	4.35	1.60	5.95
Plate glass, bronze or grey, 1/4" thick	"	6.45	2.60	9.05
Clear	"	4.95	2.60	7.55
Polished	"	5.50	2.60	8.10
Plexiglass				
1/8" thick	S.F.	1.75	2.60	4.35
1/4" thick	"	3.45	1.60	5.05
Clear, float glass				
3/16" thick	S.F.	3.35	2.40	5.75
1/4" thick	"	4.30	2.60	6.90
3/8" thick	"	7.75	3.55	11.30
Tinted glass, polished plate, twin ground				
3/16" thick	S.F.	3.60	2.40	6.00
1/4" thick	"	4.50	2.60	7.10
3/8" thick	"	8.00	3.55	11.55
Insulating glass, two lites, clear float glass				
1/2" thick	S.F.	7.20	4.75	11.95
5/8" thick	"	8.30	5.70	14.00
3/4" thick	"	9.15	7.15	16.30
7/8" thick	"	9.60	8.15	17.75
1" thick	"	10.30	9.50	19.80
Plate mirror glass				
Wall type, 1/4" thick				
15 sf	S.F.	7.30	2.85	10.15
Over 15 sf	"	6.70	2.60	9.30

09 FINISHES

SUPPORT SYSTEMS	UNIT	MAT.	INST.	TOTAL
09110.10 METAL STUDS				
Studs, non load bearing, galvanized				
2-1/2", 20 ga.				
12" o.c.	S.F.	0.48	0.54	1.02
16" o.c.	"	0.41	0.43	0.84
25 ga.				
12" o.c.	S.F.	0.35	0.54	0.89
16" o.c.	"	0.25	0.43	0.68
24" o.c.	"	0.19	0.36	0.55
3-5/8", 20 ga.				
12" o.c.	S.F.	0.51	0.64	1.15
16" o.c.	"	0.48	0.51	0.99
24" o.c.	"	0.43	0.43	0.86
25 ga.				
12" o.c.	S.F.	0.31	0.64	0.95
16" o.c.	"	0.26	0.51	0.77
24" o.c.	"	0.24	0.43	0.67
4", 20 ga.				
12" o.c.	S.F.	0.67	0.64	1.31
16" o.c.	"	0.57	0.51	1.08
24" o.c.	"	0.48	0.43	0.91
25 ga.				
12" o.c.	S.F.	0.36	0.64	1.00
16" o.c.	"	0.34	0.51	0.85
24" o.c.	"	0.28	0.43	0.71
6", 20 ga.				
12" o.c.	S.F.	0.81	0.80	1.61
16" o.c.	"	0.69	0.64	1.33
24" o.c.	"	0.57	0.54	1.11
25 ga.				
12" o.c.	S.F.	0.45	0.80	1.25
16" o.c.	"	0.41	0.64	1.05
24" o.c.	"	0.36	0.54	0.90
Load bearing studs, galvanized				
3-5/8", 16 ga.				
12" o.c.	S.F.	1.35	0.64	1.99
16" o.c.	"	1.25	0.51	1.76
18 ga.				
12" o.c.	S.F.	1.15	0.43	1.58
16" o.c.	"	1.05	0.51	1.56
4", 16 ga.				
12" o.c.	S.F.	1.50	0.64	2.14
16" o.c.	"	1.20	0.51	1.71
6", 16 ga.				
12" o.c.	S.F.	1.60	0.80	2.40
16" o.c.	"	1.50	0.64	2.14
Furring, 16" o.c.				
Installed on solid walls				
3/4" channels	S.F.	0.32	0.99	1.31
1-1/2" channels	"	0.52	1.05	1.57
Installed on columns and beams				
7/8" channel	L.F.	0.31	1.70	2.01
1-5/8" channel	"	0.52	1.70	2.22

09 FINISHES

SUPPORT SYSTEMS

SUPPORT SYSTEMS	UNIT	MAT.	INST.	TOTAL
09110.10 METAL STUDS				
Furring on ceilings				
3/4" furring channels				
12" o.c.	S.F.	0.35	1.85	2.20
16" o.c.	"	0.29	1.70	1.99
1-1/2" furring channels, 24" o.c.	"	0.25	1.45	1.70

LATH AND PLASTER

LATH AND PLASTER	UNIT	MAT.	INST.	TOTAL
09205.10 GYPSUM LATH				
Gypsum lath, 1/2" thick				
Clipped	S.Y.	4.40	1.45	5.85
Nailed	"	4.05	1.60	5.65
09205.20 METAL LATH				
Stucco lath				
1.8 lb.	S.Y.	2.90	3.20	6.10
3.6 lb.	"	3.30	3.20	6.50
Paper backed				
Minimum	S.Y.	3.40	2.55	5.95
Maximum	"	3.85	3.65	7.50
09210.10 PLASTER				
Gypsum plaster, trowel finish, 2 coats				
Ceilings	S.Y.	3.65	6.10	9.75
Walls	"	3.65	5.65	9.30
3 coats				
Ceilings	S.Y.	5.05	8.50	13.55
Walls	"	5.05	7.30	12.35
09220.10 PORTLAND CEMENT PLASTER				
Stucco, portland, gray, 3 coat, 1" thick				
Sand finish	S.Y.	3.80	11.10	14.90
Trowel finish	"	3.80	11.60	15.40
White cement				
Sand finish	S.Y.	4.35	11.60	15.95
Trowel finish	"	4.35	12.75	17.10
Scratch coat				
For ceramic tile	S.Y.	1.35	2.55	3.90
For quarry tile	"	1.35	2.55	3.90
Portland cement plaster				
2 coats, 1/2"	S.F.	0.26	0.57	0.83
3 coats, 7/8"	"	0.36	0.73	1.09

09 FINISHES

LATH AND PLASTER

09250.10 GYPSUM BOARD	UNIT	MAT.	INST.	TOTAL
Drywall, plasterboard, 3/8" clipped to				
Metal furred ceiling	S.F.	0.25	0.29	0.54
Columns and beams	"	0.25	0.64	0.89
Walls	"	0.25	0.26	0.51
Nailed or screwed to				
Wood framed ceiling	S.F.	0.25	0.26	0.51
Columns and beams	"	0.25	0.57	0.82
Walls	"	0.25	0.23	0.48
1/2", clipped to				
Metal furred ceiling	S.F.	0.31	0.29	0.60
Columns and beams	"	0.31	0.64	0.95
Walls	"	0.31	0.26	0.57
Nailed or screwed to				
Wood framed ceiling	S.F.	0.31	0.26	0.57
Columns and beams	"	0.31	0.57	0.88
Walls	"	0.31	0.23	0.54
5/8", clipped to				
Metal furred ceiling	S.F.	0.34	0.32	0.66
Columns and beams	"	0.34	0.71	1.05
Walls	"	0.34	0.29	0.63
Nailed or screwed to				
Wood framed ceiling	S.F.	0.34	0.32	0.66
Columns and beams	"	0.34	0.71	1.05
Walls	"	0.34	0.29	0.63
Taping and finishing joints	"	0.03	0.17	0.20

TILE

09310.10 CERAMIC TILE	UNIT	MAT.	INST.	TOTAL
Glazed wall tile, 4-1/4" x 4-1/4"				
Minimum	S.F.	1.50	1.80	3.30
Average	"	2.35	2.10	4.45
Maximum	"	6.15	2.50	8.65
Unglazed floor tile				
Portland cement bed, cushion edge, face mounted				
1" x 1"	S.F.	4.55	2.30	6.85
1" x 2"	"	7.30	2.20	9.50
2" x 2"	"	4.80	2.10	6.90
Adhesive bed, with white grout				
1" x 1"	S.F.	4.05	2.30	6.35
1" x 2"	"	4.15	2.20	6.35
2" x 2"	"	4.20	2.10	6.30

09 FINISHES

TILE

TILE	UNIT	MAT.	INST.	TOTAL
09330.10 QUARRY TILE				
Floor				
4 x 4 x 1/2"	S.F.	3.40	3.35	6.75
6 x 6 x 1/2"	"	3.45	3.15	6.60
6 x 6 x 3/4"	"	3.95	3.15	7.10
Wall, applied to 3/4" portland cement bed				
4 x 4 x 1/2"	S.F.	3.05	5.05	8.10
6 x 6 x 3/4"	"	3.80	4.20	8.00
Cove base				
5 x 6 x 1/2" straight top	L.F.	2.95	4.20	7.15
6 x 6 x 3/4" round top	"	3.15	4.20	7.35
09410.10 TERRAZZO				
Floors bonded to concrete, 1-3/4" thick, 5/8" topping				
Gray cement	S.F.	2.60	3.65	6.25
White cement	"	2.85	3.65	6.50
Not bonded, 3" thick, 5/8" top, 1/4" sand cushion				
Gray cement	S.F.	3.10	4.25	7.35
White cement	"	3.45	4.25	7.70
Monolithic terrazzo, 3-1/2" base slab, 5/8" topping	"	2.20	3.20	5.40
Terrazzo tiles, non-slip surface				
9" x 9" x 1" thick	S.F.	9.75	3.65	13.40
12" x 12"				
1" thick	S.F.	10.70	3.40	14.10
1-1/2" thick	"	11.15	3.65	14.80
18" x 18" x 1-1/2" thick	"	14.50	3.65	18.15
24" x 24" x 1-1/2" thick	"	18.90	3.00	21.90

ACOUSTICAL TREATMENT

ACOUSTICAL TREATMENT	UNIT	MAT.	INST.	TOTAL
09510.10 CEILINGS AND WALLS				
Acoustical panels, suspension system not included				
Fiberglass panels				
5/8" thick				
2' x 2'	S.F.	0.54	0.29	0.83
2' x 4'	"	0.54	0.26	0.80
3/4" thick				
2' x 2'	S.F.	0.79	0.29	1.08
2' x 4'	"	0.79	0.26	1.05
Mineral fiber panels				
5/8" thick				
2' x 2'	S.F.	0.59	0.29	0.88
2' x 4'	"	0.59	0.26	0.85
3/4" thick				
2' x 2'	S.F.	0.74	0.29	1.03

09 FINISHES

ACOUSTICAL TREATMENT

09510.10 CEILINGS AND WALLS	UNIT	MAT.	INST.	TOTAL
2' x 4'	S.F.	0.74	0.26	1.00
Ceiling suspension systems				
T bar system				
2' x 4'	S.F.	1.25	0.26	1.51
2' x 2'	"	1.45	0.29	1.74

FLOORING

09550.10 WOOD FLOORING	UNIT	MAT.	INST.	TOTAL
Wood strip flooring, unfinished				
Fir floor				
C and better				
Vertical grain	S.F.	2.00	0.86	2.86
Flat grain	"	1.90	0.86	2.76
Oak floor				
Minimum	S.F.	2.45	1.20	3.65
Maximum	"	3.45	1.20	4.65
Maple floor				
Minimum	S.F.	2.35	1.20	3.55
Maximum	"	2.95	1.20	4.15
Parquet, 5/16", white oak				
Finished	S.F.	5.60	1.30	6.90
Unfinished	"	1.85	1.30	3.15
Finishing, sand, fill, finish, and wax	"	0.41	0.64	1.05
Refinish sand, seal, and 2 coats of polyurethane	"	0.71	0.86	1.57
Clean and wax floors	"	0.12	0.13	0.25

09630.10 UNIT MASONRY FLOORING	UNIT	MAT.	INST.	TOTAL
Clay brick				
9 x 4-1/2 x 3" thick				
Glazed	S.F.	4.80	2.15	6.95
Unglazed	"	4.75	2.15	6.90
8 x 4 x 3/4" thick				
Glazed	S.F.	4.75	2.25	7.00
Unglazed	"	4.70	2.25	6.95

09660.10 RESILIENT TILE FLOORING	UNIT	MAT.	INST.	TOTAL
Solid vinyl tile, 1/8" thick, 12" x 12"				
Marble patterns	S.F.	1.85	0.64	2.49
Solid colors	"	1.90	0.64	2.54
Travertine patterns	"	2.30	0.64	2.94

09 FINISHES

FLOORING	UNIT	MAT.	INST.	TOTAL
09665.10 RESILIENT SHEET FLOORING				
Vinyl sheet flooring				
Minimum	S.F.	2.10	0.26	2.36
Average	"	2.60	0.31	2.91
Maximum	"	4.60	0.43	5.03
Cove, to 6"	L.F.	0.58	0.51	1.09
09682.10 CARPET PADDING				
Carpet padding				
Foam rubber, waffle type, 0.3" thick	S.Y.	3.65	1.30	4.95
Jute padding				
Minimum	S.Y.	2.65	1.15	3.80
Average	"	3.20	1.30	4.50
Maximum	"	3.95	1.45	5.40
Sponge rubber cushion				
Minimum	S.Y.	3.30	1.15	4.45
Average	"	3.50	1.30	4.80
Maximum	"	3.75	1.45	5.20
Urethane cushion, 3/8" thick				
Minimum	S.Y.	2.10	1.15	3.25
Average	"	2.40	1.30	3.70
Maximum	"	2.65	1.45	4.10
09685.10 CARPET				
Carpet, acrylic				
24 oz., light traffic	S.Y.	17.35	1.45	18.80
28 oz., medium traffic	"	21.95	1.45	23.40
Residential				
Nylon				
15 oz., light traffic	S.Y.	12.45	1.45	13.90
28 oz., medium traffic	"	14.95	1.45	16.40
Commercial				
Nylon				
28 oz., medium traffic	S.Y.	15.95	1.45	17.40
35 oz., heavy traffic	"	19.05	1.45	20.50
Wool				
30 oz., medium traffic	S.Y.	26.00	1.45	27.45
36 oz., medium traffic	"	27.40	1.45	28.85
42 oz., heavy traffic	"	29.90	1.45	31.35
Carpet tile				
Foam backed	S.F.	2.30	0.26	2.56
Tufted loop or shag	"	2.55	0.26	2.81
Clean and vacuum carpet				
Minimum	S.Y.	0.18	0.10	0.28
Average	"	0.29	0.17	0.46
Maximum	"	0.35	0.26	0.61
09700.10 SPECIAL FLOORING				
Epoxy flooring, marble chips				
Epoxy with colored quartz chips in 1/4" base	S.F.	6.35	1.45	7.80
Heavy duty epoxy topping, 3/16" thick	"	5.50	1.45	6.95

09 FINISHES

PAINTING

PAINTING	UNIT	MAT.	INST.	TOTAL
09910.10 EXTERIOR PAINTING				
Exterior painting				
Wood surfaces, 1 coat primer, two coats paint				
Door and frame	EA.	3.05	43.70	46.75
Windows	S.F.	0.06	0.65	0.71
Wood trim	"	0.14	0.65	0.79
Wood siding	"	0.14	0.33	0.47
Hardboard surfaces				
One coat primer, two coats paint	S.F.	0.14	0.33	0.47
Asbestos cement surfaces				
One coat primer, two coats paint	S.F.	0.17	0.33	0.50
Galvanized surfaces, galvanized primer				
One coat primer, two coats paint	S.F.	0.15	0.31	0.46
Stucco surfaces, acrylic primer, acrylic latex paint				
One coat primer, two coats paint	S.F.	0.15	0.44	0.59
Concrete masonry unit surfaces, brush work				
One coat filler, one coat paint	S.F.	0.18	0.33	0.51
Two coats epoxy	"	0.25	0.44	0.69
Texture coating	"	0.23	0.26	0.49
Concrete surfaces				
One coat filler, one coat paint	S.F.	0.14	0.33	0.47
Two coats paint	"	0.21	0.44	0.65
Structural steel				
One field coat paint, brush work				
Light framing	S.F.	0.08	0.22	0.30
Heavy framing	"	0.08	0.13	0.21
Pipes, one coat primer, one coat paint				
4" dia.	L.F.	0.06	0.33	0.39
8" dia.	"	0.14	0.44	0.58
12" dia.	"	0.26	0.65	0.91
Miscellaneous surfaces				
Stair pipe rails				
Two rails	L.F.	0.12	0.87	0.99
One rail	"	0.07	0.52	0.59
Stair to 4' wide, including rails, per riser	EA.	0.53	3.75	4.28
Gratings and frames	S.F.	0.12	0.87	0.99
Ladders	L.F.	0.14	0.75	0.89
09920.10 INTERIOR PAINTING				
Walls, concrete and masonry, brush, primer, acrylic				
One coat primer, one coat paint	S.F.	0.08	0.33	0.41
Two coats paint	"	0.12	0.44	0.56
Plywood, paint	"	0.04	0.15	0.19
Natural finish	"	0.06	0.16	0.22
Wood, paint	"	0.06	0.16	0.22
Natural finish	"	0.07	0.19	0.26
Metal				
One coat filler	S.F.	0.12	0.16	0.28
One coat primer, one coat paint	"	0.14	0.33	0.47
Two coats paint	"	0.19	0.44	0.63
Plaster or gypsum board, paint	"	0.07	0.15	0.22
Epoxy	"	0.09	0.16	0.25
Ceilings, one coat paint, wood	"	0.06	0.19	0.25

09 FINISHES

PAINTING	UNIT	MAT.	INST.	TOTAL
09920.10 INTERIOR PAINTING				
Concrete	S.F.	0.09	0.16	0.25
Plaster	"	0.06	0.15	0.21
09920.30 DOORS AND MILLWORK				
Painting, doors				
Minimum	S.F.	0.12	0.87	0.99
Average	"	0.18	1.30	1.48
Maximum	"	0.30	1.75	2.05
Cabinets, shelves, and millwork				
Minimum	S.F.	0.09	0.44	0.53
Average	"	0.12	0.75	0.87
Maximum	"	0.14	1.30	1.44
09920.60 WINDOWS				
Painting, windows				
Minimum	S.F.	0.06	0.52	0.58
Average	"	0.07	0.65	0.72
Maximum	"	0.09	1.05	1.14
09955.10 WALL COVERING				
Vinyl wall covering				
Medium duty	S.F.	0.85	0.37	1.22
Heavy duty	"	1.10	0.44	1.54
Cork wall covering				
1' x 1' squares				
1/4" thick	S.F.	1.20	0.65	1.85
1/2" thick	"	1.35	0.65	2.00
3/4" thick	"	1.50	0.65	2.15
Wall fabrics				
Natural fabrics, grass cloths				
Minimum	S.F.	0.70	0.40	1.10
Average	"	0.88	0.44	1.32
Maximum	"	2.75	0.52	3.27
09980.10 PAINTING PREPARATION				
Cleaning, light				
Wood	S.F.	0.03	0.07	0.10
Plaster or gypsum wallboard	"	0.03	0.06	0.09
Normal painting prep, masonry and concrete				
Unpainted	S.F.	0.03	0.04	0.07
Painted	"	0.03	0.07	0.10
Plaster or gypsum				
Unpainted	S.F.	0.03	0.04	0.07
Painted	"	0.03	0.07	0.10
Wood				
Unpainted	S.F.	0.03	0.04	0.07
Painted	"	0.03	0.07	0.10
Sandblasting				
Brush off blast	S.F.	0.12	0.17	0.29
Commercial blast	"	0.23	0.44	0.67

09 FINISHES

PAINTING	UNIT	MAT.	INST.	TOTAL
09980.10 PAINTING PREPARATION				
Near white metal blast	S.F.	0.33	0.75	1.08
White metal blast	"	0.44	0.87	1.31
09980.15 PAINT				
Paint, enamel				
600 sf per gal.	GAL			23.65
550 sf per gal.	"			18.25
500 sf per gal.	"			13.75
450 sf per gal.	"			12.65
350 sf per gal.	"			12.10
Latex, 400 sf per gal.	"			11.45
Aluminum				
400 sf per gal.	GAL			15.95
500 sf per gal.	"			30.80
Red lead, 350 sf per gal.	"			27.50
Primer				
400 sf per gal.	GAL			18.25
300 sf per gal.	"			18.15
Latex base, interior, white	"			15.20
Sealer and varnish				
400 sf per gal.	GAL			14.00
425 sf per gal.	"			20.50
600 sf per gal.	"			27.50

10 SPECIALTIES

SPECIALTIES	UNIT	MAT.	INST.	TOTAL
10210.10 VENTS AND WALL LOUVERS				
Vents w/screen, 4" deep, 8" wide, 5" high				
Modular	EA.	54.50	8.95	63.45
Aluminum gable louvers	S.F.	9.80	4.75	14.55
Vent screen aluminum, 4" wide, continuous	L.F.	2.60	0.95	3.55
Wall louver, aluminum mill finish				
Under, 2 sf	S.F.	20.20	3.55	23.75
2 to 4 sf	"	17.35	3.15	20.50
5 to 10 sf	"	16.45	3.15	19.60
Galvanized steel				
Under 2 sf	S.F.	19.65	3.55	23.20
2 to 4 sf	"	13.85	3.15	17.00
5 to 10 sf	"	13.00	3.15	16.15
10225.10 DOOR LOUVERS				
Fixed, 1" thick, enameled steel				
8"x8"	EA.	31.70	3.20	34.90
12"x8"	"	35.10	3.20	38.30
12"x12"	"	39.70	3.65	43.35
20"x8"	"	64.50	3.65	68.15
10520.10 FIRE PROTECTION				
Portable fire extinguishers				
Water pump tank type				
2.5 gal.				
Red enameled galvanized	EA.	71.50	13.60	85.10
Red enameled copper	"	81.00	13.60	94.60
Carbon dioxide type, red enamel steel				
Squeeze grip with hose and horn				
2.5 lb	EA.	37.90	13.60	51.50
5 lb	"	79.00	15.70	94.70
10 lb	"	114.00	20.40	134.40
Dry chemical, pressurized type				
Red enameled steel				
2.5 lb	EA.	17.85	13.60	31.45
5 lb	"	26.20	15.70	41.90
Fire extinguisher cabinets				
Enameled steel				
8" x 12" x 27"	EA.	114.00	40.80	154.80
8" x 16" x 38"	"	146.00	40.80	186.80
10550.10 POSTAL SPECIALTIES				
Residential postal accessories				
Letter slot	EA.	62.00	12.85	74.85
Rural letter box	"	42.50	32.20	74.70
Apartment house, keyed, 3.5" x 4.5" x 16"	"	62.00	8.55	70.55
10800.10 BATH ACCESSORIES				
Grab bar, 1-1/2" dia., stainless steel, wall mounted				
24" long	EA.	31.40	12.85	44.25
36" long	"	44.90	13.55	58.45

10 SPECIALTIES

SPECIALTIES	UNIT	MAT.	INST.	TOTAL
10800.10 BATH ACCESSORIES				
1" dia., stainless steel				
12" long	EA.	24.70	11.20	35.90
24" long	"	29.20	12.85	42.05
36" long	"	37.00	14.30	51.30
Hand dryer, surface mounted, 110 volt	"	280.00	32.20	312.20
Medicine cabinet, 16 x 22, baked enamel, steel, lighted	"	56.00	10.30	66.30
With mirror, lighted	"	101.00	17.15	118.15
Mirror, 1/4" plate glass, up to 10 sf	S.F.	5.40	2.55	7.95
Mirror, stainless steel frame				
18"x24"	EA.	84.00	8.55	92.55
24"x30"	"	112.00	12.85	124.85
24"x60"	"	236.00	25.70	261.70
With shelf, 18"x24"	"	129.00	10.30	139.30
Sanitary napkin dispenser, stainless steel, wall mounted	"	309.00	17.15	326.15
Shower rod, 1" diameter				
Chrome finish over brass	EA.	50.50	12.85	63.35
Stainless steel	"	48.80	12.85	61.65
Toilet tissue dispenser, stainless, wall mounted				
Single roll	EA.	30.30	6.45	36.75
Double roll	"	47.10	7.35	54.45
Towel dispenser, stainless steel				
Flush mounted	EA.	140.00	14.30	154.30
Surface mounted	"	73.00	12.85	85.85
Combination towel dispenser and waste receptacle	"	275.00	17.15	292.15
Towel bar, stainless steel				
18" long	EA.	25.80	10.30	36.10
24" long	"	30.30	11.70	42.00
30" long	"	32.50	12.85	45.35
36" long	"	35.90	14.30	50.20
Toothbrush and tumbler holder	"	21.90	8.55	30.45
Waste receptacle, stainless steel, wall mounted	"	185.00	21.45	206.45

11 ARCHITECTURAL

EQUIPMENT	UNIT	MAT.	INST.	TOTAL
11450.10 RESIDENTIAL EQUIPMENT				
Compactor, 4 to 1 compaction	EA.	1,100	66.50	1,167
Dishwasher, built-in				
2 cycles	EA.	942.00	133.00	1,075
4 or more cycles	"	1,420	133.00	1,553
Disposal				
Garbage disposer	EA.	440.00	88.50	528.50
Heaters, electric, built-in				
Ceiling type	EA.	236.00	88.50	324.50
Wall type	"	148.00	88.50	236.50
1500 watt, wall type	"	167.00	66.50	233.50
3000 watt, wall type	"	275.00	88.50	363.50
Hood for range, 2-speed, vented				
30" wide	EA.	118.00	88.50	206.50
42" wide	"	516.00	88.50	604.50
Ice maker, automatic				
30 lb per day	EA.	752.00	37.90	789.90
50 lb per day	"	1,590	133.00	1,723
Folding access stairs, disappearing metal stair				
8' long	EA.	1,260	37.90	1,298
12' long	"	1,340	37.90	1,378
Wood frame, wood stair				
22" x 54" x 8'9" long	EA.	60.50	26.50	87.00
25" x 54" x 10' long	"	63.50	26.50	90.00
Ranges electric				
Free standing, 21", 1 oven	EA.	600.00	88.50	688.50
Built-in, 30", 1 oven	"	800.00	88.50	888.50
2 oven	"	1,200	88.50	1,289
Counter top, 4 burner, standard	"	752.00	66.50	818.50
With grill	"	1,590	66.50	1,657
Free standing 30", 1 oven	"	870.00	53.00	923.00
2 oven	"	2,500	53.00	2,553
Water softener				
30 grains per gallon	EA.	1,090	88.50	1,179
70 grains per gallon	"	1,500	133.00	1,633

12 FURNISHINGS

INTERIOR	UNIT	MAT.	INST.	TOTAL
12302.10 CASEWORK				
Kitchen base cabinet, prefinished, 24" deep, 35" high				
12"wide	EA.	108.00	25.70	133.70
24" wide	"	144.00	28.60	172.60
36" wide	"	196.00	32.20	228.20
48" wide	"	224.00	32.20	256.20
Corner cabinet, 36" wide	"	151.00	32.20	183.20
Wall cabinet, 12" deep, 12" high				
30" wide	EA.	86.00	25.70	111.70
36" wide	"	91.00	25.70	116.70
15" high				
30" wide	EA.	91.00	28.60	119.60
36" wide	"	98.50	28.60	127.10
24" high				
30" wide	EA.	108.00	28.60	136.60
36" wide	"	132.00	28.60	160.60
30" high				
12" wide	EA.	82.50	32.20	114.70
24" wide	"	101.00	32.20	133.20
36" wide	"	142.00	36.70	178.70
Corner cabinet, 30" high				
24" wide	EA.	132.00	42.90	174.90
36" wide	"	176.00	42.90	218.90
Vanity with top, laminated plastic				
30" wide	EA.	309.00	64.50	373.50
48" wide	"	372.00	103.00	475.00
12390.10 COUNTER TOPS				
Stainless steel, counter top, with backsplash	S.F.	66.00	6.45	72.45
Acid-proof, kemrock surface	"	17.60	4.30	21.90
12500.10 WINDOW TREATMENT				
Drapery tracks, wall or ceiling mounted				
Basic traverse rod				
50 to 90"	EA.	25.70	12.85	38.55
84 to 156"	"	39.50	14.30	53.80
12510.10 BLINDS				
Venetian blinds				
2" slats	S.F.	2.40	0.64	3.04
1" slats	"	4.75	0.64	5.39

15 MECHANICAL

BASIC MATERIALS

BASIC MATERIALS	UNIT	MAT.	INST.	TOTAL
15120.10 BACKFLOW PREVENTERS				
Backflow preventer, flanged, cast iron, with valves				
3" pipe	EA.	1,560	143.00	1,703
4" pipe	"	2,250	159.00	2,409
15140.11 PIPE HANGERS, LIGHT				
A band, black iron				
1/2"	EA.	0.42	2.05	2.47
1"	"	0.53	2.10	2.63
1-1/4"	"	0.58	2.20	2.78
Copper				
1/2"	EA.	0.48	2.05	2.53
3/4"	"	0.48	2.10	2.58
1"	"	0.51	2.10	2.61
2 hole clips, galvanized				
3/4"	EA.	0.14	1.90	2.04
1"	"	0.17	1.95	2.12
PVC coated hangers, galvanized, 28 ga.				
1-1/2" x 12"	EA.	0.70	1.90	2.60
2" x 12"	"	0.78	2.05	2.83
Wire hook hangers				
Black wire, 1/2" x				
4"	EA.	0.15	1.45	1.60
6"	"	0.19	1.50	1.69
15290.10 DUCTWORK INSULATION				
Fiberglass duct insulation, plain blanket				
1-1/2" thick	S.F.	0.21	0.36	0.57
2" thick	"	0.25	0.48	0.73

PLUMBING

PLUMBING	UNIT	MAT.	INST.	TOTAL
15410.05 C.I. PIPE, ABOVE GROUND				
No hub pipe				
1-1/2" pipe	L.F.	2.25	2.05	4.30
2" pipe	"	2.50	2.40	4.90
3" pipe	"	2.70	2.85	5.55
4" pipe	"	3.50	4.75	8.25
15410.10 COPPER PIPE				
Type "K" copper				
1/2"	L.F.	0.74	0.89	1.63

15 MECHANICAL

PLUMBING	UNIT	MAT.	INST.	TOTAL
15410.10 COPPER PIPE				
3/4"	L.F.	2.30	0.95	3.25
1"	"	3.10	1.00	4.10
DWV, copper				
1-1/4"	L.F.	5.00	1.20	6.20
1-1/2"	"	5.80	1.30	7.10
2"	"	8.15	1.45	9.60
3"	"	14.65	1.60	16.25
4"	"	25.50	1.80	27.30
15410.30 PVC/CPVC PIPE				
PVC schedule 40				
1/2" pipe	L.F.	0.68	1.20	1.88
3/4" pipe	"	0.86	1.30	2.16
1" pipe	"	1.25	1.45	2.70
1-1/4" pipe	"	1.30	1.60	2.90
1-1/2" pipe	"	1.40	1.80	3.20
2" pipe	"	1.85	2.05	3.90
2-1/2" pipe	"	3.30	2.40	5.70
3" pipe	"	3.75	2.85	6.60
4" pipe	"	5.25	3.55	8.80
15430.23 CLEANOUTS				
Cleanout, wall				
2"	EA.	51.00	19.05	70.05
3"	"	57.00	19.05	76.05
4"	"	76.00	23.80	99.80
15430.25 HOSE BIBBS				
Hose bibb				
1/2"	EA.	4.45	9.50	13.95
3/4"	"	4.70	9.50	14.20
15430.60 VALVES				
Gate valve, 125 lb, bronze, soldered				
1/2"	EA.	8.25	7.15	15.40
3/4"	"	11.10	7.15	18.25
Threaded				
1/2"				
3/4"				
Ball valve, bronze, 250 lb, threaded				
1/2"	EA.	6.75	11.40	18.15
3/4"	"	11.20	11.40	22.60
Radiator temp control valve, with control and sensor				
1/2" valve	EA.	51.50	17.85	69.35
1" valve	"	60.50	17.85	78.35
Solar water temperature regulating valve				
3/4"	EA.	265.00	23.80	288.80
1"	"	271.00	28.60	299.60

15 MECHANICAL

PLUMBING

15430.70 DRAINS, ROOF & FLOOR	UNIT	MAT.	INST.	TOTAL
Floor drain, cast iron, with cast iron top				
2"	EA.	67.00	23.80	90.80
3"	"	67.00	23.80	90.80
4"	"	67.00	23.80	90.80
Roof drain, cast iron				
2"	EA.	196.00	23.80	219.80
3"	"	196.00	23.80	219.80
4"	"	196.00	23.80	219.80

PLUMBING FIXTURES

15440.10 BATHS	UNIT	MAT.	INST.	TOTAL
Bath tub, 5' long				
Minimum	EA.	323.00	95.00	418.00
Average	"	681.00	143.00	824.00
Maximum	"	1,020	286.00	1,306
6' long				
Minimum	EA.	370.00	95.00	465.00
Average	"	716.00	143.00	859.00
Maximum	"	1,120	286.00	1,406
Square tub, whirlpool, 4'x4'				
Minimum	EA.	1,120	143.00	1,263
Average	"	1,390	286.00	1,676
Maximum	"	2,990	357.00	3,347
5'x5'				
Minimum	EA.	1,140	143.00	1,283
Average	"	1,620	286.00	1,906
Maximum	"	3,120	357.00	3,477
6'x6'				
Minimum	EA.	1,330	143.00	1,473
Average	"	1,820	286.00	2,106
Maximum	"	3,810	357.00	4,167
For trim and rough-in				
Minimum	EA.	98.00	95.00	193.00
Average	"	139.00	143.00	282.00
Maximum	"	202.00	286.00	488.00
15440.12 DISPOSALS & ACCESSORIES				
Continuous feed				
Minimum	EA.	43.90	57.00	100.90
Maximum	"	219.00	95.00	314.00
Batch feed, 1/2 hp				
Minimum	EA.	161.00	57.00	218.00
Maximum	"	260.00	95.00	355.00

15 MECHANICAL

PLUMBING FIXTURES	UNIT	MAT.	INST.	TOTAL
15440.15 FAUCETS				
Kitchen				
Minimum	EA.	86.50	47.60	134.10
Average	"	139.00	57.00	196.00
Maximum	"	167.00	71.50	238.50
Bath				
Minimum	EA.	139.00	47.60	186.60
Average	"	203.00	57.00	260.00
Maximum	"	219.00	71.50	290.50
Lavatory, domestic				
Minimum	EA.	89.00	47.60	136.60
Average	"	185.00	57.00	242.00
Maximum	"	277.00	71.50	348.50
Shower				
Minimum	EA.	104.00	47.60	151.60
Average	"	185.00	57.00	242.00
Maximum	"	289.00	71.50	360.50
For trim and rough-in				
Minimum	EA.	46.20	57.00	103.20
Average	"	69.50	71.50	141.00
Maximum	"	104.00	143.00	247.00
15440.20 LAVATORIES				
Lavatory, counter top, porcelain enamel on cast iron				
Minimum	EA.	113.00	57.00	170.00
Average	"	167.00	71.50	238.50
Maximum	"	243.00	95.00	338.00
Wall hung, china				
Minimum	EA.	127.00	57.00	184.00
Average	"	173.00	71.50	244.50
Maximum	"	462.00	95.00	557.00
For trim and rough-in				
Minimum	EA.	110.00	71.50	181.50
Average	"	133.00	95.00	228.00
Maximum	"	231.00	143.00	374.00
15440.30 SHOWERS				
Shower, fiberglass, 36"x34"x84"				
Minimum	EA.	450.00	204.00	654.00
Average	"	624.00	286.00	910.00
Maximum	"	895.00	286.00	1,181
Steel, 1 piece, 36"x36"				
Minimum	EA.	416.00	204.00	620.00
Average	"	612.00	286.00	898.00
Maximum	"	705.00	286.00	991.00
Receptor, molded stone, 36"x36"				
Minimum	EA.	139.00	95.00	234.00
Average	"	225.00	143.00	368.00
Maximum	"	346.00	238.00	584.00
For trim and rough-in				
Minimum	EA.	106.00	130.00	236.00
Average	"	133.00	159.00	292.00
Maximum	"	162.00	286.00	448.00

15 MECHANICAL

PLUMBING FIXTURES	UNIT	MAT.	INST.	TOTAL
15440.40 SINKS				
Kitchen sink, single, stainless steel, single bowl				
Minimum	EA.	121.00	57.00	178.00
Average	"	162.00	71.50	233.50
Maximum	"	229.00	95.00	324.00
Double bowl				
Minimum	EA.	162.00	71.50	233.50
Average	"	185.00	95.00	280.00
Maximum	"	248.00	143.00	391.00
Porcelain enamel, cast iron, single bowl				
Minimum	EA.	122.00	57.00	179.00
Average	"	146.00	71.50	217.50
Maximum	"	200.00	95.00	295.00
Double bowl				
Minimum	EA.	167.00	71.50	238.50
Average	"	191.00	95.00	286.00
Maximum	"	254.00	143.00	397.00
Washing machine box				
Minimum	EA.	104.00	71.50	175.50
Average	"	139.00	95.00	234.00
Maximum	"	185.00	143.00	328.00
For trim and rough-in				
Minimum	EA.	162.00	95.00	257.00
Average	"	231.00	143.00	374.00
Maximum	"	289.00	190.00	479.00
15440.60 WATER CLOSETS				
Water closet flush tank, floor mounted				
Minimum	EA.	187.00	71.50	258.50
Average	"	420.00	95.00	515.00
Maximum	"	723.00	143.00	866.00
For trim and rough-in				
Minimum	EA.	99.00	71.50	170.50
Average	"	117.00	95.00	212.00
Maximum	"	146.00	143.00	289.00
15440.70 WATER HEATERS				
Water heater, electric				
10 gal	EA.	145.00	47.60	192.60
20 gal	"	187.00	57.00	244.00
30 gal	"	195.00	57.00	252.00
40 gal	"	197.00	57.00	254.00
Oil fired				
20 gal	EA.	605.00	143.00	748.00
50 gal	"	935.00	204.00	1,139

15 MECHANICAL

HEATING & VENTILATING	UNIT	MAT.	INST.	TOTAL
15555.10 BOILERS				
Cast iron, gas fired, hot water				
115 mbh	EA.	1,060	917.00	1,977
175 mbh	"	1,290	1,000	2,290
235 mbh	"	1,910	1,100	3,010
Electric, hot water				
115 mbh	EA.	3,120	550.00	3,670
175 mbh	"	3,700	550.00	4,250
235 mbh	"	4,390	550.00	4,940
Oil fired, hot water				
115 mbh	EA.	1,730	733.00	2,463
175 mbh	"	2,190	846.00	3,036
235 mbh	"	2,540	1,000	3,540
15610.10 FURNACES				
Electric, hot air				
40 mbh	EA.	520.00	143.00	663.00
60 mbh	"	606.00	150.00	756.00
80 mbh	"	664.00	159.00	823.00
100 mbh	"	901.00	168.00	1,069
125 mbh	"	993.00	173.00	1,166
Gas fired hot air				
40 mbh	EA.	520.00	143.00	663.00
60 mbh	"	549.00	150.00	699.00
80 mbh	"	635.00	159.00	794.00
100 mbh	"	664.00	168.00	832.00
125 mbh	"	722.00	173.00	895.00
Oil fired hot air				
40 mbh	EA.	635.00	143.00	778.00
60 mbh	"	791.00	150.00	941.00
80 mbh	"	866.00	159.00	1,025
100 mbh	"	1,010	168.00	1,178
125 mbh	"	1,130	173.00	1,303

REFRIGERATION	UNIT	MAT.	INST.	TOTAL
15670.10 CONDENSING UNITS				
Air cooled condenser, single circuit				
3 ton	EA.	1,320	47.60	1,368
5 ton	"	2,200	47.60	2,248
With low ambient dampers				
3 ton	EA.	1,540	71.50	1,612
5 ton	"	2,420	71.50	2,492

15 MECHANICAL

REFRIGERATION	UNIT	MAT.	INST.	TOTAL
15780.20 ROOFTOP UNITS				
Packaged, single zone rooftop unit, with roof curb				
2 ton	EA.	1,240	286.00	1,526
3 ton	"	1,770	286.00	2,056
4 ton	"	2,350	357.00	2,707
15830.10 RADIATION UNITS				
Baseboard radiation unit				
1.7 mbh/lf	L.F.	39.90	11.40	51.30
2.1 mbh/lf	"	52.50	14.30	66.80
15830.70 UNIT HEATERS				
Steam unit heater, horizontal				
12,500 btuh, 200 cfm	EA.	185.00	47.60	232.60
17,000 btuh, 300 cfm	"	214.00	47.60	261.60

AIR HANDLING	UNIT	MAT.	INST.	TOTAL
15855.10 AIR HANDLING UNITS				
Air handling unit, medium pressure, single zone				
1500 cfm	EA.	1,980	178.00	2,158
3000 cfm	"	2,540	317.00	2,857
Rooftop air handling units				
4950 cfm	EA.	6,930	317.00	7,247
7370 cfm	"	7,840	408.00	8,248

AIR DISTRIBUTION	UNIT	MAT.	INST.	TOTAL
15890.10 METAL DUCTWORK				
Rectangular duct				
Galvanized steel				
Minimum	Lb.	2.95	2.60	5.55
Average	"	3.30	3.15	6.45
Maximum	"	4.60	4.75	9.35
Aluminum				

15 MECHANICAL

AIR DISTRIBUTION	UNIT	MAT.	INST.	TOTAL
15890.10 METAL DUCTWORK				
Minimum	Lb.	6.25	5.70	11.95
Average	"	7.25	7.15	14.40
Maximum	"	10.90	9.50	20.40
Fittings				
Minimum	EA.	2.65	9.50	12.15
Average	"	5.30	14.30	19.60
Maximum	"	13.20	28.60	41.80
15890.30 FLEXIBLE DUCTWORK				
Flexible duct, 1.25" fiberglass				
5" dia.	L.F.	1.15	1.45	2.60
6" dia.	"	1.20	1.60	2.80
15910.10 DAMPERS				
Horizontal parallel aluminum backdraft damper				
12" x 12"	EA.	28.90	7.15	36.05
16" x 16"	"	40.40	8.15	48.55
20" x 20"	"	52.00	10.20	62.20
15940.10 DIFFUSERS				
Ceiling diffusers, round, baked enamel finish				
6" dia.	EA.	28.90	9.50	38.40
8" dia.	"	34.70	11.90	46.60
Rectangular				
6x6"	EA.	23.10	9.50	32.60
9x9"	"	27.70	14.30	42.00
12x12"	"	42.70	14.30	57.00
15x15"	"	59.00	14.30	73.30
18x18"	"	81.00	14.30	95.30
15940.40 REGISTERS AND GRILLES				
Lay in flush mounted, perforated face, return				
6x6/24x24	EA.	24.25	11.40	35.65
8x8/24x24	"	24.25	11.40	35.65
9x9/24x24	"	24.25	11.40	35.65
10x10/24x24	"	24.25	11.40	35.65

16 ELECTRICAL

BASIC MATERIALS

	UNIT	MAT.	INST.	TOTAL
16050.30 BUS DUCT				
Bus duct, 100a, plug-in				
10', 600v	EA.	154.00	91.50	245.50
With ground	"	204.00	140.00	344.00
10', 277/480v	"	198.00	91.50	289.50
With ground	"	243.00	140.00	383.00
16110.12 CABLE TRAY				
Cable tray, 6"	L.F.	9.75	1.95	11.70
Ventilated cover	"	3.95	1.00	4.95
Solid cover	"	3.10	1.00	4.10
16110.21 ALUMINUM CONDUIT				
Aluminum conduit				
1/2"	L.F.	0.76	1.00	1.76
3/4"	"	0.99	1.35	2.34
1"	"	1.00	1.65	2.65
16110.22 EMT CONDUIT				
EMT conduit				
1/2"	L.F.	0.17	1.00	1.17
3/4"	"	0.23	1.35	1.58
1"	"	0.37	1.65	2.02
16110.23 FLEXIBLE CONDUIT				
Flexible conduit, steel				
1/2	L.F.	0.19	1.00	1.19
3/4"	"	0.26	1.35	1.61
1"	"	0.53	1.35	1.88
16110.24 GALVANIZED CONDUIT				
Galvanized rigid steel conduit				
1/2"	L.F.	0.76	1.35	2.11
3/4"	"	0.95	1.65	2.60
1"	"	1.30	1.95	3.25
16110.25 PLASTIC CONDUIT				
PVC conduit, schedule 40				
1/2"	L.F.	0.20	1.00	1.20
3/4"	"	0.25	1.00	1.25
1"	"	0.37	1.35	1.72
16110.27 PLASTIC COATED CONDUIT				
Rigid steel conduit, plastic coated				
1/2"	L.F.	2.15	1.65	3.80
3/4"	"	2.50	1.95	4.45
1"	"	3.25	2.65	5.90

16 ELECTRICAL

BASIC MATERIALS	UNIT	MAT.	INST.	TOTAL
16110.28 STEEL CONDUIT				
Intermediate metal conduit (IMC)				
1/2"	L.F.	0.71	1.00	1.71
3/4"	"	0.85	1.35	2.20
1"	"	1.15	1.65	2.80
16110.80 WIREWAYS				
Wireway, hinge cover type				
2-1/2" x 2-1/2"				
1' section	EA.	7.50	5.10	12.60
2'	"	10.65	6.30	16.95
3'	"	14.45	8.30	22.75
16120.41 ALUMINUM CONDUCTORS				
Type XHHW, stranded aluminum, 600v				
#8	L.F.	0.11	0.17	0.28
#6	"	0.17	0.20	0.37
#4	"	0.22	0.27	0.49
16120.43 COPPER CONDUCTORS				
Copper conductors, type THW, solid				
#14	L.F.	0.04	0.13	0.17
#12	"	0.07	0.17	0.24
#10	"	0.09	0.20	0.29
Type "BX" solid armored cable				
#14/2	L.F.	0.32	0.83	1.15
#14/3	"	0.40	0.93	1.33
#14/4	"	0.54	1.00	1.54
#12/2	"	0.34	0.93	1.27
#12/3	"	0.50	1.00	1.50
#12/4	"	0.70	1.15	1.85
16120.45 FLAT CONDUCTOR CABLE				
Flat conductor cable, with shield, 3 conductor				
#12 awg	L.F.	3.40	1.95	5.35
#10 awg	"	4.00	1.95	5.95
16120.47 NON-METALLIC SHEATHED CABLE				
Non-metallic sheathed cable				
Type NM cable with ground				
#14/2	L.F.	0.12	0.50	0.62
#12/2	"	0.18	0.53	0.71
#10/2	"	0.29	0.59	0.88
#8/2	"	0.59	0.66	1.25
#6/2	"	0.88	0.83	1.71
#14/3	"	0.20	0.86	1.06
#12/3	"	0.29	0.88	1.17
#10/3	"	0.43	0.90	1.33
#8/3	"	0.91	0.91	1.82

16 ELECTRICAL

BASIC MATERIALS	UNIT	MAT.	INST.	TOTAL
16120.47 NON-METALLIC SHEATHED CABLE				
#6/3	L.F.	1.25	0.93	2.18
#4/3	"	1.85	1.05	2.90
#2/3	"	2.75	1.15	3.90
16130.40 BOXES				
Round cast box, type SEH				
1/2"	EA.	12.70	11.55	24.25
3/4"	"	13.85	13.95	27.80
SEHC				
1/2"	EA.	15.95	11.55	27.50
3/4"	"	16.75	13.95	30.70
Rectangle, type FS, 2 gang boxes				
1/2"	EA.	11.55	11.55	23.10
3/4"	"	12.40	13.25	25.65
1"	"	13.65	16.60	30.25
Weatherproof cast aluminum boxes, 1 gang, 3 outlets				
1/2"	EA.	3.30	13.25	16.55
3/4"	"	3.60	16.60	20.20
2 gang, 3 outlets				
1/2"	EA.	6.30	16.60	22.90
3/4"	"	6.60	17.70	24.30
16130.45 EXPLOSION PROOF FITTINGS				
Flexible couplings with female unions				
1/2" x 18"	EA.	72.00	6.65	78.65
3/4" x 18"	"	91.00	9.15	100.15
1" x 18"	"	152.00	11.55	163.55
16130.60 PULL AND JUNCTION BOXES				
4"				
Octagon box	EA.	1.05	3.80	4.85
Box extension	"	1.50	1.95	3.45
Plaster ring	"	0.80	1.95	2.75
Cover blank	"	0.34	1.95	2.29
Square box	"	1.25	3.80	5.05
Box extension	"	1.35	1.95	3.30
Plaster ring	"	0.63	1.95	2.58
Cover blank	"	0.40	1.95	2.35
16130.65 PULL BOXES AND CABINETS				
Galvanized pull boxes, screw cover				
4x4x4	EA.	3.45	6.30	9.75
4x6x4	"	4.30	6.30	10.60
16130.80 RECEPTACLES				
125 volt, 20a, duplex, grounding type, standard grade	EA.	4.65	6.65	11.30
Ground fault interrupter type	"	36.00	9.80	45.80
250 volt, 20a, 2 pole, single receptacle, ground type	"	5.40	6.65	12.05

16 ELECTRICAL

BASIC MATERIALS

BASIC MATERIALS	UNIT	MAT.	INST.	TOTAL
16130.80 RECEPTACLES				
120/208v, 4 pole, single receptacle, twist lock				
20a	EA.	11.60	11.55	23.15
Dryer receptacle, 250v, 30a/50a, 3 wire	"	14.20	9.80	24.00
Clock receptacle, 2 pole, grounding type	"	5.95	6.65	12.60
16350.10 CIRCUIT BREAKERS				
Molded case, 240v, 15-60a, bolt-on				
1 pole	EA.	7.20	8.30	15.50
2 pole	"	16.00	11.55	27.55
70-100a, 2 pole	"	42.30	17.70	60.00
15-60a, 3 pole	"	52.00	13.25	65.25
70-100a, 3 pole	"	75.50	20.40	95.90
16395.10 GROUNDING				
Ground rods, copper clad, 1/2" x				
6'	EA.	6.30	22.10	28.40
8'	"	8.15	24.10	32.25

SERVICE AND DISTRIBUTION

SERVICE AND DISTRIBUTION	UNIT	MAT.	INST.	TOTAL
16470.10 PANELBOARDS				
120/208v, flush, 3 ph., 4 wire, main only				
100a				
12 circuits	EA.	315.00	169.00	484.00
20 circuits	"	434.00	209.00	643.00
30 circuits	"	629.00	233.00	862.00
225a				
30 circuits	EA.	658.00	257.00	915.00
42 circuits	"	835.00	316.00	1,151

LIGHTING

LIGHTING	UNIT	MAT.	INST.	TOTAL
16510.05 INTERIOR LIGHTING				
Recessed fluorescent fixtures, 2'x2'				
2 lamp	EA.	44.00	24.10	68.10

16 ELECTRICAL

LIGHTING

LIGHTING	UNIT	MAT.	INST.	TOTAL
16510.05 INTERIOR LIGHTING				
4 lamp	EA.	59.00	24.10	83.10
Surface mounted incandescent fixtures				
40w	EA.	40.00	22.10	62.10
75w	"	43.50	22.10	65.60
100w	"	51.50	22.10	73.60
Recessed incandescent fixtures				
40w	EA.	73.50	50.00	123.50
75w	"	77.00	50.00	127.00
100w	"	79.00	50.00	129.00
Light track single circuit				
2'	EA.	19.75	16.60	36.35
4'	"	36.80	16.60	53.40
8'	"	66.00	33.20	99.20
Fixtures, square				
R-20	EA.	52.50	4.80	57.30
R-30	"	55.00	4.80	59.80
Mini spot	"	72.50	4.80	77.30
16670.10 LIGHTNING PROTECTION				
Lightning protection				
Copper point, nickel plated, 12'				
1/2" dia.	EA.	25.40	33.20	58.60
5/8" dia.	"	30.00	33.20	63.20

RESISTANCE HEATING

RESISTANCE HEATING	UNIT	MAT.	INST.	TOTAL
16850.10 ELECTRIC HEATING				
Baseboard heater				
2', 375w	EA.	34.30	33.20	67.50
3', 500w	"	42.30	33.20	75.50
4', 750w	"	52.50	37.90	90.40
5', 935w	"	70.00	44.20	114.20
6', 1125w	"	78.00	53.00	131.00
7', 1310w	"	97.00	60.50	157.50
8', 1500w	"	109.00	66.50	175.50
9', 1680w	"	120.00	73.50	193.50
10', 1875w	"	125.00	76.00	201.00
Unit heater wall mounted				
1500w	EA.	160.00	53.00	213.00
Thermostat				
Integral	EA.	26.30	16.60	42.90

- G -

- H -

- I -

- J -

- K -

- L -

- M -

- N -

- O -

- P -

Special Bonus Software Offer

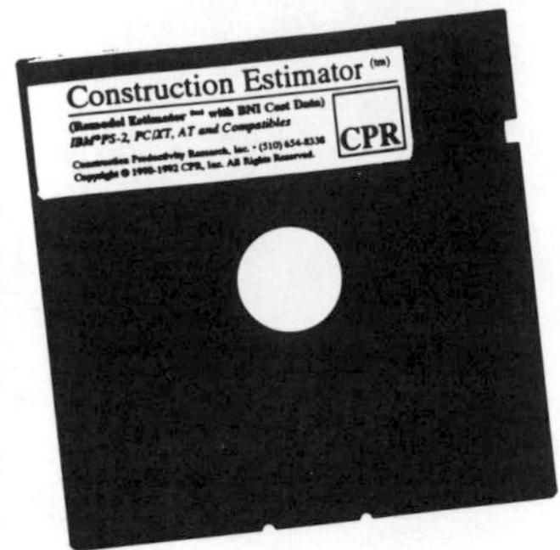

As A Buyer Of A Building News 1992 Costbook You Are Eligible To Receive

— AT NO COST! —

CONSTRUCTION ESTIMATOR

The Complete, Stand Alone, Easy-To-Use, Construction Estimating System

- This program provides the basic tools to develop accurate, comprehensive and organized cost estimates.
- The reliable cost data can be used to supplement your own records and provides a basis for accurate estimating.
- IBM Compatible — 5¼″ diskette.
- Immediate on-screen access to data through "Look-up" windows. "Pull-down" menus.
- Easy to learn and master — very user-friendly.
- Different markups can be applied to each estimate.

Act NOW And Receive – FREE – An Electronic Database With Over 1,000 Lines Of Building News Costbook Data

Order Form

NAME ____________________

COMPANY ____________________

ADDRESS ____________________

CITY, STATE, ZIP ____________________

TELEPHONE ____________________

Simply fill out this form, read and sign the statement below and send this complete page to our East Coast office:

Building News Bookstore
77 Wexford Street
Needham Heights, MA 02194

I purchased my 1992 Costbook at: ____________________ STORE ____________________ CITY, ____________________ STATE

If you have received the Bonus Software through our mail offering, there is no need to order another. You may copy and share the software and data with co-workers and associates.

Bonus Software Qualifications

The PC-ESTIMATOR™ is a software product developed, produced and distributed by CPR International, Inc., 3195 Adeline Street, Suite A, Berkeley, CA 94703, (415) 654-8338. The electronic cost data provided with the PC-ESTIMATOR is derived from the Building News 1992 Construction Costbooks.

CPR International has no affiliation with BNI Publications Inc. (Building News). All questions regarding the software should be directed to CPR International, Inc.

BNI Publications Inc., its authors and editors, do not warrant or guarantee the correctness of the data or information contained in the costbooks. BNI Publications Inc., and its authors and editors, do hereby disclaim any responsibility or liability in connection with the use of data in electronic or printed form published by BNI Publications Inc., or other information in the database or costbooks.

I have read and agree to the above information.

NAME - PLEASE SIGN ____________________

NAME - PLEASE PRINT ____________________

INDEX

Plans are available in standard blueline prints, mylar sepia or vellum prints. Plan prices are subject to change one month after date of publication.
To charge on American Express, MasterCard or Visa, call Toll Free 1-800-323-7379 (outside the United States call 708-635-8800) or send check to:

Professional Builder & Remodeler
1350 E. Touhy Avenue,
P.O. Box 5080
Des Plaines, IL 60017-5080

A house plan order will include the following:

- General specification design notes.
- Foundation and floor plans; basement plans included only where applicable.
- Exterior elevations of all four views.
- Building sections and details as required to construct individual design.
- Interior elevation of cabinets and walls with unique conditions.
- Schematic electrical plans with suggested switch, outlet and light fixture conditions.
- Some, but not all, plans have a list of building materials. (List is not recommended for use to order materials, but is generally helpful in acquiring an estimated construction price.)

Mechanical and plumbing drawings are not included. Mechanical and plumbing codes and regulations vary widely across the country; therefore, this portion of the design is left to the contractor.
Allow three weeks for processing and mailing. Plans are non-returnable. **Express mail delivery is available for an extra charge of $15. Canada express service at a cost of $20. One day overnight service is available for an extra charge of $40. Canada overnight service at a cost of $50. This charge is per each architect. Handling charge payable on all orders at a cost of $5.**

□ Check □ Bill American Express □ Bill MasterCard □ Bill Visa

I understand I will receive either 5 sets of bluelines, or a reproducible mylar or vellum. (Please refer to plan page to see which is available, mylar or vellum.) I would like to order the following plan numbers (homes under 2000 sq. ft. are a flat fee of $300.00).

__________ Plan Number __________ Total sq. ft. × $0.15 = $__________

□ 5 bluelines □ mylars □ vellums

__________ Plan Number __________ Total sq. ft. × $0.15 = $__________

□ 5 bluelines □ mylars □ vellums

__________ Plan Number __________ Total sq. ft. × $0.15 = $__________

□ 5 bluelines □ mylars □ vellums

Special mailing charges (per each architect): = $__________
Handling charges payable on all orders = $ 5.00
Total of order $__________

Name__________

Company name__________

Address__________
(cannot be delivered to a Post Office Box)

City/State/Zip Code__________

Daytime phone with area code__________

Credit card number__________

Expiration date__________

- -

Plans are available in standard blueline prints, mylar sepia or vellum prints. Plan prices are subject to change one month after date of publication.
To charge on American Express, MasterCard or Visa, call Toll Free 1-800-323-7379 (outside the United States call 708-635-8800) or send check to:

Professional Builder & Remodeler
1350 E. Touhy Avenue,
P.O. Box 5080
Des Plaines, IL 60017-5080

A house plan order will include the following:

- General specification design notes.
- Foundation and floor plans; basement plans included only where applicable.
- Exterior elevations of all four views.
- Building sections and details as required to construct individual design.
- Interior elevation of cabinets and walls with unique conditions.
- Schematic electrical plans with suggested switch, outlet and light fixture conditions.
- Some, but not all, plans have a list of building materials. (List is not recommended for use to order materials, but is generally helpful in acquiring an estimated construction price.)

Mechanical and plumbing drawings are not included. Mechanical and plumbing codes and regulations vary widely across the country; therefore, this portion of the design is left to the contractor.
Allow three weeks for processing and mailing. Plans are non-returnable. **Express mail delivery is available for an extra charge of $15. Canada express service at a cost of $20. One day overnight service is available for an extra charge of $40. Canada overnight service at a cost of $50. This charge is per each architect. Handling charge payable on all orders at a cost of $5.**

□ Check □ Bill American Express □ Bill MasterCard □ Bill Visa

I understand I will receive either 5 sets of bluelines, or a reproducible mylar or vellum. (Please refer to plan page to see which is available, mylar or vellum.) I would like to order the following plan numbers (homes under 2000 sq. ft. are a flat fee of $300.00).

__________ Plan Number __________ Total sq. ft. × $0.15 = $__________

□ 5 bluelines □ mylars □ vellums

__________ Plan Number __________ Total sq. ft. × $0.15 = $__________

□ 5 bluelines □ mylars □ vellums

__________ Plan Number __________ Total sq. ft. × $0.15 = $__________

□ 5 bluelines □ mylars □ vellums

Special mailing charges (per each architect): = $__________
Handling charges payable on all orders = $ 5.00
Total of order $__________

Name__________

Company name__________

Address__________
(cannot be delivered to a Post Office Box)

City/State/Zip Code__________

Daytime phone with area code__________

Credit card number__________

Expiration date__________

INDEX

Plans are available in standard blueline prints, mylar sepia or vellum prints. Plan prices are subject to change one month after date of publication.
To charge on American Express, MasterCard or Visa, call Toll Free 1-800-323-7379 (outside the United States call 708-635-8800) or send check to:

Professional Builder & Remodeler
1350 E. Touhy Avenue,
P.O. Box 5080
Des Plaines, IL 60017-5080

A house plan order will include the following:

- General specification design notes.
- Foundation and floor plans; basement plans included only where applicable.
- Exterior elevations of all four views.
- Building sections and details as required to construct individual design.
- Interior elevation of cabinets and walls with unique conditions.
- Schematic electrical plans with suggested switch, outlet and light fixture conditions.
- Some, but not all, plans have a list of building materials. (List is not recommended for use to order materials, but is generally helpful in acquiring an estimated construction price.)

Mechanical and plumbing drawings are not included. Mechanical and plumbing codes and regulations vary widely across the country; therefore, this portion of the design is left to the contractor.
Allow three weeks for processing and mailing. Plans are non-returnable. **Express mail delivery is available for an extra charge of $15. Canada express service at a cost of $20. One day overnight service is available for an extra charge of $40. Canada overnight service at a cost of $50. This charge is per each architect. Handling charge payable on all orders at a cost of $5.**

☐ Check ☐ Bill American Express ☐ Bill MasterCard ☐ Bill Visa

I understand I will receive either 5 sets of bluelines, or a reproducible mylar or vellum. (Please refer to plan page to see which is available, mylar or vellum.) I would like to order the following plan numbers (homes under 2000 sq. ft. are a flat fee of $300.00).

______________ ______________ × $0.15 = $__________
Plan Number Total sq. ft.

☐ 5 bluelines ☐ mylars ☐ vellums

______________ ______________ × $0.15 = $__________
Plan Number Total sq. ft.

☐ 5 bluelines ☐ mylars ☐ vellums

______________ ______________ × $0.15 = $__________
Plan Number Total sq. ft.

☐ 5 bluelines ☐ mylars ☐ vellums

Special mailing charges (per each architect): = $__________
Handling charges payable on all orders = $ 5.00
Total of order $__________

Name______________________________

Company name______________________________

Address______________________________
(cannot be delivered to a Post Office Box)

City/State/Zip Code______________________________

Daytime phone with area code______________________________

Credit card number______________________________

Expiration date______________________________

- -

Plans are available in standard blueline prints, mylar sepia or vellum prints. Plan prices are subject to change one month after date of publication.
To charge on American Express, MasterCard or Visa, call Toll Free 1-800-323-7379 (outside the United States call 708-635-8800) or send check to:

Professional Builder & Remodeler
1350 E. Touhy Avenue,
P.O. Box 5080
Des Plaines, IL 60017-5080

A house plan order will include the following:

- General specification design notes.
- Foundation and floor plans; basement plans included only where applicable.
- Exterior elevations of all four views.
- Building sections and details as required to construct individual design.
- Interior elevation of cabinets and walls with unique conditions.
- Schematic electrical plans with suggested switch, outlet and light fixture conditions.
- Some, but not all, plans have a list of building materials. (List is not recommended for use to order materials, but is generally helpful in acquiring an estimated construction price.)

Mechanical and plumbing drawings are not included. Mechanical and plumbing codes and regulations vary widely across the country; therefore, this portion of the design is left to the contractor.
Allow three weeks for processing and mailing. Plans are non-returnable. **Express mail delivery is available for an extra charge of $15. Canada express service at a cost of $20. One day overnight service is available for an extra charge of $40. Canada overnight service at a cost of $50. This charge is per each architect. Handling charge payable on all orders at a cost of $5.**

☐ Check ☐ Bill American Express ☐ Bill MasterCard ☐ Bill Visa

I understand I will receive either 5 sets of bluelines, or a reproducible mylar or vellum. (Please refer to plan page to see which is available, mylar or vellum.) I would like to order the following plan numbers (homes under 2000 sq. ft. are a flat fee of $300.00).

______________ ______________ × $0.15 = $__________
Plan Number Total sq. ft.

☐ 5 bluelines ☐ mylars ☐ vellums

______________ ______________ × $0.15 = $__________
Plan Number Total sq. ft.

☐ 5 bluelines ☐ mylars ☐ vellums

______________ ______________ × $0.15 = $__________
Plan Number Total sq. ft.

☐ 5 bluelines ☐ mylars ☐ vellums

Special mailing charges (per each architect): = $__________
Handling charges payable on all orders = $ 5.00
Total of order $__________

Name______________________________

Company name______________________________

Address______________________________
(cannot be delivered to a Post Office Box)

City/State/Zip Code______________________________

Daytime phone with area code______________________________

Credit card number______________________________

Expiration date______________________________